CW00691198

Walking on Water

God's Ongoing Faithfulness at Diospi Suyana Hospital

Klaus-Dieter John

instant apostle

First published in Great Britain in 2024

Instant Apostle
104A The Drive
Rickmansworth
Herts
WD3 4DU

Copyright © Klaus Dieter-John 2024

The author has asserted his rights under Section 77 of the Copyright, Designs and Patents Act, 1988, to be identified as the author of the work.

All rights reserved. No portion of this book may be reproduced or transmitted in any form or by any means, electronic or mechanical, including photocopying and recording, or by any information storage and retrieval system, without permission in writing from the publisher.

Unless otherwise indicated, all Scripture quotations are taken from the Holy Bible, New International Version® Anglicised, NIV® Copyright © 1979, 1984, 2011 by Biblica, Inc.® Used by permission. All rights reserved worldwide.

Every effort has been made to seek permission to use copyright material reproduced in this book. The publisher apologises for those cases where permission might not have been sought and, if notified, will formally seek permission at the earliest opportunity.

The views and opinions expressed in this work are those of the author and do not necessarily reflect the views and opinions of the publisher.

British Library Cataloguing-in-Publication Data

A catalogue record for this book is available from the British Library.

This book and all other Instant Apostle books are available from Instant Apostle:

Website: www.instantapostle.com

Email: info@instantapostle.com

ISBN 978-1-912726-84-4

Printed in Great Britain.

Dedication

This book is dedicated to all who doubt God and wonder whether there is any real basis for faith, hope and love.

The author would like to thank Janet Yachoua and Jenn Baldwin for translating the text into English.

Also available

I Have Seen God: The Miraculous Story of the Diospi Suyana Hospital in Peru by Klaus-Dieter John (2014). ISBN: 978-0857215741

God Has Seen Us: Diospi Suyana – A Story Shared Around the World by Klaus-Dieter John (2019). ISBN: 978-0857219442

Klaus-Dieter John: Hope in the Land of the Incas by Janet Benge and Geoff Benge (2014). ISBN: 978-1576587553

Author's note

The author has described events to the best of his knowledge and extensive personal documentation. While timelines and locations are presented as accurately as possible, some names have been altered to protect the privacy of the individuals involved.

Contents

Foreword

I was dining with a few friends at the Deli Huasi café in Curahuasi when I was approached by a Peruvian man who had been hanging out near the café door. While I did not recognise the man, he certainly seemed to know me.

'Dr John!' he began with a directness not in line with the South American cultural mores I had become accustomed to. 'If you ever write another book, you need to call it *Walking on Water*.'

Without another word, he turned and was gone. But his advice was sound. He clearly understood the reality and significance of our work at Diospi Suyana.

Perhaps you have heard the story of the three clergy members who had to cross a river …

First was a Catholic priest. 'Jesus said we could walk on water, so let's do it!' he called as he carefully placed one foot in front of the other, traversing the surface of the water to the other side. His colleagues applauded his accomplishment.

Next came a Protestant minister. Taking a run-up, he launched himself full speed at the river bank – and landed with a huge bellyflop. His feet found the bottom of the river, and he trudged through water up to his hips until he reached the other side. Cold, wet and humiliated, he pulled himself out of the river.

An Orthodox priest pulled up the rear. He hoisted his rucksack onto his shoulder and marched across the water without a word or fuss. Clearly, this was no big deal.

As the Protestant minister retreated some distance to change out of his wet clothing, the Catholic priest chuckled somewhat sympathetically to his Orthodox brother, stating, 'To be fair, we really should have told him where the stones were.'

'What stones?' replied the Orthodox priest.

While this story was created to make people smile, there is a lesson here. When we put our faith in God and attempt the 'impossible' – such as walking on water – we will encounter one of these three scenarios.

Perhaps, like the Catholic priest, we put our faith in elements other than divine intervention. Instead of the stones in the story, we may rely on our own efforts, connections, psychology, etc – at least as a backup plan.

Or maybe we step out in faith and end up in a proverbial 'bellyflop' because God did not intervene in the way we expected. Does that mean He doesn't care, doesn't exist or just prefers to stay out of our business? Will our 'failure' be simply an inconvenience and embarrassment, or will there be more severe consequences?

Then there is the question, or rather, the possibility, of real-life divine intervention – *a miracle*. Even walking on water. The concept of 'walking on water' has been of great existential significance to me for many years. Not in a sensationalist manner, but as evidence of the Bible's claim that the Almighty God is deeply interested and involved in our lives, giving us meaning, love and hope.

Diospi Suyana is an extensive experience with God. People from all over the world have been a part of this incredible journey over the last two decades. The tales of our adventures have been carefully researched and documented so that they may be presented to you as an accurate account of events.

So can a person ever *really* hope to walk on water? I leave that to you, dear reader, to decide …

Klaus-Dieter John

1

An early morning shock

'Please give me a minute to call my lawyer,' the former president said as he headed to the stairs.

The police officers nodded in assent and made themselves comfortable in the elegant seating of the lounge. They had been tasked by the state to bring Alan García into custody, pending trial. The past two-term leader of Peru had been under investigation for years – what were ten more minutes?

The corruption and scandal surrounding the Odebrecht construction corporation were about to claim yet another celebrity victim. Close associates of the erstwhile Head of State had pocketed US$4 million in kickbacks from the Brazilian firm. Since it had been García himself who had awarded Odebrecht the lucrative contract to build an electric railway in the capital city of Peru, he could not protest his innocence with any degree of credibility.

Checkmate, as TV presenter Jaime Bayly later reported in his special broadcast.

A loud 'bang' echoed throughout the opulent dwelling. The officers ran upstairs and broke through the locked bedroom door to find Alan García sitting in a chair with blood gushing from his right temple. A revolver lay on the floor nearby. García's shot had been well calculated; even immediate emergency surgery could not have saved his life. Shortly after 10am on Wednesday 17th April 2019, the media announced the death of Alan García.

Dr Jens Haßfeld broke the news to me at the hospital. I rushed to my office and pulled up the RPP website. Peru's leading news source reflected the massive shock waves sweeping the nation as news of García's suicide spread.

I could not help but think back to the events of 26th February 2008.

My wife and I were waiting, along with Dr David Brady, Diospi Suyana urologist, and Dr Chorrea, a high-ranking member of the presidential, social-democratic APRA political party, in the exquisite conference chamber of the Government Palace. A door opened. President Alan García and his wife, Pilar Nores, entered, stepping into the glow of the chandeliers.

After the customary exchange of pleasantries, I guided my attentive audience through a presentation on the history of Diospi Suyana. I led with the dream my wife, Tina, and I had had back in high school of spending our lives together, serving as doctors to those in need. In 2002, Tina and I put our glorious vision down on paper – a hundred pages of it. We were determined to build a state-of-the-art hospital for the descendants of the Incas, high up in the Andes mountains of southern Peru. And the most unbelievable part? We resolved to do all of this without the aid of bank loans, the government or Bill Gates.

It all came down to faith. Only with God's help could this dream become a reality.

The President and First Lady focused on the small screen of my laptop as I recounted numerous examples of God's provision and miraculous intervention as He led us along this winding path to our goal. I told them how a man named Udo Klemenz and his wife, Barbara, had been sitting in their kitchen, discussing and praying about what God had in store for them next. At the very same moment, I was in a meeting in my home town of Wiesbaden, Germany, and heard their names for the first time. I gave them a call – their phone rang just as they ended their prayer with an 'Amen'. Udo Klemenz joined our massive project, supervising all the construction. And he charged us nothing.

Of course, I had to tell the story of how we had sought help directly from Pilar Nores just two years earlier when a state agency wanted to shut down our construction and fine us US$700,000 over a missing licence. In our panic, we decided to reach out to the newly elected presidential couple. Everyone told us we were wasting our time. Even the German Ambassador said we had no chance of success.

And yet, three weeks later, Pilar Nores granted us a seventy-minute audience in her office. At the conclusion, she agreed to become the patron of Diospi Suyana.

'You know, Mr President,' I began as I clicked to the next slide, 'in December 2005, my projector – the one I use for my presentations all over the world – was confiscated by Peruvian Customs at the airport. I needed a replacement as soon as possible. While I was trying one out at a small store in Lima, the head of the Impsat telecommunications company "just happened" to be standing behind me, watching all the pictures of the Diospi Suyana story that flitted across the screen. He ended up donating a satellite dish that would give us telephone and internet service. This generous gift was reported in the weekly magazine *Somos*. A mine owner read about it and donated all the steel we would need for the facility roof. And then TV Channel 2 got wind of what was going on and featured Diospi Suyana in a special report, *Hospital of Hope*.'

For a moment, there was stunned silence. Then García cleared his throat, leaned over and said to me, 'Dr John, you are a lot closer to God than I am!'

That was quite a presumptuous statement, as no one can know and pass judgement on another's relationship with God. In the depths of our hearts, battles often rage undetected by those around us. But, as Jesus Himself promised His disciples, 'a mustard seed of faith' is enough to move mountains. God knows we are transient beings, tossed between hope and fear, faith and doubt. And yet, all we are asked to do is cry out to God to experience His awesome and very real power.

Almost exactly eleven years had passed between that first meeting and García's death. During that time, Diospi Suyana had grown from little more than an idea to a functional facility with a staff of 270. It was never easy. So many times we took two steps forward, only to take a step back. Sometimes it was even the other way around. We made great progress, then suffered setbacks. We celebrated victories, then descended into valleys of tears. But throughout this journey, God's hand has been so evident, I see it as my mission in life to share these experiences.

I would have loved to have another opportunity to share my testimony of faith with this remarkable leader. I would have loved to assure him that, in any situation, even in our darkest moments, we can rest in the shadow of the Most High.

Unfortunately, that opportunity never came. Alan García was buried on Good Friday in 2019.

2

We have come from a long way away

The sun cast its last rays through the dull window panes of the tiny adobe home. Daniel Ticona looked across the table at his nephew.

'I have so much pain with these two hernias, and they are getting bigger.' The Aymara Indian coughed, then continued, 'Constantino, you told me your mother received such good treatment at that Diospi Suyana hospital. Maybe the doctors there can help me!'

Constantino slowly shook his head. 'Uncle, it is such a long way from our village to the hospital. You would have to change coaches more than once. Would you be able to cope with the stress of such a journey?'

'Of course, I can! God has given me strength!' Daniel's eyes showed his deep resolve. 'I might be over eighty, but I can handle a coach trip!'

'Uncle, I will come with you. We can leave this week if you like!'

Daniel's weathered countenance brightened. 'My nephew, I thank you. May God watch over us through our travels!'

The older man stuck his wrinkled hands into the pockets of his faded trousers, as if this gesture would give him courage, for he certainly would need some. He had no way of knowing that political unrest was gathering like dark storm clouds over the state of Cusco.

Sometimes it is better not to know what is coming, to be able to lie down and rest in ignorance. Fear and uncertainty can have such a paralysing effect, tormenting and draining our last drop of strength. Daniel's body was wracked with pain, his endurance all but spent. There was a government hospital in his city of Puno, but its reputation was poor. Most doctors showed no kindness or respect when treating Indio patients. Getting an appointment took weeks, and an operation even longer. Although private care was more efficient, it was financially beyond the means of Daniel and his family. The only alternative was to seek help further afield.

So on a Wednesday afternoon in February, in the middle of the rainy season, Daniel and Constantino boarded a minibus in their village of Ilave that would take them along the bumpy tracks to the central Puno station. Daniel had had some experience with long coach trips for medical treatment in the past. On a couple of occasions he had travelled south, around Lake Titicaca and into Bolivia to a clinic in the city of La Paz. This usually took seven or eight hours, provided there were no incidents at the Peru–Bolivia border, no flat tyres, etc. On this journey, however, Daniel would be heading north. He was familiar with Cusco, the old capital of the Inca empire, but Constantino explained that Diospi Suyana was even farther away, beyond the horizon, somewhere in the state of Apurímac.

The hectic atmosphere was unsettling to Daniel. So many people shouting and hurrying. His eyes swept the scene, constantly looking over to Constantino. Without his nephew, he would be lost entirely in a place like this.

Soon the pair were standing in the queue for tickets. When they arrived at the window, Constantino purchased two tickets for Cusco. They would depart at 22:30.

Thoughts of all the risks and dangers they might encounter flooded Daniel's mind. Would the driver stay awake at the wheel? Would he drive safely? Daniel was always hearing stories about horrific highway collisions. Armed robberies were not uncommon either, carried out by masked men hiding in darkness, waiting to ambush an unsuspecting vehicle, then disappearing with their loot into the bushes lining the road.

Daniel breathed a quiet prayer. He knew God would be with him and Constantino, all the way to Cusco and even beyond that. He resolved to take courage and put his trust in God.

It took the coach about eight hours to cover the 400-kilometre stretch of highway to Cusco. Thank heavens there were no incidents. Shortly after dawn, the men took a taxi through the streets of Cusco, then picked up a minibus for the three-hour drive to Curahuasi. For the last leg of their trip, they climbed into a three-wheeled mototaxi that struggled at a walking pace past the guesthouses and restaurants on the way to the hospital.

The entrance to Diospi Suyana bustled with street traders and food vendors offering sweets, sandwiches and even hot meals. The highly sought-after admissions tickets, called 'coupons', had long since been distributed. People queued outside all night long for the opportunity to receive one. Those not so fortunate were standing around dejectedly, undecided as to whether they should try again the next day.

The mototaxi stopped at the guards' station. Two Indios in black uniforms approached the vehicle. Daniel and his nephew could see on the wall ahead, written in large letters, 'Hospital Diospi Suyana – Welcome!'

This brought hope to both their hearts, but looking further, they saw the masses of people gathered in the courtyard – so many milling about, looking as though they had been invited then forgotten. The numbers clearly exceeded the capacity of the hospital. Would Daniel share their fate and face bitter disappointment?

'We have no coupons left for today,' one of the guards explained sympathetically.

Constantino was not willing to give up hope. 'We have just travelled fifteen hours from Puno! My uncle is eighty-two years old and in terrible pain!'

'If that is so,' the guard replied, 'we will admit you as an emergency case!'

The two weary travellers heaved a massive sigh of relief. Another hurdle cleared. They slowly walked the path to the hospital doors. To the right, children climbed and played on the playground swings, seemingly without a care in the world. Daniel and Constantino entered the lobby, apprehensive as to what awaited them. The waiting area was huge and overflowing, as one might expect. About 120 patients, predominantly Quechua Indios, sat on orange-coloured benches. Others crowded around the reception desk, hoping for good news.

'We have come from such a long way,' one *campesino* pleaded. 'Can a doctor possibly see my mother this afternoon?'

The receptionist shook her head. 'I am afraid not. Perhaps tomorrow.'

Daniel and his nephew followed signs directing them down the corridor between the pharmacy and laboratories to a small waiting area, then through double doors into A&E. Several nurses at the desk welcomed the pair.

'How can we help you?' a diminutive Peruvian woman asked, introducing herself as Maribel.

Since his uncle could only speak broken Spanish, Constantino answered. 'We travelled all night to get here. My uncle is in pain. He has a lot of swelling on both sides of his groin, and something is wrong with his prostate too.'

Maribel invited them to have a seat. She told them she would need to take some notes, and then get pulse and blood pressure readings.

Daniel did not reply, but his gratitude shone through his eyes. What a gift to be looked after with such care and even a smile. The nurse had a foreign accent and it was soon clear she was serving at Diospi Suyana as a missionary. Whatever trouble they had gone through to get here became worth it in a single moment.

A short time later, Daniel was directed to a bed behind a folding privacy screen. Constantino sat in an adjacent chair.

'I am so grateful we got in,' whispered Daniel. 'When I think of all those people we passed who waited all night, who are still waiting – we are very lucky!'

Constantino nodded in agreement.

A young female doctor with sparkling dark eyes swept in after about ten minutes.

'My name is Dr Karla Aguilar, and I would like to help you. First, I have a few questions, then we will do a thorough physical examination.'

Daniel was amazed at the efficiency of it all. After the exam, a nurse came in to collect blood and urine samples. A little while later, he was taken all the way to the other side of the hospital for an ultrasound scan. As the foreign medic pressed a plastic stick-shaped object against Daniel's abdomen, he smiled and explained that this would help him see inside Daniel's body.

'Your prostate is really swollen and you have hernias as well!' the medic declared.

When the ultrasound was complete, Daniel and Constantino returned to the waiting area. Before they left the building that afternoon, all lab results were in, all pertinent information, including diagnosis, was filed, and Daniel had an appointment scheduled with a urologist for the following morning. Word was that this doctor from Austria really knew his stuff. Daniel would be in good hands. They found cheap lodging across the road at one of the many establishments catering to Diospi Suyana guests.

After a much-needed good night's rest, Daniel and Constantino returned to the hospital in the morning and made themselves comfortable in the crowded waiting area. Suddenly, at 8.30am, large double doors swung open, revealing a sanctuary with white walls and stained-glass windows. On a platform towards the front, young people were playing modern worship music. The patients in the waiting area rose almost as one and filed into the chapel. Daniel and Constantino followed, not knowing exactly what to expect. When Daniel looked behind him, he could see that more than 250 people had made their way into the two storeys of the chapel. A simple wooden cross hung at the front. Rays of sunshine streamed through the coloured glass, casting vibrant reflections across the walls and floor.

After the assembly had sung two songs, a pastor who looked to be about seventy years of age took the floor. He addressed the people in both Spanish and Quechua. Daniel knew instinctively that this man was the 'real deal'. Instead of spouting platitudes, he spoke from his heart about God, creator of the universe, who loves all people, old and young, healthy and sick. The man's words were a healing balm to the worried patients who had come to Curahuasi with their physical pain and troubled souls, driven by the desperate need to find relief and restoration. It comes as no surprise that the Quechua word *Curahuasi* actually means 'house of healing', and the literal translation of *Diospi Suyana* is 'God is our hope'.

At 10.30am, the urologist called for Daniel. Dr David Brady was a tall, slim man who towered over most of his patients by at least a foot. After carefully reading Daniel's file, he stated that it was very clear that Daniel would require an operation to repair his hernias, and asked if he would like to have the procedure done at Diospi Suyana. Constantino translated each sentence into Aymara for his uncle.

Daniel nodded assent and asked if the operation could be completed before the dry season in May. He was shocked when Dr Brady responded that he could schedule the procedure for the following Tuesday, 12th February.

Only a few days to wait! That afternoon, Daniel and Constantino travelled to Cusco to spend the weekend with some acquaintances there. Only one more weekend of pain! Daniel was ecstatic.

Daniel understood how precious this opportunity was. There was no way he was going to miss it. He would be back at Diospi Suyana bright and early Monday morning, whatever the cost.

3

Where there's a will, there's a way

It was early in the morning on Monday 11th February. Daniel and Constantino were already at the bus stop in Arcopata, where minibuses departed for Curahuasi about every twenty minutes. There weren't many people out, but that didn't register as unusual. They hadn't heard that the regional farmers had called for a general strike that day. The *campesinos* wanted the government to declare a state of emergency owing to the poor harvest and to provide bailouts to the farmers who had lost so much money. Tensions were high and people were desperate. It wouldn't take much to ignite violence in such an emotional powder keg. Most people chose to remain in the safety of their homes.

'We're on strike – nobody gets through!' announced the *campesinos* who barricaded the roads.

Daniel and Constantino remained oblivious to the burgeoning drama. They gazed through the windows of the nine-passenger Hyundai vehicle as it churned up the hill to Cusco. Dilapidated old adobe homes and cement constructions in process lined both sides of the road. Steel rods jutting into the sky indicated owners' intentions to add another storey or two as soon as they had the money to do so. The pavement was strewn with piles of rubbish where stray dogs rummaged and fought for something to eat.

The minibus had travelled about twenty kilometres and they could see the outskirts of Izcuchaca just ahead. Suddenly, the driver slammed on the brakes. A large mass of vehicles of various sizes was completely blocking the road.

'This is the end of the line,' the driver called out. 'We'll never get through this barricade.'

Some of the passengers began to grumble. 'Damn strikes never achieve anything except causing problems for the rest of us,' growled a well-dressed man sitting up front.

'What's happening?' Constantino asked another passenger.

'You haven't heard about the strike?' The Indio woman sitting behind him was amazed he didn't know. The capital city of Anta is normally bustling with life by nine in the morning. Mototaxis race round the corners of busy streets, appearing to come out of nowhere. Pedestrians hurry to their various destinations while dogs dash through the crowds and traffic. But not on this day. The streets were empty. Shops and businesses were closed. The eerie silence was unsettling. Locals understood the current instability. If the police took action, widespread violence could erupt in an instant. There are no winners in a Peruvian street fight, only injured and dead.

The passengers disembarked and walked towards the barricade, passing other vehicles trapped on the road.

The protesters were certainly not playing around. In addition to blocking the road with cars and trucks, they had felled trees and placed piles of stones to ensure no one could pass. Fumes from burning tyres filled the air, irritating the eyes and lungs of all unfortunate enough to be downwind.

A group of protestors had set up camp at the side of the road, and some were arguing vehemently with vehicle drivers attempting to circumvent the massive blockade.

'We're not letting anyone through,' a dark figure bellowed. 'And if you try, we'll smash your faces in!'

Constantino and Daniel looked at each other apprehensively and took a step backwards.

'Come on, let's wait over there,' Constantino suggested, taking his uncle by the hand and leading him towards a nearby fence. They sat down and ate some of the potatoes and cheese they had bought from street vendors.

'We have to get to Curahuasi *today*! I cannot miss my operation!' Daniel's voice trembled with emotion.

Hours passed. The situation remained unchanged; the air hung heavy with threat, and increasing levels of alcohol certainly did nothing to calm anyone down.

The men waited and worried. Had all their efforts been in vain? They closed their eyes, bowed their heads and brought their need to God in prayer.

'Father in heaven, please help us get to Curahuasi,' they pleaded. 'You always make a way when there seems to be no way!'

'*Hermano*, brother, how long do you think it would take to get around the barricades on foot? It certainly doesn't look like any cars will be let through today.'

The man Constantino had addressed looked sympathetically at Daniel. 'Probably about eight hours. It's thirty kilometres to Ancahuasi – maybe you can get a taxi there.'

None of that sounded promising to Constantino and Daniel. They decided to wait a bit longer for their miracle. As dusk fell, they knew there was no more time left to waste – it was now or never!

The men gathered up their courage and their luggage. A rain shower had just blown in over Izcuchaca. Undeterred, they buttoned their coats up, pulled their hats down and set out, giving a wide berth to the barricades and angry men who still might try to stop them. They were not alone, as they were joined by a surprising number of Peruvians who had had enough of sitting still and were now moving ahead, silently, under the protective cover of darkness.

Indios from the highlands are used to walking long distances, but at night and in the rain – this was torture. Before long, they were soaked to the skin.

'We need to keep moving, or we'll catch our death of cold,' Daniel exhorted, marching forward.

It was about ten hours later, in the grey light of dawn, the two frozen and exhausted men dragged themselves across the town square in Ancahuasi. An incredible achievement, no doubt, but they could not rest. Curahuasi was still eighty kilometres away.

No taxi driver was willing to take them to Limatambo. Some said it was relatively safe as far as the toll station, eight kilometres away, but after that the road spiralled down through hairpin turns into the valley below. During protests such as the one in progress, *campesinos* had been known to throw rocks down the hillside onto passing cars, considering broken windows and other damage a fair price for strike-breakers to pay. It just wasn't worth the risk.

Daniel and Constantino remembered they were not alone. They knelt again to pray for a solution. It wasn't long in coming, appearing in the shape of a bicycle.

Constantino lost no time in approaching the man riding towards them on his bike. '*Señor*, would you sell us your bicycle?'

The man smelled a good deal. 'How much?'

Within minutes, they had agreed upon the price of 100 *soles*. Constantino was now the proud owner of an old 'boneshaker' bicycle.

'Uncle, sit on the luggage rack and I'll pedal!'

Not a couple of kids playing around; these were two men already suffering from hypothermia, simply trying to find a way to travel faster than they could walk. Although physically spent, they both had an iron resolve. Daniel struggled onto the back of the bike and wrapped his arms around his nephew's waist.

There probably aren't too many Europeans or Americans who could manage such a trip at eighty-two years of age. Tackling thirty-seven kilometres on a battered bicycle *after* trekking all night through the rain would be a challenge for even the most athletic. Call it endurance, tenacity, 'mettle' – or faith. Christians often cling to this promise from the book of Isaiah:

> But those who hope in the LORD
> will renew their strength.
> They will soar on wings like eagles;
> they will run and not grow weary,
> they will walk and not be faint.
> (Isaiah 40:31)

At two o'clock that afternoon, the pair rode into Limatambo, discovering with great delight a taxi parked just ahead. What a blessing!

Within the hour, the bone-weary travellers crossed the threshold of the Diospi Suyana hospital. Their journey of 125 kilometres had taken thirty-two harrowing hours.

After a hot shower and a hearty dish of soup, Daniel snuggled into his dry hospital bed. He and Constantino had made it! Admittedly a day late, but who could have denied him the needed operation with all he had been through?

Certainly not Dr Brady. He operated on the hernias the next morning. Daniel was released from the hospital two days later. Miraculously, neither Daniel nor Constantino became ill after their excruciating – and wet – overnight travel experience. They gave thanks to God for His keeping and joyfully began their journey home. All went smoothly – the strike had ended the previous Tuesday.

What Daniel undertook in order to be treated at Diospi Suyana is remarkable but not entirely unusual. During intake procedures, staff learn that approximately 80 per cent of our patients have travelled a long distance for our help. These patients pass state hospitals and private clinics to queue in front of Diospi Suyana. They invest their time and money with no guarantee that they will receive one of the coveted treatment coupons.

Many factors have contributed to Diospi Suyana's legendary reputation. Peru's healthcare system has been marked by corruption and incompetence, yet many media reports have sung praises of our hospital, declaring it a model of success. The combination of kindness, good treatment results and low prices contributes to this positive view, but it is not everything. In my opinion, our faith is an absolutely essential component. Everyone who attends our morning worship services understands that we are not in this for the money. We want to share our faith in the living God in a practical and loving way, with expertise and passion in equal measure.

As Jesus once said, 'Whatever you did for one of the least of these brothers and sisters of mine, you did for me' (Matthew 25:40).

4

Blood, sweat, tears and drama

It's understandable why most people prefer to avoid hospitals. In addition to all the associated body fluids, such as blood and urine, hospitals tend to remind us of the temporal nature of our lives. Unlike a scary film that we can switch off with the touch of a button, the grim realities of our own mortality are not as easy to escape. Feelings of horror and disgust can cling to us. One might think medical professionals are so accustomed to suffering and death that they are less affected than others. But still, the sight of an emaciated cancer patient or the yellow face of someone suffering from cirrhosis will haunt even the most experienced healer and follow us home.

Despite the common aversion to hospitals, there is still gratitude for the existence of a place where suffering is eased and lives are prolonged. Nearly everyone will require such care at some point in their lives, surrounded by others in need.

In the mountains of Peru, the Quechua people have extremely limited access to quality healthcare, which is why so many, young and old, set out on such daunting journeys to be treated at the Diospi Suyana hospital. Daniel Ticona had very compelling reasons for walking all night through the rain to get here.

Pablo Human, however, was not able to walk at all. His five adult children had to carry the fifty-five-year-old over the hospital threshold. An Indio from southern Peru, Pablo was suffering from an aortal aneurysm, a dangerous weakening and subsequent swelling of the body's major artery. This type of aneurysm is comparable to a ticking time bomb. It could burst without warning, causing an individual to bleed to death internally within minutes. In Pablo's case, the aneurysm was compounded by multiple blood clots, impeding blood flow in both of his legs. His right thigh was cold to the touch and his foot had turned completely black. His left leg looked a bit better, but he had already lost sensation in his big toe, so there was an urgent need for action. If all of that were not enough, the necrotic tissue was infected and sepsis had set in. As a previous heart attack survivor, Pablo was hardly an ideal candidate for surgery; in fact, other doctors had refused to help him because the chance of success was so low.

As Pablo's children gently set him down on the consulting room table, they all looked expectantly at the vascular surgeon, Dr Thomas Tielmann.

'Doctor, please do something,' they implored. 'We cannot lose our father!'

Dr Tielmann conducted a thorough physical examination and ordered a series of further tests. When the results were in, he informed Pablo and his family that he was willing to operate but was clear that, 'God alone knows whether or not he will come through it.'

Moved by the doctor's kindness, the children spontaneously wrapped their arms around him in a hug, a gesture that expressed more than words ever could. In his understanding and acceptance, Dr Tielmann had given them a tiny seed of hope.

When was the last time you hugged your GP? It's probably been a while ...

Pablo wept as Dr Tielmann said a prayer, surrendering the next few days into God's hands. Pablo's life was on the line, but it would be God, not chance, that would determine his fate.

The operation itself also began with a prayer. Dr Tielmann opened the abdominal wall and clamped the renal arteries. He cautiously cut into the aneurysm and inserted a stent. He then extracted the blood clots in the pelvic arteries using a balloon catheter. Pablo's legs became warm as blood flow was restored. Because of the necrosis, Pablo's right leg unfortunately needed to be amputated. The whole procedure took about four hours to complete. Despite the extreme risk, the operation was successful and saved Pablo's life. At some point in the future, Pablo would be fitted with a leg prosthesis to restore his mobility. Praise God we have such options!

In addition to providing medical care through our highly qualified mission staff, Diospi Suyana provides training to junior doctors and young nurses. For medical students from all over the world, the experience with Diospi Suyana is almost always life changing. Here we see issues at more advanced stages than usually encountered in Europe or the US, where medical care is more readily available.

My wife Tina whirled through A&E in her usual fashion. All seven beds were occupied, and the waiting room was overflowing.

'Rebekka, please see to the pregnant lady there and get her medical history.' Tina gestured towards a young woman with a distended belly.

The Swiss medical student grabbed her clipboard and approached the patient, drawing the privacy curtain behind her. Within minutes she emerged, announcing, 'This woman is not pregnant – she has brought an ultrasound report with her from another doctor. It says she has a large tumour!'

The twenty-nine-year-old patient, Alicia Carbajal, was immediately referred to our gynaecologist, Dr Jens Haßfeld. Ultrasound and CT scans both confirmed the presence of a giant ovarian cyst. The very next day, the patient was on the operating table, where Dr Haßfeld removed a tumour weighing more than thirty pounds.

Alicia made it through the night with no complications. The next morning, she was on her feet, walking through the ward, in good spirits with noticeable great relief. The biopsy of the tumour revealed no sign of cancer, so the operation itself was all that was needed to provide healing to this mother of two.

As for Rebekka, our medical student, this is a case she will remember for as long as she lives.

Unpredictability is a simple fact of life in South America, and it is certainly no different at Diospi Suyana. We deal with each moment as it comes, and flexibility is critical. At the hospital, there is usually only one person covering each speciality – one urologist, one traumatologist, one general surgeon and so on. If the phone rings or a patient is rolled into A&E and a particular expertise is needed, you do your duty. It's as simple as that.

Take, for example, the Friday evening when Dr Tim Boeker was just settling into an enjoyable weekend with his family, complete with a campfire and film. When the call came that a young man had just mangled his forearm on a rotary saw, Dr Boeker abandoned his plans, bid his children goodnight and rushed to the hospital.

The lad's arm was almost completely severed, held on only one side by some tissue and the ulnar bone. The electric saw had sliced through arteries, veins, nerves, bones and most of the tendons. There were only two options: Dr Boeker could amputate the forearm completely, stitch up the wound and go back to his family; or he could spend the night attempting the arduous task of restoring the arm.

Dr Boeker chose the latter. Assisted by Dr Brady, the operation took six hours but was considered a success as blood flow and sensation gradually returned to the patient's arm. What a joyful gift to be able to use his right hand again!

As I share the story of Diospi Suyana around the world, I am often asked what role prayer plays as we care for our patients. Our medical staff have received excellent training and are experts in their field, but as Christians, we know we are only human. We know our endeavours are nothing without God's blessing. His is LORD over life and death. That is why we pray

– not just in our morning worship services, but throughout our work, in the operating theatres, at the bedsides, everywhere. Our patients gratefully receive this aspect of our ministry. And sometimes we experience results that the laws of medicine cannot explain …

It was Friday 30th November. Tina and I had just arrived home, exhausted after a particularly gruelling twelve-hour day at the hospital. Tina was fighting a cold after her recent trip to Germany for her father's eighty-third birthday. Cusco–Lima–Madrid–Frankfurt and back within seven days, then right back to her patients. The jetlag compounded her chronic lack of sleep, and I was especially concerned about her cough.

'Is there anything that absolutely has to be done this evening?' I asked.

'No, not really,' she replied, heading to the kitchen to stew some apples.

I settled down with a sudoku puzzle in the bedroom. Suddenly I registered the sound of a distant ambulance siren. As the siren grew louder, I heard our garage door open and the car engine start.

'I'll come with you!' I called as I ran outside. Too late: Tina had already rounded the corner on her way. I closed the door slowly, wondering what the emergency could be this time.

Despite the late hour, I found a mototaxi that would take me to the hospital. There I found Tina, Dr Ana Delgado and several nurses in the X-ray department. She filled me in on the tragic situation, a perfect example of how harm can come out of nowhere when we least expect it.

Twelve-year-old José and his little brother Pedro were playing near the Apurímac River when it happened. José tripped and fell head first down a deep, narrow hole in the ground. He struggled wildly in an effort to break free, but only succeeded in loosening the surrounding sand, which rained down upon him from all sides, burying his head. With every panicked breath, José drew grit and soil into his lungs. Pedro pulled on José's legs but could not budge him, so he ran to get help. Time passed. A long time. To anyone buried alive as José was, time is of the essence. Brain cells will begin to die within ten minutes of such oxygen deprivation. A neighbour finally came and was able to free José, but his face was already an ominous deep blue. It was in this dire condition that the family brought him to the Diospi Suyana hospital.

The situation was grim – that much was written all over the faces of the attending staff. José's central nervous system had sustained massive damage owing to the prolonged lack of oxygen. His muscles began to contract in violent spasms. Everyone in the room had to hold him tight so that medication to halt the seizures could be injected.

We did a CT scan of José's head as well as an X-ray of his lungs. At 9pm I picked up our anaesthesiologist, Dr Leslie Ichocan – we needed reinforcements! At this point, we had no idea if any of the boy's brain function could be restored.

There was great concentration in the intensive care unit as we went through the typical procedures of putting our patient on a ventilator, inserting a gastric tube and urinary catheter, and putting in a line for intravenous medication. And yet we felt we must prepare for the worst.

'We don't know if your son will ever regain consciousness,' Tina broke the news to José's distraught parents as gently as possible. They were paralysed with shock. Just that afternoon, he had been an active and happy boy; now their son was nearly unrecognisable, attached to all kinds of cables and tubes in an attempt to heal and bring relief. How did God allow this to happen?

At 11pm that fateful Friday night, we finally left the hospital and fell exhausted into bed. At 1am we would receive a phone update on the boy's condition.

The next morning brought no improvement. Clinical assessments showed irreversible brain damage. And then Gladys Illesca, former head of our Kids' Clubs, stepped onto the ward and knelt at José's bedside.

'God, if this boy is able to leave the hospital on his own two feet,' she prayed aloud, 'I will personally organise his next birthday party.' It was a heartfelt cry for help for a boy medicine said could no longer be helped.

On Monday morning, José awoke from the coma. At about 11am, he told my wife, '*Gracias*,' 'Thank you.'

José was talking and responding as if nothing had happened. Cognitively there was no deficit, and he was able to move his arms and legs normally. For us doctors, it was nothing short of a miracle.

Nearly nine months later, on 25th August, José celebrated his thirteenth birthday at the Diospi Suyana Kids' Club House. As promised, Gladys took care of all the arrangements.

Today, José is entirely healthy and has no residual damage from his dramatic brush with death. None of us doctors had the faith to pray for his healing, but Gladys did. Despite catastrophic clinical findings, God was at work, and José was given a second chance at life!

In this chapter, I have shared the stories of just four patients, but we see up to 250 each day – that is approximately five thousand each month! We do our best for each of them. Our treatment often helps, but not always. Most of our patients are grateful, but some are not. We serve out of love, not a desire for financial gain. We get tired, even exhausted, but we never doubt that we are doing the right thing.

5

Colégio Diospi Suyana – an exemplary school

A television crew was filming for ZDF, a German television station, and the three reporters wanted to take a look at the Diospi Suyana school in addition to the hospital. As they meandered through the classrooms, including the art and science rooms, the team leader remarked, 'This school is nicer than mine was in Berlin!'

The Colégio Diospi Suyana is no posh preparatory school, such as might be attended by the children of the social elite in Munich or of diplomats in Lima. On the contrary, it serves and shapes a generation growing up in the hardships often associated with poverty. Many of our students come from broken or dysfunctional Quechua families and experience extreme neglect. Somehow our teachers manage to take children from all kinds of backgrounds – including the children of our foreign missionary staff – and create strong connections in classrooms where all students not only know that they are accepted, but also receive educational training second to none in the Peruvian Highlands.

In December 2023, we celebrated our tenth year of operation. We started with just 176 students, but by 2024 we had 573 students enrolled, from kindergarten to high school. Christian and Verena Begalke, whose background I discuss in

God Has Seen Us,[1] headed up the school along with local national Nicolas Sierra. All the staff consider their school leadership a ministry to which they are greatly committed. In May 2018, Peru's largest weekly magazine, *Somos*, ran an article on this *Educacion de Altura* – 'High-level Education' – which referred to the exceptional quality of the school, as well as the altitude of its location!

Editor Ana Nuñez and her photographer spent two days observing and becoming familiar with our operations at the school. She marvelled, 'It is difficult to imagine that a school like this could exist in the village of Curahuasi, in a remote area between Cusco and Abancay, nearly a thousand kilometres from the capital of Lima! Everything in this mountain school has been donated, from the money for the land, the cement for the walls, the musical instruments and even the science lab materials!'

But perhaps the following stories will provide a clearer picture of Colégio Diospi Suyana's true impact on families in crisis, saying so much more than accounting sheets and media reports could ever really convey.

The mother of Ana Maria (class 7) and Fiorela (class 4) suffered from depression and struggled to provide structure and consistency for her children. An understandable repercussion of living in such a chaotic environment, both girls struggled academically. Fiorela did not meet the learning requirements for her class and so was held back to repeat it. After consultation with the local authorities, our social workers Carolin Klett and Debora Centner became involved with the family, as official case workers. They not only assisted with needs identified in the home but were also able to coordinate a network of support through local churches. Now the mother has a steady job and actively participates in parent training opportunities, where she learns alongside others how to navigate the challenges of raising her daughters.

---

[1] Klaus-Dieter John, *God Has Seen Us* (Oxford: Lion, 2019).

Ana Maria and Fiorela are different children now. Not only can one sense that by observing or chatting with them, but they have turned around academically as well. The girls work hard at school and demonstrate good potential for future success.

Anyeli (class 5) and Gino (class 1) have been attending the Colégio since March 2019. The family had learned about the school on the radio, and Anyeli had even prayed that God would make it possible for her to attend.

Anyeli's stepfather was in deep depression owing at least in part to insurmountable debt. The home environment was cold and unfeeling, with marital discord a flag of impending separation. The family's geographic location also posed a challenge. Their simple dwelling was in the village of Trancapata, forty-five minutes away. But our staff was undeterred and welcomed the children with open arms.

The school fees and taxi fares for the children were completely covered through our sponsorship programme. Debora Centner was able to resource school materials and snacks. She, the classroom teachers and the school pastors have developed a close relationship with the family, and this seed has borne fruit. The stepfather is now on medication which allows him to function and maintain a job so that he can provide for his family. Both parents are attending seminars and learning to work as a cohesive team, improving their relationship with each other as well as with their children. Anyeli and Gino love going to school and are also benefiting from extra tutoring to help them catch up with their peers.

And finally, I would like to introduce you to four-year-old Giselle Solange. She attends the kindergarten at Diospi Suyana. Giselle's home life was extremely unstable. Her parents fought violently and often. She herself was a regular recipient of physical and emotional maltreatment. Giselle's father was a day labourer on various construction sites, but his earnings frequently didn't make it home past the bar on the corner. As often occurs with children in families dealing with similar stressors, Giselle experienced a significant lack of supervision, stimulation and demonstration of love. On top of everything else, Giselle had a speech impediment. Her mother's small shop did not bring in enough profit to even consider speech therapy. The family situation continued on a downward spiral until Giselle's father finally left.

In modern Western culture, mention of faith in the face of such difficult circumstances is often met with disdain, if not outright hostility. But in this particular case, it was the Bible, prayer and counselling that made all the difference. Our speech therapist, Nelli Klassen, provided Giselle with excellent treatment, but even more than that, she began to read the Bible with Giselle's mother. It wasn't long before Giselle's mother began attending a local church, learning first-hand about the awesome power of prayer. She began to pray for the healing of her marriage. Two weeks later, her husband returned home and reintegrated into family life. He now spends quality time with Giselle; they even come to the school library each week to read together.

Naturally, progress is often two steps forward and one step back, but the school pastor works alongside the family to support them through the rough patches. In summer 2019, Giselle's mother told Debora Centner, 'We always used to yell at each other and say such hurtful things. Now, if there is a disagreement, I'll go outside. My husband often comes out too and asks for forgiveness. We talk through the problem and come up with a solution together. This would never have happened before!' Her statements were especially noteworthy against the pervasive backdrop of Latin American machismo.

The tales of these three families represent hundreds of others. Colégio Diospi Suyana isn't just about acquiring academic knowledge and passing exams. Here we look to educate and restore hope to the families of our students through a 'wraparound' approach. Our teachers, psychologists and social workers don't just 'talk the talk'; they also work to provide encouragement and comfort in the name of faith.

6

Addicts, party animals and millionaires

A stable family background, a rigorous education and exemplary character – unsurprisingly, these attributes apply to so many of our staff. But not to all. And it's precisely these 'exceptions to the rules', those who have come so far through seemingly insurmountable obstacles, who often fill roles at Diospi Suyana that no one else can. One such walking miracle is Marco. What he lacked in height, he made up for with an abundance of bushy black dreadlocks.

Marco was a pretty easy-going kind of guy, used to making his own rules and doing as he pleased. He played guitar in a band and could often be found on the streets of Abancay. Marco shunned the idea of a career and had no regular work. He much preferred the company of his bandmates over general society. Their time together was often spent getting high on cocaine or weed. Marco could roll a joint in a matter of seconds, his fingers stained from frequent contact with the dried cannabis. After a few drags, Marco would feel like a new man, floating higher and higher above the cares of this world as the drugs coursed through his body. It never lasted long, though, and Marco found himself living from one fix to the next.

Like every 'pothead', Marco needed a regular supply of marijuana and paper. While at his parents' home back in 2009, Marco found a thick book consisting of about a thousand pages of wonderfully fine paper – perfect for rolling and enough to last for weeks! He tore out the back page and got to work. In no time at all, he was inhaling deeply and feeling relaxed. Five and a half pages met a similar fate. Marco reached for another page, but this time, he went to the very front of the book. Instead of ripping out a page, he began to read: 'In the beginning God created the heavens and the earth.'

'Interesting,' mused Marco, scanning the next few lines of text.

Marco later shared that it was as though the book started talking to him. He sat outside on the grass in Abancay and just drank it in, every single word. Each sentence became seared into his mind. When Marco finished reading through the entire Bible a few weeks later, he was no longer the same person as when he started. He knew he was wasting his life and needed help. He desperately wanted forgiveness and purpose.

'God, help me! Set me free!' The cry of Marco's heart was answered more quickly than he could have ever imagined.

From that moment, Marco was freed of his addiction. He never used again. In the New Testament, Marco had read Jesus' words, 'Let anyone who is thirsty come to me and drink. Whoever believes in me, as Scripture has said, rivers of living water will flow from within them' (John 7:37-38). No drug could beat that!

Marco's inner transformation was evident on the outside as well. His friends could see the new joy and light in his eyes. Marco even cut off his dreadlocks to signify his conversion, and he enrolled in a four-year theology course in Lima.

Marco's brother was an alcoholic and his father a radical extremist, and yet they were so impressed by the change they saw in him that they too came to faith in God. While they had never been particularly close before, they soon began to attend church together as a family every Sunday.

In August 2014, I shared my presentation about Diospi Suyana in an auditorium at Abancay University. Approximately two hundred young people were in the audience. Marco was one of them. Immediately after the presentation, Marco came up and introduced himself to me. In December of the same year, this recovered addict and I were signing an employment contract. Since then, Marco has been serving as our itinerant pastor across southern Peru, visiting those who have been patients at Diospi Suyana. He humbly follows in the steps of his Master, showing love to thousands of the poor and despised, predominantly Quechua Indios and Mestizos of the Andes.

In May 2018, Marco sent me photos of a visit he had made to an Indio village. In one, he is holding a tattered Bible, standing next to the simple coffin of a young woman who had lost her battle with cancer. Her relatives and neighbours came to pay their respects and support the family, just as they would in Western secular culture. Most of them were not believers and would not darken the door of any church on Sundays. Still, they stayed and they listened as Marco delivered the eulogy at the *camposanto*, the Spanish word for cemetery that literally means 'holy ground'.

There is something about a cemetery that raises questions – often uncomfortable ones – about the meaning of life and what happens after death. Even those who claim no faith, even mocking believers, are often silenced in this space.

'Was Jesus right when He said that one day we would all have to give account before God? Can this Risen One really forgive our sins and give us eternal life?' These questions in Marco's sermon are equally relevant for the entire world. Our confidence is in the resurrection of Christ. There is no alternative.

I often receive updates from Marco about his work. He is honest about the challenges he faces in his ministry.

'Not everything I experience is a garden of roses,' he admits. 'I really need God's power and presence all the time. Sometimes I experience extremes of heat and cold, sometimes I am left in the rain with no shelter. I eat whatever I am offered. There are times when I cannot find the patients I am looking for. I get discouraged and wonder if my work is pointless. Some of my journeys are dangerous, on narrow roads with reckless drivers. I am constantly praying for God's protection and provision. But with His help, I know that there is no hardship I cannot overcome. I really can do all things through Christ who strengthens me.'[2]

From reefers to ravers, we move on to a Hamburg nightclub where the air is thick enough to slice and the pulsating bass rhythms literally 'rock the house'.

Matthias Rehder was studying natural sciences at university. He was considered a 'bright spark' with loads of potential. His father was a professor of chemistry at the same university. Matthias clearly got his intelligence through both the nature and nurture channels. If that were not enough, Matthias was also good-looking – that enviable combination making him a prime candidate for success in modern Western European society. Two years later, he passed his degree programmes in Maths and Chemistry with distinction.

Matthias had no need for God and looked down on those who used that 'crutch' to get through life. He had not been brought up in a religious home, was neither baptised nor confirmed, and saw no reason to change. He was young, talented, happy, healthy – and managing just fine on his own, thank you very much.

One day, Matthias watched a film about the Thirty Years' War. He picked up a copy of the New Testament afterwards, curious to learn more about the issues that had led to such destruction and bloodshed across Europe 350 years ago. As he read, he was surprised to find that the story of Jesus was presented four times, once in each of the Gospels. Matthias had a copy of the Luther Bible, very old and difficult to read, but he persevered through all 400 pages.

It was 11th November 2011, the beginning of the Carnival season in Hamburg. While the local festivities certainly were not as elaborate as those Cologne is typically known for, it was still a good excuse to go out for a beer in the evening. Twenty-seven-year-old Matthias began chatting with an attractive young

---

[2] See Philippians 4:13.

woman named Jennifer Serec. Their conversation quickly turned to a completely unexpected subject – faith in a personal God.

Matthias had never met anyone quite like Jennifer. As they continued getting to know one another, standing by the dance floor, he could not help but notice how her eyes shone as she shared her experiences of God. She was a university student, completing a course in Social Pedagogy, but she seemed like someone from a different world. He certainly hadn't seen this coming. Two hours later, Matthias and Jennifer were still talking. He was quite taken with her and trying to wrap his brain around the incredible things that she was telling him, things that she so obviously believed with her whole heart. As he fell into bed later that night, he shook his head in bewilderment. Science had provided more than enough answers to the universe. Could there be room for God as well?

Matthias was hooked. Jennifer was clearly someone very special, and besides, he was always up for a good philosophical debate. They continued to see each other and deliberate the finer points of the Christian faith. What was the deal with Jesus Christ? Did he actually rise from the dead? Seriously? Matthias began investigating further on his own as well. He started reading works by famous Oxford professor C S Lewis as well as American author Timothy Keller. Bit by bit, Matthias was learning about this strange way of life. Eventually, he met some believers who invited him to a worship service. There were actually others like Jennifer who loved God and trusted His active involvement in their lives!

Following his probationary teaching, Matthias and Jennifer travelled to visit a Christian community in southern India. It was here that the former agnostic and sceptic surrendered his heart to God. He was baptised in the Indian Ocean on Christmas Day, 2013. He and Jennifer were married the following year.

The young couple certainly did not follow a typical trajectory. In autumn 2017, they began teaching at a mission school in Nepal, a temporary opportunity until permanent teachers could be found. Shortly after starting this ministry, another volunteer told them about Diospi Suyana. They checked out the YouTube video about this 'Hospital of Faith' high in the Andes and simply could not stop thinking about it. Jennifer ordered the first book, *I Have Seen God*,[3] online. She discovered the second, *God Has Seen Us*, on her ailing mother's nightstand when she went home to visit.

Applications began to come in for the teaching slots they had been covering. Their commitment in Nepal was ending. On 2nd January 2019, the small family – which now included son Janne Paul – arrived at Lima Airport. The two educators had grand plans for the Diospi Suyana school. They were certain they were travelling the path God had laid out for them, a journey that started in a nightclub with a young woman unafraid to share her faith.

As we draw to the end of this chapter, I will share just one more story. It begins in southwestern Germany, in the Baden-Württemberg district of Lörrach. There, not far from the *Großer Feldberg*, or 'Great Field Mountain', lies the town of Todtnau. Although this present-day ski resort area has existed for nearly a thousand years, being listed in the records of German Emperor Conrad II in 1025 AD, it maintains a remarkably small population of about five thousand. One of those inhabitants is Dr Georg Steinfurth, an all-around wonder: doctor, entrepreneur, philosopher, part-time scientist – and writer. In the last few years, Dr Steinfurth has amassed huge profits. It would not be a stretch by any means to call this man a millionaire.

Georg was a slim, good-looking guy in high school but had always been more interested in books than girls. Reading was easily his favourite pastime. Some people only read to prep for exams or perhaps when they are bored. Others find reading enjoyable and educational, and it has a profound impact on both their character and their worldview. Books gained enormous

---

[3] Klaus-Dieter John, *I Have Seen God* (Oxford: Lion, 2014).

importance for Georg in 1979, when as a sixteen-year-old, he wrestled with his own humanity and the meaning of life in the wake of the death of a dear friend. The news of Edgar's death hit Georg hard. Wasn't it only two days earlier that they had matched wits over a chess board? And now he was gone?

Four strong men lowered Edgar's coffin into the waiting earth. But what was actually in the box? Human remains of a too-short life? It certainly wasn't 'Edgar' as Georg had known him. What would happen when the body decomposed? Would Edgar's identity be wiped out? Georg pondered these questions, but the answers were elusive. Was there an afterlife? Clever minds have been puzzling over this for millennia.

Georg began to seek answers in literature and history. As soon as he finished lunch each day, he retreated to his bedroom and immersed himself in physics texts and *The Tibetan Book of the Dead*. He explored Indian Sanskrit and parapsychology as well. Finally, he purchased a six-volume series covering the history of philosophy. He spent two years in private study, also consulting other relevant works.

It was 18th April 1981, a day Georg would never forget. The teen was lying on his bed and had just finished the last page of yet another book, his search for meaning concluding in nothingness. 'There is no truth,' he muttered. 'Everything is subjective and nothing really matters.' Georg's descent into existential nihilism left him feeling empty and depressed as he considered what had ultimately become of his friend.

'I AM the Truth.'

Georg quite clearly heard the voice but had no idea where it had come from. He was perplexed but launched into cautious debate anyway. 'No, life is just a cosmic accident. It has no meaning or purpose.'

'I AM the Truth.'

After hearing the voice a second time, Georg remembered years earlier when he had served as an altar boy in the Catholic Church. Didn't the priest use to say something like that about

God? Despite the vast array of books overflowing the shelves in Georg's home, a Bible was remarkably not among them.

The very next day, Georg got a lift into Freiberg and bought a copy of the New Testament. He read it all the way home and was reminded that Jesus was the One who claimed to be the Truth – now he just needed to find out why.

About two weeks later, another strange event occurred. He dreamt of seeing a flock of sheep heading towards his parents' home. A man in a white robe was leading them. The man looked Georg right in the eye and said, 'I am the Good Shepherd. Follow me!'

Georg sensed immediately that he did not belong with this flock. Jesus was for 'good' people, people with noble intentions – not for him. In his dream, Georg ran away as fast as he could but found that he could not escape the sheep, which eventually enfolded him.

George awoke with a start and made a decision that would change the course of his life forever: He would follow the Good Shepherd. He would follow the Truth.

Georg confessed his sins and sought forgiveness from everyone he had wronged. He gave away what little money he had to the poor on the street. He completely turned his life around as he pursued the truth of Christ. Not a typical sequence of events for one preparing for high school graduation exams, but effective nonetheless. On 23rd May 1982, Georg graduated top of his class with multiple additional honours.

So now what? Georg's parents, nominal Catholics, were not enthused when he toyed with the idea of becoming a pastor. Or perhaps teaching should be his path? The newspapers were full of reports that the education job market was saturated and it would be difficult to find a place. Georg prayed and asked God for direction. After all, the Good Shepherd had offered to lead him in his dream – now he needed precisely that.

Before long, Georg came across a *Stern* magazine article featuring an interview with Mother Teresa in which she described her ministry in Calcutta and appealed for doctors to join in service to the sick and dying. Georg took this as the sign he was looking for. He would study medicine so he too could provide compassion and care to the most needy and marginalised in society.

Many young people have the dream of saving the world through medicine, but the required training is nothing short of brutal, and fewer and fewer stay the course during each subsequent academic term. But Georg was no quitter. He stayed true to his calling as a doctor, working at the Freiburg University Clinic and specialising in emergency and palliative care on the oncology and intensive care units. Georg toiled for up to four hundred hours a month to serve the diseased and dying, leaving scarce time for his wife Kerstin and their three little ones.

After careful consideration, the couple determined a change was in order. In 2003, they moved to tiny Todtnau and opened a Christian family practice. But unlike any such centre known at that time, they wanted to include mental health services (counselling and psychotherapy) under the same roof. They named this concept and resulting practice *s'Doc-Hüsli* – a dialectical approximation of 'The Doc's House'.

It was a brilliant idea, and the practice rocketed to success. One office became two, two became four. Additional staff were onboarded and patient numbers increased exponentially. The media got wind of this ground-breaking holistic approach to healthcare. Print and radio reports spread awareness across the country, precipitating even further growth.

In 2016, Georg and his wife, who had managed the practice tirelessly through its progressive stages, were invited to Berlin to receive a prestigious award from Springer Medicine, recognising *s'Doc-Hüsli* as the most innovative German medical practice of the year. This honour could be considered equivalent to an Academy Award in the medical field. The Steinfurths were featured on the front page of the *Ärzte-Zeitung* medical journal and catapulted into the spotlight of German healthcare politics.

From a worldly view, Dr Steinfurth and his wife had 'arrived'. With such popularity, such a platform, such *power*, the world was now their proverbial oyster!

Power is seductive. Most people who have power will fight to keep what they have. Many will seek to grow their sphere of influence and privilege, never being content with the status quo. Money is much the same. There are endless tragic tales of individuals with insatiable appetites who meet their untimely destruction through the endless pursuit of 'more'. Thomas Middelhoff, former head of the Bertelsmann media company, describes such a moral spiralling in his sensational and provoking autobiographical best-seller, *Schuldig* ('Guilty').[4]

But Georg and Kerstin Steinfurth were cut from a different cloth. Following their public accolades and rise to 'stardom', they did a radical 'about face'. They sold their practices and two apartments and donated much of the proceeds to various ministries in Germany as well as to Cubans who had lost everything in Hurricane Irma. After that, they still had €300,000 in their account, waiting for a purpose. They considered buying a house, maybe taking over an old farm. Nothing seemed exactly right. Failing to reach a consensus, they ended up dividing the money into thirds, one-third each for the children, Kerstin and Georg.

Right around this time, someone gave Georg a book for young people about a mission hospital in Peru, titled *Hope in the Land of the Incas*.[5] Georg began to read this incredible tale of faith and wanted to know more.

On 10th May 2016, such an opportunity presented itself. A group of students had invited me to speak at the University of Karlsruhe. The coordinator of the event, Christian van Reensen, was just about to leave Germany to join the Diospi Suyana team in Peru as an IT specialist. He enthusiastically strove to fill the auditorium to capacity, but on the day, only sixty showed up for

---

[4] Thomas Middelhoff, *Schuldig* (Wetzlar: Adeo, 2019).

[5] Janet and Geoff Benge, *Klause-Dieter John: Hope in the Land of the Incas* (Seattle: YWAM, 2015).

my presentation. Georg and Kerstin Steinfurth were two of them. The Diospi Suyana story not only spoke to Georg's heart, but it apparently also spoke to his wallet. Six days later, a donation of €100,000 appeared in the Diospi Suyana bank account.

As a young man, Georg had searched for Truth and found it in the Good Shepherd, Jesus Christ. As a successful doctor, he remained true to his faith. For the Steinfurths, money was simply a tool entrusted to them by God to be used for the needs of the kingdom. This man from Todtnau valued dependency on God over the supposed security of a full bank account.

'Georg, I am very impressed by your unwavering faith in God,' I said to him once during a phone call.

'But Klaus, He has been so faithful to *me*,' he enthused, sharing how his life's journey, however unpredictable, always follows the lead of the Shepherd.

7

Over the mountains with the best news ever

The Diospi Suyana school gives hundreds of children the opportunity for a positive future. The hospital treats and heals thousands of patients each year as well. These are figures to be proud of, but we want to reach out and promote positive change in even more lives. There is really only one way to do that: the media.

Maybe some of you are frowning at this point. General distrust of the media? Aversion to the concepts of faith and marketing used in the same paragraph? A sense of seduction and manipulation of the public? All are completely understandable initial reactions, but I ask you to hear me out.

I am a passionate advocate of the use of media to spread information and assistance. Here are some numbers to explain why reaching a broad audience is so critical.

According to a 2008 report in *El Comercio*, Peru's leading daily newspaper, more than 63 per cent of Peruvian women between fifteen and forty-nine years of age have been victims of physical, mental and/or sexual abuse. But it's not just females who are dealing with maltreatment. In 2015, the State Institute of Statistics (INEI) published the results of a study that found nearly 66 per cent of all adolescents aged between twelve and seventeen had experienced violence in the home. These numbers are staggering.

In the mountain villages of the Andes, violence within the home is strongly correlated with excessive alcohol consumption, which itself is strongly correlated with socioeconomic factors such as unemployment/ underemployment and poverty. Add a lack of education and a culture of superstition and you end up with a perfect storm for producing the disturbing statistics above.

Can a twenty-four-hour radio programme combat such challenges? I believe it can.

To clarify beyond the shadow of a doubt, we at Diospi Suyana are believing Christians. We consider the best news ever to be the gospel of Jesus Christ. According to Oxford atheist Richards Dawkins, our universe is massive, unfeeling and meaningless. Our lives have no purpose. I simply cannot accept that depressing – and baseless – worldview. The Christian faith itself is diametrically opposed to such fatalism. Jesus Christ loved each human being so much that He chose to die on a cross so that we could live. My life was bought with His precious blood – proof of my value and purpose.

People might try to argue that the sacrifice of Jesus two thousand years ago has little bearing on the here and now. That would be a monumental mistake. I would like to call Matthew Parris as my 'chief witness'. Parris is one of the best-known journalists in England, his work appearing in many publications, including *The Times*. He served as a member of Parliament in the House of Commons for many years. And he is a staunch atheist.

On 27th December 2008, *The Times Online* published a rather surprising essay written by Parris. The title was, 'As an atheist, I truly believe Africa needs God'. Bear in mind that Parris knows what he is talking about here, having been born and spent much of his childhood in Africa. He leads with the view that missionaries rather than aid workers are the solution to Africa's greatest problem, defining that problem as overwhelming apathy. He goes on to explain:

Now a confirmed atheist, I've become convinced of the enormous contribution that Christian evangelism makes in Africa: sharply distinct from the work of secular NGOs, government projects and international aid efforts. These alone will not do. Education and training alone will not do. In Africa Christianity changes people's hearts. It brings a spiritual transformation. The rebirth is real. The change is good.[6]

Parris provides an illustration from his childhood:

We had friends who were missionaries, and as a child I often stayed with them; I also stayed, alone with my little brother, in a traditional rural African village. In the city we had working for us Africans who had converted and were strong believers. The Christians were always different. Far from having cowed or confined its converts, their faith appeared to have liberated and relaxed them. There was a liveliness, a curiosity, an engagement with the world – a directness in their dealings with others – that seemed to be missing in traditional African life. They stood tall.[7]

God's love is what allows us to live and breathe. The sins of the past are forgiven, and our present is filled with God's kindness, purpose and care. Our future abounds with eternal hope. This is the message I want people to hear; it is the best news ever. This is why I am a fervent supporter of Christian programming in all forms of modern media.

During our years in Ecuador, my wife and I experienced the impact of local radio stations first-hand. We had always hoped that Diospi Suyana would eventually start its own broadcasts.

---

[6] Matthew Parris, 'As an atheist, I truly believe Africa needs God', *The Times*, 27th December 2008, www.thetimes.co.uk/article/as-an-atheist-i-truly-believe-africa-needs-god-3xj9bm80h8m (accessed 21st February 2024).

[7] Parris, 'As an atheist, I truly believe Africa needs God'.

At first, we were only considering access for the local area around Curahuasi.

In autumn 2011, Diospi Suyana received a significant financial gift earmarked for establishing a radio station. For two long years, the money sat in an account in Germany while we tackled other projects. Our construction team, led by Udo Klemenz, was in the important process of building our Kids' Clubs facility in the middle of Curahuasi. This was followed by the even more ambitious objective of creating a school for six hundred students. The planning, the fundraising, the acquisition of materials and the construction itself – so much to do! Thirty-six months of constant activity left little room for anything else. The media idea would just have to wait.

Put on hold but not forgotten. Every now and then, I would casually eye a space behind the hospital, a semicircular patch situated between the operating theatres and the embankment. With a little imagination, this could be the perfect place to build a radio station. One day, I met with Christian Oswald from our IT department to measure the available area. I carefully noted all the dimensions on a slip of paper, which I placed in my diary. It stayed there for weeks. And then, one day, it was gone.

In June 2013, I had an appointment with notary Nohemi Aparicio to make some amendments to our Peruvian organisational charter and bylaws.

'Ms Aparicio,' I explained pointedly, 'Diospi Suyana is more than medicine and education. We have a message to share and would like to start our own radio station.'

Without missing a beat, she responded, 'Right, then we will also include the goal of a TV station in the statutes.'

The dear woman had clearly misunderstood me.

'No, no – just a radio station. That's all.' Despite my Peruvian passport, my German upbringing demanded accuracy in the details.

'OK, we will include one radio station and one TV station then,' she replied.

Perplexed, I considered her rather adamant proposal. Maybe she was right. All our projects had somehow turned out much more extensive than we initially envisioned – maybe this one would too?

I gave in. 'Fine. We'll put in a TV station as well.'

In the summer of 2014, engineer Johannes Bahr was putting the final touches to the school. Udo Klemenz had returned to Germany for what we thought was the last time. With his current project nearly complete, Johannes began dropping hints about the next.

'Klaus, the school will be done in three months – but I could spend another year here …'

Johannes' 'hints' became less and less subtle – quite uncharacteristic of him – until one day, he finally blurted out, 'When are we going to get started on the broadcast media station?!'

I mumbled some vague response, but by 28th October 2014, I could escape no longer. Cornered at my desk, I grabbed a sheet of paper and a pencil. I began to sketch a preliminary vision of the station, including a generous foyer at the entrance and a press room on the first floor. Of course, we would need offices, a kitchen, toilets, a special room to house the servers …

When done, I waved the piece of paper in his face triumphantly. 'Johannes, here's the first draft – what do you think?'

'That might work,' the young engineer responded dryly. 'I'll get started on the measurements.'

I forwarded our plan to media experts on three continents – Edinburgh, Scotland; Ascunción, Paraguay; and Elkhart, Indiana, USA. All three came back with resounding approval: 'Looks good – go for it!'

8

The email from Sydney

As far as media matters go, I was only planning to 'bake small bread rolls'. For those readers who did not grow up in a family of bakers as I did, I simply mean that I was only thinking basic, small, functional. No grand aspirations here. But that went out the window on 27th March 2015 when I received a surprise email from Sydney, Australia. It popped up on my laptop screen while I was giving a presentation in England and immediately grabbed my attention.

The message was from a man named Chris Welch, who was writing to express interest in assisting with our broadcasting ambitions. Welch was employed as an engineer for TX Australia Limited, the joint venture company responsible for radio and television transmission, marketing and maintenance across all five major mainland metropolitan areas of the continent. His attached CV was impressive, indicating twenty-five years of experience in the field.

All quite remarkable, but it was his next sentence that catapulted our vision to new heights. Welch continued, 'Moreover, I have practical experience with large satellite networks in extensive regions of Asia and the Pacific.'

Later on, as I sat at the desk in my hotel room and reread the email, I couldn't help but wonder if we would be punching above our weight with this guy. He had a wide range of specialist skills and a great deal of experience with satellite broadcasting, and all we had were four alpacas grazing in the grassy space where we had vague dreams of building some kind of mass media station.

I could not bring myself to answer Welch's email that night, but his incredible offer was on my mind as I switched off the light and settled under the bedcovers. I wondered if I would ever meet this man from 'down under', literally half a world away.

To rewind a few years, on 13th January 1996, warm sunshine flooded Australia's east coast. It was an unforgettable day for Chris and Sandi, as the tall satellite technician and his tiny acoustician fiancée were about to say, 'I do!' They were primed for success – a good-looking, healthy couple of high achievers. Chris' starting salary was generous, and before long the family was joyfully expecting some new little additions. The future was looking bright.

In 2001, the Welches moved to Wahroonga, purchasing a home with a pool and garden in the upscale suburb of Sydney. They had no difficulty securing a mortgage for this prime real estate with their current assets. To all intents and purposes, the Welch family had arrived.

It is human nature to strive, to be discontent. We always want more. We look for fulfilment in 'better' – 'bigger', 'faster', 'higher', 'further', etc. Soon one car is not enough. A house soon replaces the apartment we were once so happy to have, and by the time we move in, we are already hoping for a larger one. Maybe this universal longing is indicative of a hole we feel inside, that we are unable to fill ourselves.

So when 2009 came around, it was no surprise that the Welches were ready to sell their lovely bungalow at 26 Leuna Avenue. But no one expected them to move into the much smaller dwelling next door, at 28 Leuna Avenue. Watching the movers carry their worldly possessions fifteen metres from one front door to another, surely anyone would wonder what on earth the Welches were thinking. But this decision had not been a random or a reckless one. Chris and Sandi were acting with deep conviction.

As believing Christians, they had decided they wanted to be ready for anything at any time. If God were to call them to do something special, they did not want to be delayed or deterred by any kind of debt, including a mortgage. For them, freedom came from having less, not more. People with this outlook are indeed a rare breed, and hard to find, whether in a bustling metropolis such as Sydney or the vast Siberian expanses of Russia.

Over the 2014 Easter holidays, Chris and his oldest son, Jake, served on a short-term mission in Cambodia through the US Christian relief organisation Samaritan's Purse, well known across Europe for its Operation Christmas Child shoebox distribution. The two Australians were astounded as they witnessed such widespread human suffering up close.

From the comfort of one's couch, photos of poverty and desperation are easy to dismiss as they flash momentarily across our TV. Uncomfortable? Just change the channel, and the disturbing images disappear.

But in person is quite another experience. There is so much to process and absolutely no escape. The heat; the smells of poor sanitation, sickness and death; countless pitiable figures simply trying to survive – all of this stayed with Jake and Chris. But rather than being overwhelmed with despair, they saw hope. In addition to seeing remarkable efficiency, they were amazed by the love demonstrated by the missionaries as they sought to provide relief from the indescribable suffering. Upon their return home, the Welches resolved to join the ranks of those who are 'doers of the Word'.

They applied to numerous mission organisations. They wrote letters and emails, made phone calls and even had interviews. No matter how many doors they knocked on, none would open. While frustrating, it was also understandable. The Welch family had grown to now include seven children. Financing such a large family would be very expensive, and no mission was either willing or able to make such an investment.

In the summer of 2014, Youth with a Mission (YWAM) released a book about me and my wife. *Hope in the Andes* was written by New Zealanders Janet and Geoff Benge, part of a series targeted at teenage readers. The English language version could be found in family bookcases across North America, Australia and England.

At the beginning of 2015, Sandi was gifted the book by her friend, Lili Wilkinson. 'Sandi, you've got to read this! It is the perfect book for your family!' Lili encouraged.

Most of us are open to a good read, but if we're honest, so many books we are given go straight to the shelf, never to be touched again. We never have time to tackle all the literary recommendations well-meaning friends share. Sandi, mother to half a football team, was certainly no different in this respect.

In March, Lili phoned not once but twice to see how Sandi was getting on with the book, impatient for Sandi to catch her enthusiasm.

'Ermmm, I've not started it yet,' Sandi admitted reluctantly.

Lili wasn't going to let it go. 'You *have* to read this book!'

Several days later, circumstances aligned to support Lili's impassioned endeavour. Sandi developed an ingrown toenail, which required surgery on 23rd March to alleviate the pain. Sandi was now relegated to the couch, essentially 'benched'. All the chores would need to be done by the kids, her loving husband or somebody else – *anybody else*. With so much responsibility taken off her plate, Sandi had to find another way to occupy her time. She heard Lili's voice in her head and reached for her copy of *Hope in the Andes*.

Her three days of 'enforced relaxation' were enough. After skimming the first page, Sandi was drawn in and devoured the stories of answered prayer and God's intervention in far-away Peru. On page 214, the tale became even more exciting – life-changing, in fact. In our interview, author Janet Benge had asked me about upcoming projects. Off the cuff, I had chatted at length about the enormous benefits of having a radio station.

'Chris! CHRIS!' Sandi accosted her husband when he came home from work that evening. 'You've got to check this out – they are going to build a Christian family radio station in Peru, and they are looking for people like you!'

Chris had scarcely glanced at the book before he sent me that email. But things started moving. My packed itinerary in Great Britain meant that I could only shoot back a quick response, promising to be back in touch again later. There really was no hurry; after all, our broadcasting centre didn't even exist!

In 2014, the Australian government mandated that all transmission towers, satellite connections and receivers be checked in preparation for an upgrade, a massive undertaking that would vastly improve the quality of radio and TV broadcasting across the entire continent. To that end, the government had purchased twenty-nine sets of testing equipment, each costing A$250,000. After a virtual army of technicians had satisfactorily completed this mammoth task, the government planned to auction off the used supplies.

Sandi and Chris were torn. If they were ever to work for Diospi Suyana, this equipment would prove very useful. But so far, they had only a brief email from me acknowledging receipt of Chris' CV. That was it.

As the sun rose on 31st March 2015, the Welches had made a decision that would seem premature to some and downright insane to others. They would take a huge risk and bid in the second round of the auction – with their own money. Buoyed by their conviction, they entered their bid on the government auction webpage. The bidding stood at A$25,865 – hardly small change. Seconds later, they were the proud owners of thirteen boxes of telecommunications equipment.

What had they done? This incredible step of faith surely couldn't end well, could it? After all the letters of rejection they had received thus far, did they really think Diospi Suyana would be different? That they would welcome them enthusiastically with open arms, saying, 'Oh, you have seven children? You're just who we have been waiting for!'

Regardless of worldview, faith or any other personal beliefs, most people would agree that what Sandi and Chris had done defied all logic and common sense. But when Christians place their all at God's disposal, fully trusting in Him, they see the Holy Spirit move. God knows our hearts. He tests our motives. When we desire His will above all else, He will guide us along His path, however unconventional it may be.

A week later, on 7th April, Chris picked up the equipment from a storage facility in Sydney. Sandi and the older kids helped him carry the boxes into the living room. The extraordinary amount of gear piled on the carpet was indeed something to behold, and had come at quite a cost, relieving the couple of about A$25,000.

With that task done, Chris and Sandi had a moment to consider the complete absurdity of their actions. Chris went into the kitchen to fetch them each a cup of tea. He was just about to get comfortable on the sofa when his mobile rang. It was almost ten o'clock in the morning. Chris picked up and heard an unfamiliar voice with a foreign accent.

I had returned home to Peru some time earlier and was in the process of sorting through everything that had accumulated during my time in Europe. It was Monday evening, 6th April. I was just planning to leave work when a strange thought bounced into my head – maybe I should try calling that satellite guy from Australia. After all, it had been about ten days since I had received his email. I did a quick time zone check via Google and found that it was already Tuesday on the east coast of Australia, and 10am – not a bad time for a phone call.

'This is Chris Welch; with whom do I have the pleasure of speaking?'

Within less than a minute, we were on the same wavelength, our conversation friendly, detailed and productive. I realised immediately that this technician could expand our broadcasting capabilities far beyond what we had originally dreamed. Our radio programmes would be received not just by the thirty thousand residents of Curahuasi, but likely by thousands, if not millions, of Peruvians across the country.

Chris hung up the phone and looked at his wife. Without a word, both understood what had just happened. God had confirmed and blessed their selfless action. It looked like they would be relocating to South America in the not-too-distant future.

9

Australia

Following this pivotal conversation, Chris and I had frequent communication via email and telephone. People who step out in faith as the Welches had done are an excellent fit for Diospi Suyana. I contemplated Australia on my globe. So far away, but oh so tempting …

The British publisher Lion Hudson released my first book, *I Have Seen God*, at the beginning of 2015, and I soon learned that the Christian book chain Koorong was selling loads of copies. The time was right for the Diospi presentation tour to hit its fifth continent! I rang up one of the Koorong executives and inquired when the weather might be most suitable for a road tour, which of course showed how little I actually knew.

'The weather is always great here,' came the bemused response. 'Come whenever you want!'

On 21st October 2015, I boarded a Singapore Airlines flight from Frankfurt to Sydney via Singapore. I could not wait to meet the Welch family in person! They had taken on the daunting task of arranging the details of this tour, packed with thirty-six presentations and interviews. Upon landing, I picked up a rental car from the airport and drove to the Welches' home, taking good care to drive as prescribed by the laws of the land: on the left!

'Welcome!' The Welch family bid me cross the threshold into the 'organised chaos' of their large family. Sandi was actually expecting their *eighth* child at this time, but wasn't yet showing. I looked around their humble home which radiated warmth and love. Seven children, each as precious as the next, regarded me closely. So *this* was the man from Peru who was about to turn their lives upside down ... We had a thoroughly enjoyable visit together, my first ever introduction to Australian hospitality, and I returned to my hotel rather late in the evening.

On my long-haul trips, I do my best to ignore the jetlag. I force myself to go with whatever the local time is, often jumping in to work immediately. I had no idea what time a European 'should' feel tired after arriving in Australia, but I didn't have time for that indulgence anyway. Rather than dozing in a hotel room, I began the itinerary Chris had set up for me – a radio interview at a studio in Sydney and two more by phone with stations in Brisbane and Melbourne. Because he and Sandi had done all the coordination, Chris often accompanied me on the road to various presentations and meetings. We never ran out of things to talk about in the car, and what he shared with me about his family background was truly amazing.

At the age of sixteen, Chris' father had left England on his own, without so much as a 'goodbye' to his friends and family. He boarded a ship and reached Australia two months later. When World War 2 broke out shortly afterwards, he lied about his age in order to join the military and was subsequently deployed to Palestine. The atrocities of war left their mark on the young man, and he returned to Australia shell-shocked, with what we would likely call post-traumatic stress disorder (PTSD) today.

Listening to such stories, I could not help but wonder if Chris was cut from the same cloth as his father. Chris presented as much more relaxed, not really a 'daredevil'. I could not imagine him making the same choices as his father, and yet he clearly must have inherited comparable courage to take risks.

My three-week adventure on the world's largest island took me through the major metropolitan areas on the east coast. I shared the story of Diospi Suyana with churches, businesses and even care homes. The audience members listened attentively and often appeared captivated by the details of God's provision.

Following my presentation at the Plains Retirement Centre near Brisbane, a gentleman by the name of Neville Tayler approached me.

'Dr John, your story is truly extraordinary,' the nonagenarian proclaimed jovially. 'It's a perfect example of the old adage that the truth is stranger than fiction!'

I nodded. The wise old man had it exactly right. God's ways are sometimes so unexpected, so astonishing, so preposterous even – like what we might read about in a brilliant work of fantasy or even science fiction. But our inability to foresee or comprehend something does not make it any less real.

These are the kinds of encounters that keep me encouraged. Being on the road or on my own in a new city can be exhausting and lonely. But there are rewarding moments along the way that make it all worth it; events so special, they are impossible to forget. Meeting the Berry family is a perfect example.

Gary and Jane Berry live in Melbourne with their children, Sara and Josh. They read *Hope of the Andes* together a few months before my arrival. Ever since, Josh had reminded his mother at least once a week that he wanted to visit Diospi Suyana.

No doubt providentially, on 23rd October, the Berry family heard my interview on the radio.

'Hey, isn't that the doctor from that book?' Jane immediately got online and started searching. If I happened to be in Sydney, the Berry family was more than game to drive to see me. A round trip of a mere eighteen hundred kilometres, but what did that matter when doing something for your children? A once-in-a-lifetime opportunity! Jane and her husband are certainly persistent. After digging a bit, they learned that I would be giving a presentation in Melbourne the following Sunday morning at the German Lutheran church – practically right outside their front door.

Within three short days, the Berrys arranged an additional presentation for that afternoon. They publicised the event via Facebook, and thirty people showed up. It was a pleasant engagement, culminating with a group photo. Everything went well, but the part I will never forget was meeting Josh Berry, aged nine.

Most kids that age are into TV, video games, mobile phones, etc. But Josh had heard that there were 23,000 homeless people in his home territory of Victoria, and he decided he wanted to do something to help. He was determined to give two pairs of socks to anyone without a roof over their head, so he created a long-term plan to acquire and distribute 50,000 pairs of socks. He created his own website: www.2pairseach.com.au and got to work. By September 2023, Josh had collected 40,362 pairs of socks.

How does a child his age come up with something like this?

Josh's parents are Christians. Sure, they have shared the parable of the Good Samaritan with their children many times, underscoring Jesus' call to love and serve others. Josh has heard these words with his whole heart, not just because they were spoken two thousand years ago, but because he sees his parents living them out on a daily basis. Every member of the Berry family is a living testament to the truth that faith in God means love in action.

That aspect of faith is not often highlighted in the media. I suppose such stories just don't sell as well as those involving scandals and other drama, but it would be unfortunate to overlook the enormous potential Christians have to make a positive change in the world. In the Middle Ages, it was often Christians who cared for victims of the Great Plague, at great risk to their own health and well-being. Christians often take responsibility for the welfare of widows and orphans. And even in modern times, Christians minister in prisons, refugee camps and many other places where human suffering can be found – all in the name of sharing God's love, being the hands and feet of Jesus.

In the cut-throat world of competitive business, many consider faith in God little more than a crutch for the weak or those otherwise unable to cope with the realities of life. The outlook of the RFS (Radio Frequency Systems) company in Melbourne was no exception – at least initially.

On Monday 9th September, Chris Welch and I were presenting the vision of Diospi Suyana to a totally secular audience. As the name would suggest, RFS is a telecommunications company. Welch had had a working relationship with them for about twenty years and was well known to the members of our audience. They had heard that this father of seven was about to pick up and move across the globe for some mission project. What on earth was he thinking? Had he lost his mind? They showed up out of sheer curiosity, exchanging smirks and raised eyebrows as we prepared to begin.

I jumped in as I always do – open, honest and straight to the point.

'We believe that with God's help, all things are possible!' I proclaimed. 'But I admit this is sometimes a difficult principle to live by.'

The audience was speechless, hanging on every word we said. When had I ever experienced this level of attention? The atmosphere was electric. Nobody had ever spoken about God in that room before, and here we were, sharing stories of God at work in our present world, a world dominated by stock markets and the individual pursuit of profit. God lives here? Indeed, He does.

People talked about Diospi Suyana for days afterwards. One member of staff who had previously mocked believers changed his tune and had nothing but praises to sing for the work we were doing among the Quechua Indios of the Andes.

Australia is expensive. Extremely expensive. The cost of living is practically daylight robbery. Of course, I was careful with my money, but I did need to eat at least. Bread roll for breakfast, yoghurt for lunch, a small bar of chocolate for an energy boost enabling me to drive another three thousand kilometres – even snacks are so costly in Australia, it's enough to make one lose their appetite! Despite my efforts at frugality, my food was costing me approximately A\$50 each day.

My transportation and accommodation are covered by Diospi Suyana. The financial donations received during a tour usually amount to about ten times more than what is spent. But I always pick up the tab for my own food. Usually, it is not a big deal. But in Australia, it suddenly became one. Based on the exchange rate at that time, I had spent €600 on food in just three weeks. While I was used to paying out of my own pocket, the depths to which I needed to dig here, while spending weeks away from my wife, were really starting to irk me.

On Monday 16th November, I had just returned my rental car and was waiting in the long queue to clear airport security, grateful that my first trip to Australia had gone well. Suddenly, my mobile phone vibrated, indicating receipt of a text message. It was from a lady in leadership at the Life Source Church, where I had presented twice the previous weekend.

'We would like to send some financial support,' I read on the screen. 'Please send us your bank details.'

I phoned the woman and told her where to find the financial information on the Diospi Suyana flier I had left at the church. 'You can transfer your gift to that account, and the money will come safely to Peru,' I assured her.

'No, this time we are not looking to support Diospi Suyana; we want to give to you personally,' she responded amiably.

Before long, the transfer was received in my German bank account. The gift of A$1,000 was almost exactly what I had spent on food during my tour. Nobody had asked about my personal finances, but God knew. And He Himself paid for my hamburgers, muesli and juice – right down to the last penny.

10

A family goes for broke

I landed in Frankfurt on Tuesday 17th November 2015 after twenty-six hours of travelling. Back in cold, dreary Europe at 6.20 in the morning. The next day, I shared the Hospital of Faith story with 230 students in Tübingen, then returned to Wiesbaden the same evening to pack my bags and prepare for my upcoming trip to Timişoara, Romania. I would leave early Saturday morning for Romania, where twenty presentations and interviews had been arranged, down to the last detail, by publisher Casa Cartii. A driver and interpreter would accompany me on my whirlwind tour of this country by the Black Sea.

Looking back, my itinerary was insane, with physical demands that pushed me to the limit. Hopping from one hemisphere to the next, eschewing much-needed sleep, spending long hours on the road – any one of these factors could have been way too much for me. But somehow, they weren't. God gave me strength for each requirement, and I sensed His blessing on both me and my audience in every presentation. This wasn't my tour; it was His.

As stressed as I was, it was nothing compared to what the Welch family was going through, 15,000 kilometres away. They were facing possibly the biggest decision of their lives, the implications of which we could not even begin to fathom. Should they really give up their stability and set out for Peru with their seven – no, make that *eight* – children? No secured income for those few years. No guarantee that any of them would return unscathed. Could they even learn the language? Would they be able to find a comfortable home to accommodate a family of their exceptional size? The questions were endless.

It's easy to make grand plans from the comfort of your own garden, especially when you know no one is likely to hold you accountable for them. Perhaps those ideas make for scintillating conversation at parties, but so often they never materialise because the cost of following through is so dear.

'Of course, one day, I'm going to take a team to the summit of K2 or paddle a canoe up the Nile! And just as soon as I retire, I'll be off to Africa to help the poor!' Joking aside, I cannot tell you how many times people have shared statements such as these with me. There is a massive difference between a fantasy and an actual game plan.

The Welches certainly understood this. Chris and Sandi had been preparing for this moment for years. The move from the larger house to the smaller one, eliminating all debt, the mission to Cambodia, and all the many prayers had brought them to this place of spiritual readiness. And together they said, 'Yes, we'll go!'

Jesus once said that whoever puts his hand to the plough and looks back is not worthy of the kingdom of God (Luke 9:62). He meant we need to take courage and focus on what lies ahead on His path, rather than allowing our own desires and insecurities to get in the way. Most people would find this extreme, but the truth is that we cannot experience the reality of God without radical obedience. Being a Christian is so much more than going to church at Christmas or occasionally giving to charity. A middle-aged lady once assured me that she was religious because whenever she goes on holiday and explores a church as a tourist, she always lights a candle. But is this the kind of faith that can carry us through life?

Following Christ is so much more. God's will is more important than my own desire for comfort, security, luxury, etc. I long with all my heart to be His instrument, for Him to use me in His way to make the world a better place. It is not an easy path, and few choose to walk it. None of us is spared sweat and tears, but we know we are not alone. We start to see God at work and we experience things we never thought possible – even 'walking on water'. I'm sure even an atheist would agree with me here – if you want to walk on water, you need to get out of the boat.[8] And that is the hardest bit. Will God really keep me from going under? Will I sink to the bottom in full view of my friends and family? Will people think I'm crazy? Please understand, I am not advocating random reckless or irresponsible behaviour. But if you know that God is calling you to do something, no matter how strange it might seem or look to others, it's time to move in obedience.

The Welch family understood this well.

It was 28th November, a Saturday, and the Welches were holding a sale in their back garden. Yard sales can be fun when you're just getting rid of clutter. Freeing up space and even making some money from old junk can be quite satisfying. But this event was of a different nature. The Welches weren't just offloading surplus; they were selling their worldly possessions. Kitchen appliances, gardening tools, piles of clothing and linen – even the children were selling many of their toys. This was a real sacrifice.

Chris and Sandi's adrenaline levels were at an all-time high. Inner tension over the magnitude of their decision haunted them in their sleep. They watched with heavy hearts as complete strangers walked away with personal belongings they had once held dear. Their neighbours must have thought they had lost their minds. Were they right?

Chris glanced towards the driveway where a car was just pulling in. An older, bald man got out of the car and made a beeline for Chris, not even glancing at the tables filled with goods for sale. Chris knew instinctively something important was about to happen, and he braced himself in anticipation.

---

[8] The title of a book by John Ortberg (reprint edition; Grand Rapids: Zondervan, 2008).

This stranger who had shown up out of the blue was clearly on a mission. His countenance was quite serious and he seemed to have difficulty finding the right words.

'Mr Welch, I heard about your plans to go to Peru,' the man began in a measured tone. 'I have come to tell you something.'

The man took a deep breath and straightened up. 'Thirty years ago, God called me to mission in Rwanda, but I never went. I simply stayed at home.' The man's eyes began to fill with tears and he swallowed hard. 'I've come to encourage you. Go and do what you have been called to do. Don't lose confidence. God is with you!'

With these few words, the stranger turned back to his car. Chris was stunned. This was the confirmation he needed, at just the right time. There was no doubt that God had spoken to him through this man, through the words of this unknown citizen of Sydney.

11

Romania: an unknown land

I have a tremendous amount of respect for people who refuse to give up on their goals. John Lentink, our sonographer from the Netherlands, is the perfect example. While on a mission trip to Romania, he met a biologist named Viola, who became the love of his life. The couple joined our team in 2011, and soon after, John was knocking at my door.

'Klaus, we need to get the Diospi Suyana book translated into Romanian, and you must go there to share the story!'

I'll admit I was pretty ambivalent. Maybe it was a good idea, maybe not – either way, I didn't move on it. John, on the other hand, wouldn't let it go. He began phoning and emailing old contacts until he met with success – a publishing house in Cluj translated my first book, printed several thousand copies and organised a short speaking tour in the northwestern part of the country.

Prior to this trip, if you had asked me what I thought of Romania, I would not have had anything positive to say. I knew there was some castle in Transylvania where the bloodthirsty Count Dracula had lived, right? Nice. What about those gangs from Romania that robbed whole neighbourhoods in Germany, Austria and Switzerland? Again, not really a selling point for me. Even when discussing football in my youth, the Romanians were generally considered to 'play dirty'. And, of course, who could forget Nicolae Ceauşescu, who ruled the country with an iron fist for nearly a quarter of a century. While he and his wife Elena enjoyed every luxury and indulgence at the expense of the people, thousands of children languished miserably in underfunded state-run institutions. I will never forget the shocking pictures of such squalor broadcast on German TV after the Iron Curtain finally fell.

In short, I viewed Romania as a place of poverty, violence, corruption and suffering. Perfect holiday destination? No, thank you. I carried this prejudice with me as I disembarked from the aircraft on that dreary November day and made my way to the arrivals hall at Timişoara airport. Two Romanians who spoke some English came to pick me up, and darkness fell shortly afterwards. My first official presentation in Romania would be the next morning at a Protestant church called *Biserica Poarta Cerului*, which means 'The Gate of Heaven Church'.

By 9am, the large sanctuary was filled, primarily with young people. Of the 660 seats available, only a few remained vacant in the first row and choir stalls. The Sunday worship 'pre-service' lasted two hours, alternating between prayers and singing. I sat behind the pulpit with three clergy, which gave me the perfect vantage point for people-watching. I could see men and women from all walks of life. What they held in common, however, was great sincerity. They were not here out of a sense of duty, social expectation or habit. Everyone drank in every song, every word, genuinely thirsty for the Living Water.

Just after 11am, it was my turn. Pastor Laurentiu Pascuti translated sentence by sentence. For forty-five minutes, the audience was silent as I clicked through my 150 slides. I wondered if my words were reaching their hearts at all.

When I was finished, Pastor Nelu Filip took the microphone and said, 'We weren't actually planning to take up an offering for Diospi Suyana, but during the presentation, someone handed me a note asking me to pass around the collection plates!'

Ten minutes later, the sum collected was announced. The pastor struggled to maintain his composure as he read out the figure with a trembling voice. The young people in the sanctuary that day, who earned only a fraction of their counterparts in

Western Europe, had just given €2,700 for the work of Diospi Suyana! That is about what ten doctors would earn in Romania in a month!

After three hours, the service was finally drawing to a close. I had the opportunity to shake hands and look into the shining eyes of many who had attended. On that day, I experienced the meaning of the word 'generosity' in a way I never had before. Those Romanian believers were returning to their everyday lives, lives full of struggle and uncertainty. Earlier that month, following the Colectiv nightclub fire, widespread protests and allegations of government corruption had occurred. Prime Minister Victor Ponta and others in leadership had stepped down, and the nation's future was uncertain. And yet, despite their own problems and needs, these people had opened their wallets and given to help people they did not know who lived so far away. Why? God's Spirit was at work at the 'Gate of Heaven'. Although I had not initially been excited about coming to Romania, I was disappointed that my time at the church was coming to an end so quickly.

Five days later, I posted the following report on the Diospi Suyana web page:

> From Bistitra we drove through the snow-covered Carpathian Mountains to Botosani, on the border with Moldova. That evening, I talked about our experiences at Diospi Suyana in a church where 150 people came to listen. I could see in their eyes that they were all engaged. After the pastor's closing remarks, they all stood and sang a final hymn. Just a few bars in, I sensed the passion of the song, even though I did not understand the words. '*Există Dumnezeu!*'

'Hey, Lucian,' I whispered to my interpreter, 'does *Există Dumnezeu* mean "God exists"?'

Lucian nodded. 'The man who wrote it was imprisoned by the Communists for his faith. I remember how chills used to run down my spine when we sang this song back when I was a child.'

The second verse talks about how we are not animals living in shadows, driven only by a whip. We have a spirit and we are free. And our hearts beat for heaven. Then it repeats the affirmation that God really exists!

We moved on to another church, this time in Dumbraveni, where the service was scheduled to start at 5pm, but by 4pm the building was already packed with eight hundred people.

The pastor took the microphone and announced, 'If nobody minds, we'll start a little earlier!'

The songs the choir sang were the kind that could melt the hardest of hearts. The Romanians sang with a fervour I had never encountered in American or European churches.

'Pastor, why do Romanian choirs sing with such intense emotion?' I inquired of an elderly vicar in the town of Vicovu de Sus.

'It's like this, Klaus,' he explained with compassionate authority, 'anyone can sing. But singing like *that* comes only from a changed and sanctified life.'

The phrase 'sanctified life' might be unfamiliar to some readers. It means loving God with all our heart, soul, mind and strength. It means giving Him all of our lives – our time, money, relationships, everything – so that we might be pleasing to Him.

Since 2004, I have been to numerous different countries and shared the story of Diospi Suyana with people of every race and skin colour. I have driven 535,000 kilometres and flown at least two million kilometres (by very conservative estimates!) on just about every size and type of aeroplane. Not one of my previous journeys had the same personal impact as my first eight days in Romania. Now, whenever I think of this country in south-eastern Europe, my heart is full of gratitude, respect and love.

12
The invisible project

The Diospi Suyana Hospital has always been striking to behold, even from the air. Planes have taken razor-sharp photos at 10,000 metres showing the expanse of our campus. And for fans of Google Earth, our large, red-roofed buildings are easy to pick out – just scroll slightly left of Machu Picchu and you can't miss us.

What was not as clearly visible was the fire risk posed by the expanse between those conspicuous red roofs and the suspended ceilings several metres below – space that would allow a fire from the lab or radiology department to whoosh through to the next building in no time at all. Those two thousand square metres equalled one massive safety hazard. I had asked experts to come and survey the situation, but even after careful inspection, none could offer a workable solution. Thank God we were spared a catastrophe.

On 6th April 2015, I was accompanying yet another expert through the dark and dusty heights of the hospital. Jürgen Waltersbacher heads up a surveyor's office in Hambühren and had written to me in December 2014, offering to advise me on matters of fire safety. With no idea of what he actually planned to do, I invited him to Diospi Suyana, where he was now crawling along the planks under the roof, critically examining every nook and cranny, repeatedly probing angles never before seen by the human eye.

'We need to place panels up here!' he announced once he had finished his analysis.

'Panels ...' I repeated the word thoughtfully. Now at an age where I can unashamedly reveal my ignorance about some things, I probed, 'What exactly do you mean by that?'

'They are plates of rock wool, basically a natural product,' Waltersbacher explained patiently. 'They will help in a number of ways – they protect against fire, damp, heat and noise, and you can use the surfaces for extra storage.'

A solution that kills *five* birds with one stone? Waltersbacher had my full attention.

'So what's the damage?' I asked, concerned that the expense would derail our efforts.

'I'll measure the area, work out how many panels you need and email you an estimate.'

Waltersbacher was not a man who rushed into things or made rash decisions – I could see that about him immediately. And yet he was very willing to help us. His son, Jonas, was volunteering at our school for a year, and the family on the whole was very supportive of the Diospi Suyana cause.

Over the course of the next year, our hard-working German friend emailed me not once but thirty-nine times. He spent many long hours calculating all the materials we would need. At the same time, he kept an eye out for special offers that would save Diospi Suyana money. His efforts were rewarded when he found a top-grade product on offer from an Austrian company at a bargain price.

Seven twelve-metre containers would be needed to transport the 63.7 metric tonnes of steel and steel wool from Hamburg to Lima. The cost of the materials alone was about €50,000, marine transport €15,000, and ground transport via seven articulated lorries a further €20,000. In US dollars, the total project cost would be around $100,000 – no small change to a mission like Diospi Suyana. We were going to need a break if this was ever going to work.

The first piece of good news came from Waltersbacher's own office as he promised a five-figure cash injection. The substantial rise in our bank balance a couple weeks later confirmed he was indeed a man of his word. He also offered to come to Curahuasi for two weeks in order to personally supervise the start of the project, adding that he would assume financial responsibility for his own travel. We were off to a great start – but we would still require more help.

I enquired at the DHL Logistics Centre in Hamburg to see if there might be a shipping company willing to assist in our time of need. After all, it was nearly Christmas – generosity increases as the chocolate in our Advent calendars decreases.

A message from Lukas Zurawski, Global Forwarding Manager at DHL, caused me to quite literally jump for joy. He closed his email by confirming that the CMA shipping company had agreed to transport all our project materials free of charge! This generosity extended by a few French managers saved Diospi Suyana a sum of money in the region of €15,000.

At the end of November 2015, Waltersbacher travelled to Hamburg for the loading of the seven shipping containers. He sent impressive photos for me to publish on the Diospi Suyana website. At the beginning of December, the Dublin Express set out to sea. If all went according to plan and no tropical storm sent everything overboard, our precious cargo would arrive in the port of Callao sometime during the first week of January.

Advent was approaching. Naturally, this season feels very different in Peru, where it is 20°C in the shade, a sharp contrast to the European cold. Still, our missionary families kept some beloved traditions, such as exchanging Christmas cookie recipes and decorating something vaguely resembling a Christmas tree.

Despite the generous assistance we had already received, the remaining financial obligation was still more than Diospi Suyana could manage alone, and I began to feel uneasy. In the past, the Peruvian company Neptunia had always covered our ground transportation costs from Lima to Curahuasi and back, a distance of about twelve hundred miles. However, when our long-time ally General Director Carlos Vargas was promoted to the board of the *Andino* Investments Holding, the Neptunia subsidiary was sold off and all support to Diospi Suyana ended abruptly. The cost for one articulated lorry to make the necessary round trip through the mountains would be about US$3,500.

We were going to need *seven* lorries, and that amount of money was enough to make anyone nervous. I needed to take action, no matter how hopeless the situation might seem.

Although I had just returned to Curahuasi from Lima with Tina on 18th December I flew back on 21st December, driven by a vague hope that Carlos Vargas might be around and willing to meet with me. I had sent a short message requesting an appointment, but the email address I had for him was old. I had no idea if he would even receive my message, let alone be open to helping us. I was ecstatic to receive a reply just before boarding my flight. It was short and to the point: 'Meet tomorrow, Tuesday, 3pm.'

Since my wife and I now have Peruvian citizenship, at times we have relaxed our ingrained German habits regarding punctuality – but not when large sums of money are at stake.

Dressed up for the occasion, I sat in the waiting room on Tuesday afternoon, just as Vargas had directed. One of the secretaries approached and informed me that Vargas was in a board meeting and would not be available after all. She offered to pass along a message for me. Inwardly, my whole being collapsed. This couldn't be happening.

'Dear Señorita,' I replied with dismay, 'I have travelled here all the way from Apurímac. I am quite happy to wait until his meeting finishes!'

The young woman regarded me carefully, then invited me to take my seat again.

Beyond the conference room wall of frosted glass, I could make out the shapes of several people engaged in lively conversation, scraps of which occasionally leaked out to the waiting area. Wouldn't it be wonderful if I could share the story of Diospi Suyana with all the executives in that room? I began to pray quietly for God's blessing.

'Mr John, I'm afraid the talks will continue for several more hours,' a smartly dressed woman whom I understood to be Vargas' personal assistant appeared and declared. 'You can tell me what it is that you need.'

I shook my head. 'Señor Vargas wrote to me himself regarding this appointment. I have time and will wait as long as necessary.'

The PA no doubt thought I was as stubborn as a mule. She returned to the conference room. I used the break in conversation to intensify my prayers.

Suddenly she was back. 'OK, Mr John, if you would like to come back at 6pm, Señor Vargas will personally meet with you then.'

I did my best to contain my inner elation, thanked her politely and left the premises.

In a nearby restaurant, I pulled out my laptop and made some adjustments to my presentation slides. My gut feeling was that this meeting was going to be pivotal. So I stayed true to my personal motto: *ora et labora* – 'pray and work'.

'Come in, Klaus!' Vargas greeted me warmly with the same first name familiarity we had enjoyed in the past. To my great delight, two more gentlemen were present at the table. I had been given the privilege of speaking to not one but *three* chief executives – and brothers – at once: Carlos Vargas of *Andino*, Luis Vargas of *Triton* and Enrique Vargas of *Cosmos*. I connected my laptop and began my presentation with a passion fuelled by faith. One of the photos I shared brought me a great deal of personal satisfaction – just five days earlier, Prime Minister Pedro Cateriano had presented Tina and me with the Order of Merit for Distinguished Service during a formal ceremony at the Government Palace. Surely that would grab the attention of my audience!

I concluded my presentation with our current need: 'Seven containers with materials for our hospital will arrive at the docks in just a few days. We need seven articulated lorries to get these materials up to Diospi Suyana.'

'No worries, Klaus,' Vargas assured me. 'You can have your seven trucks.' The brothers nodded in agreement. The conference room was suddenly enveloped in a sense of goodwill, ripe for sacrificial corporate giving.

There was just time for a quick group photo that I published on the Diospi Suyana website later than evening with the caption: 'Breaking News – *Andino* Group Finances Seven Containers!'

As my wife and I lit the candles on our tree at home on Christmas Eve – well, actually, we just plugged in the electric lights, but anyway – I mentally placed the US$24,500 of support we had just been gifted under the evergreen branches. Once again, God had blessed my efforts on behalf of Diospi Suyana. It was time to give Him thanks.

The work began on 3rd March. With each steel panel weighing more than 300 kilograms, they needed to be hoisted up by a special hydraulic crane designed by Oebele de Haan, our workshop manager. From there, strong hands and strong ropes pulled the panels through a hole and into place as people watched in amazement.

This 'invisible project' is one of my absolute favourites from the last fifteen years. It was a true masterpiece, weaving together vision, talent and generosity from a myriad of unexpected sources – from a surveyor named Jürgen Waltersbacher to a French shipping company to the *Andino* conference room in Lima. I have absolutely no doubt that God's hand guided every single step of this project. Since the summer of 2016, Diospi Suyana has not only benefited from two thousand square metres of sorely needed additional storage space, but we have also been able to mitigate the fire hazard in an effective and sustainable manner.

13

The Welch family – jumping without a parachute

It was March 2015, and the time had finally come to commence the building of the media centre. Construction engineer Johannes Bahr moved his office from the school premises to the gatehouse at the back of the hospital grounds. The workers marked out the target site with red tape, and the cacophony of construction could be heard throughout our campus once again. In keeping with the tradition of his predecessor Udo Klemenz, Bahr kept our financial supporters and other interested parties up to date on the work's progress through weekly postings on the Diospi Suyana website. The crew made swift progress, and by the end of the year a subcontractor was already installing a roof on the first floor.

Way over in Australia, the Welch family were keeping a close eye on the developments. The positive reports from Peru strengthened their resolve as they made preparations to join our team on site. Despite the fact that Chris had more than enough to do at his current job and Sandi had her hands full with seven children plus one on the way, they wholeheartedly forged ahead. The Life Source Church in Sydney would be commissioning the Welches and providing some of their financial support. Individual friends and family members pledged monthly donations as well. Despite this backing, only about 5 per cent of the funds needed were covered by the end of February 2016, virtually no increase since Christmas.

Complete dependence on the generosity of others can be a bit disconcerting at times, but to fall this far short of a fiscal target just before departure was downright worrying. As believers, we can talk about God knowing and meeting all our needs, but at the end of the day, the money needs to be in the account. In hard cash.

The Welches stood firm in their resolute refusal to directly solicit donations, despite how little money was trickling in. Instead, they turned to prayer.

'God helps those who help themselves!' so the saying goes. 'If you want something done, do it yourself!' 'Faith in God is fine for church but just isn't practical for real life!' 'God has nothing to do with budgets and deadlines!' We've all heard atheists talk like this, but sometimes people who call themselves Christians don't sound any different.

At the beginning of January, Chris gave his notice at work, and on 26th February he walked out of his office for the last time. In that moment, Chris became unemployed, a situation no one would actually want. Here he was, a man over fifty, no income, a large and growing family to feed – and pledges covering only 5 per cent of the income that the family would need to survive.

Is it faith or is it folly? What do you think?

Several decades ago, my wife and I were preparing to leave our own secure jobs. We had more questions than answers at that point, though we knew the next two weeks would reveal some direction. I remember I had to change my shirt several times each day because of all my nervous sweating. Stress, uncertainty, insomnia, fear – all these words applied to our situation.

Were the Welches feeling the same way as they headed to church two days later? How would they respond to the probing questions and incredulous looks: 'Did you really give up your job?' 'How much support have you raised?' The morning had the potential to be rather uncomfortable.

At Life Source Church, the aisles were bustling with people coming and going between the two morning services. Sandi had just taken the youngest children to Sunday school when Chris heard a familiar voice in the foyer.

'Chris, I need to talk to you. Let's find a quiet corner,' Pastor John Luliano suggested cryptically.

Chris walked over, all ears.

The pastor could hardly contain his excitement as he continued. 'Today two of our members have made the largest financial gift we have ever received! And it is earmarked for you! AUS$98,000!' (This is the equivalent of US$75,000.)

Chris blinked, taking in the miraculous news. If ever there was proof that God would accompany the Welch family in faithfulness and love, surely this was it. When Sandi learned of this new development, she burst into tears. God was with them. He would never let them down. Not here, and certainly not in Peru.

Departing for several years of missionary service is no easy feat. In addition to completely upending one's existing life, emptying one's home, etc, important arrangements need to be made for life 'on the other side'. There are a thousand and one questions to be answered: Where shall we live? When do Spanish lessons start? These details must be settled before procuring airline tickets, of which the Welch family would need ten.

Chris compared prices from several different airlines. Qantas, Australia's largest airline, wanted the questionable sum of AUS$23,000 to fly two adults and eight children – an insufferable dent in the budget of a missionary family just starting out.

'When do you want me in Peru?' Chris had asked me during my visit the previous autumn.

'May 2016 would be the best time,' I answered summarily. 'Our broadcast centre will surely be ready by then.'

What happened that May defies any logical explanation, even to this day. For some reason, Qantas offered a 55 per cent discount on flights to Peru. Of course, they had never heard of this family of ten waiting anxiously on hot coals, or rather, packed suitcases. Surely, they were just trying to attract tourists from Australia, using the opportunity to visit Machu Picchu as a selling point ...

On 31st May 2016, the entire Welch family boarded the half-empty jumbo jet and flew east over the expanse of the Pacific, crossing the International Date Line and gaining an extra day, as one might say. They were able to stretch out comfortably in their seats, buoyant in the knowledge that they had saved AUS$13,000. After a stopover in Santiago, they landed in Lima that evening. No parachute required.

14
Carabayllo

The weekend was almost here! It was Friday afternoon, 31st July 2015, and I was very much looking forward to two days off. As always, I was struggling with fatigue as I sat at my computer answering emails.

I was interrupted by a knock at the door. I answered to find a Peruvian man and his girlfriend who had stopped by to say hello. I didn't know them and was not in the mood for small talk, so I tried to draw the conversation to a close as quickly and politely as possible. Twenty minutes later, I wished my unexpected guests on their way.

'By the way, I am an estate agent for properties in Lima,' the man announced, completely at random.

What? What did he just say? He had my full attention in an instant. For years, we had been discussing the benefits of having a guesthouse in Lima. Had the time now come to create a base for Diospi Suyana in the capital?

'Where could we find an affordable place in Lima?' I asked with clear interest.

'In Carabayllo!' was his reply.

I thanked him for the information, shook his hand and bid the couple farewell. As soon as they had gone, I jumped on my computer to research this unfamiliar district. The fact that I had never heard of it was surprising, given that I had travelled to Lima on Diospi business more than three hundred times since 2003. Gazing at the map on my screen, I located Carabayllo to the north, beyond the 'slum belt' that circles the capital. I expected that the location would not work for us; nevertheless, I mentally associated Carabayllo with our future guesthouse from that point on.

I was in Lima the following week. On Tuesday 4th August, I was standing on a street corner in the Miraflores district, considering what to do next. Usually when I visit the City of Kings, as Lima is sometimes called, my schedule is so jam-packed I can barely get through everything. But on this particular occasion, I actually had ninety minutes of free time. How could I make good use of this rare gift? I prayed for God to direct my steps. At that exact moment, a bus pulled up to the kerb, a large sign in the window indicating its destination: CARABAYLLO. I recalled my recent conversation with the young estate agent. I pray every morning and evening, and before meals, but not typically on busy city street corners. In all the time I have spent in Lima, I have never once noticed a bus heading for Carabayllo.

I took the hint. I would actively pursue the acquisition of a guesthouse.

Half an hour later, I was sitting in the office of Guido del Castillo, grateful to find that he was available to meet with me. Del Castillo was a mine owner, over eighty years old, and he had already done so much for Diospi Suyana. He had helped us with contacts for both business and the press, and his monetary and material donations topped the six-figure mark.

I shook his hand respectfully and got straight to the point. 'We want a guesthouse in Lima for Diospi Suyana – we just don't know where to start looking!'

'That's a superb idea!' Del Castillo's face lit up and he summoned his employees. 'Everybody, come here! Dr John wants a guesthouse for his hospital and he needs our help!'

Within seconds, a first-class taskforce had assembled around the table. Del Castillo, several of his staff and I spent about thirty minutes brainstorming possible locations, trustworthy agents and financial considerations. I left feeling substantially more informed and prepared to go forward.

The following Wednesday, I called on Maureen and Aileen Moncur, two sisters who ran a reputable estate agency in the Molina district and who had been recommended to me by Del Castillo's team. We settled in the lounge and I began to explain the meaning of 'Diospi Suyana'. I was, of course, hoping to share my passion for our mission and that they might, as a result, see their way clear to substantially lowering their fees for a good cause.

The congenial pair immediately recalled having seen or heard a report about the hospital at some point. 'We will help you find the right place,' Maureen assured me. 'It's a good time to buy – the real estate market has recently turned and you'll find prices are much more reasonable.' I was oblivious to these convenient facts – but God wasn't. Once again, His timing was impeccable. He had brought me to the right place at the right time, and I soared to cloud nine.

Our quest took two months and involved four estate agents. I viewed a total of forty-six properties across seven districts. Udo Klemenz flew in from Germany to lend his wealth of experience to our mission. We became very methodical in our approach. On one occasion, we asked a taxi driver to take us at a 'normal' speed all the way from the southernmost district of Lima to the airport, just so we could time the ride to the minute.

The Moncur sisters proved to be both competent and dedicated. When we were about to buy a particular house situated on a hillside, they strongly advised against it, even though they would have made a substantial commission from the sale. They were genuinely interested and supportive of our cause. We had been on a first-name basis for quite a while, and as time went on we found our conversations more frequently transcending the limits of real estate to include more personal topics.

One day, I was out in the pick-up truck with Maureen, heading to view yet another house. The conversation naturally turned to God and she began to share some of her own experiences.

'Klaus, I was always sceptical so I had nothing to do with God,' she began, 'but then my family had a huge crisis. My sister Aileen's husband took off, then tried to get legal custody of their son. We were all in a panic and had no idea what to do!'

I looked over at Maureen. The anguish of that terrible time was etched on her face, even still.

'I was so desperate. One day I was sitting in my car, feeling totally helpless and heartbroken. I just cried out in the empty space of my car, "God, if You are there, please help my sister now!" At that exact moment, my phone rang. It was Aileen. I could hear the joy in her voice right away. She was calling to tell me that she had just received a letter from the court, informing her that the judge had ruled in her favour. She would keep her child!'

At the end of September, Tina accompanied me to Lima. She had her own lengthy to-do list, but planned to join the house-hunting expedition scheduled for the 24th. As we stepped over the threshold of an inviting corner abode in the Surco district, we both knew we'd finally found 'the one'.

The Estudio Olaechea legal firm supported us through the procurement process, which went on for several weeks. Three solicitors were involved with setting up contacts, drafting documents and representing us in meetings with the sellers, and they very kindly did the work for free. I was very impressed with the final sales contract – they had carefully gone over every sentence on each of the thirty-five pages in order to ensure that it was as secure as possible for us.

Before Christmas 2015, painters were already hard at work inside the house, under the close supervision of Johannes Bahr, which contributed considerably to the high standard of decorating completed. Both interior and exterior walls were given a fresh coat of paint. The woodwork shone like new. All six bathrooms were restored or replaced entirely. The building contractor refused payment. For weeks, he slept on a mattress on the floor, drafting renovation plans by the dim light of a single desk lamp bulb. His efforts have been lauded by every guest we have ever had. In March 2016, the guesthouse officially opened.

In its first seven years of operation, five thousand guests stayed at 343 *Jirón Enrique Salazar Barreto*. Our guests are always extremely complimentary, and, I have to say, whenever I step into the hallway there, it almost feels like home.

Our guesthouse offers numerous amenities. The address is in a good area of southern Lima. Police cars patrol the street several times each night, a critical security when living in a South American metropolis. The house is just minutes from the city tram, a cheap and fast means of getting to the heart of Lima. The layout of the rooms is ideal, and with a total of fifteen beds, we can accommodate as many as three families simultaneously. The wooden floors and ceilings add to the charm of the property, and there are several parks nearby for relaxation and recreation. My favourite part, though, is that while the house looks quite small and modest from the outside, the inside is an expansive 420 square metres.

A Peruvian couple manage the guesthouse and run important errands for us in Lima. Our base in the capital city is indeed heaven-sent and yet another special chapter in the history of Diospi Suyana. And it all started with a conversation I didn't want to have and a one-off prayer on a Miraflores street corner when house prices just happened to be plummeting. God is good.

15

On air at last

It was just after 2pm on 10th February 2015. We were gathered in my office to troubleshoot and determine our next steps, a 'meeting of the minds' consisting of: American radio engineer Tim Zook, civil engineer Johannes Bahr, head of logistics Agustin Landeras, and myself. If the radio antenna were to be placed on the hospital grounds, we would first need to ensure it would not interfere with any medical equipment. So, radio test – good idea. Next question – how do we do this?

Around 3pm, Agustin reached out to Rosell Ugarte, the owner of a local radio station. Without offering any other details, Agustin invited the man to the hospital to discuss a matter of importance.

Good thing Agustin hadn't let the cat out of the bag just yet. We were hoping against all hope that Ugarte would let us borrow his transistor for a while. This was a huge favour to ask, and it was extremely unlikely that he or anyone else would agree to such a request. We each took a turn to pray. And then we waited.

About an hour and a half later, Ugarte joined us at the hospital.

'Could we set up some of your broadcasting equipment here tonight?' Agustin asked. 'We would like to run some tests.'

'Absolutely not,' Ugarte replied, shaking his head in disbelief at such a preposterous appeal.

Nobody could blame him. But as the conversation continued, Ugarte suddenly had a change of heart. He called an antenna expert from Cusco on his mobile. The technician grabbed a taxi and immediately began the two-and-a-half-hour journey through the mountains to Curahuasi.

At about quarter to seven, the technician arrived and set straight to work. Ugarte's radio station was located in an open field, a good three hundred metres from the city cemetery. Darkness had long since fallen on Curahuasi and it was beginning to drizzle, but the technician scaled the massive tower to retrieve the necessary components. Less than an hour later, we were back at the hospital, watching the technician affix the transmitter to the top of a lamppost.

'It's all hooked up,' he called. 'You can switch it on!'

We tested everything we could think of. Dr Susen Dreβler ran an EKG in the operating theatre and started up a ventilator. Dr Marlen Luckow trialled her instruments in the dental clinic while Dr Ursula Buck checked the laser and ultrasound devices in Ophthalmology. In Radiology, X-ray technician Dorle Breitenbucher conducted a CT scan – of a water bottle. Everything worked perfectly, as our ad hoc lamppost radio blared music into the night sky.

An hour later, we posed in front of the lamppost for a group photo, commemorating the 'birth' of Radio Diospi Suyana.

Perhaps our jubilation that misty evening was premature. We did not yet have a radio licence, and operating without one was a criminal offence, punishable by imprisonment.

Unfortunately, all the frequencies allocated to Curahuasi had long since been claimed. I put out feelers to see if anyone was willing to sell an individual licence. This experience was something of a nightmare that haunts me to this day. One of my failed attempts led me to *TV Solar* in Abancay. The owner, Hernán Farfán, had acquired a frequency for our district but was not using it. After sharing the Diospi Suyana presentation with him, Farfán proposed that we install all the necessary equipment at Diospi Suyana's expense, then we would be permitted to share the programme time with *Solar*. This would mean that our Christian family content would be available for just a few hours each day, and the rest of the time there would be a mishmash of secular commercialism, complete with beer adverts and foul language. Not an acceptable solution by any means. I drove back to Curahuasi in a cloud of despondency.

The next 'strike' came via a shady soul who offered to rent us a frequency for US$25,000 a year. Not only was the charge exorbitant, but we would also be left with nothing once the contract ended. I declined this option as well. In the midst of the mess, I asked God to intervene. And of course, He did. Quickly.

On 29th March 2016, Hugo Orosco was sitting in my office. The gregarious Peruvian broadcaster had heard about our plight and wanted to help – not entirely altruistically, as it soon turned out. Orosco was a businessman. While some deal in wood, cars or vegetables, my unexpected guest's commodity of choice was radio airspace. He made his living off these lucrative transactions.

'Señor Orosco, before we talk business, allow me to show you who we are and what we do.'

Forty-five minutes flew by and Orosco was clearly moved by what he heard and saw, captivated by the passion and sacrifice involved in the Diospi Suyana story.

Orosco hugged me and thanked me profusely for what Diospi Suyana had done for the people of his country in the areas of education and healthcare.

'I will sell you the frequency for US$20,000!'

Compared to my last experience, this offer sounded fantastic. I shook his hand to accept, and a heavy burden fell from my shoulders.

Our next hurdle was to find skilled people to run the programme. In the months before, I had met with Doris Manco several times in Lima. This dynamic lady had served as the commercial manager at *Pacifico Radio* for ten years. She had become acquainted with Diospi Suyana back in 2007, when she filmed a forty-minute television report covering the opening of our hospital.

We didn't have much to offer her. Our volunteers from abroad receive no salary at all, and the Peruvian members of our team are paid well below the usual market rate. Working for Diospi Suyana comes at no small personal cost but leads to a huge community impact despite our limited resources. When Doris agreed to join us, I breathed a sigh of gratitude and relief.

Jesus Hertado was next to come on board. He had fifteen years of experience as a radio and TV producer. As it so happened, he also spoke fluent German, having completed a course on room acoustics in Germany.

Doris had many contacts in the industry and diligently reached out to expand our team. Carlos Aymituma had worked for nearly twenty years as a television producer and cameraman, but this family man had reservations about moving to the mountains and taking a massive pay cut.

'Do you need this man for Diospi Suyana's broadcast work?' a friend asked Doris at church one day.

'Absolutely,' came her reply. 'But the cost of moving house all the way to the mountains is probably too much for him.'

'Don't worry about it,' her friend reassured her. 'I'll pay for the plane tickets – for Carlos, his wife and their three children.'

Doris' friend kept her word and transferred the money for a family she had never even met. Learning of this generosity was the turning point for the Aymituma family. They took the leap from their familiar urban home in the capital to start an adventure 2,650 metres above sea level in Curahuasi.

José Sáenz migrated to Diospi Suyana from northern Peru. He had just completed his studies in mass communication and was eager to apply his newly acquired knowledge.

From 31st May, Chris Welch was our own resident satellite expert. When Radio Diospi Suyana went on air on 19th July, there were a few hiccups, yet another important milestone had been reached.

At the end of August, on a bright and sunny day which also happened to be the ninth anniversary of the hospital itself, we celebrated the kick-off of our media presence on the lawn in front of the broadcast centre. Long-time First Lady of Peru Pilar Nores joined us for our ceremony, full of spoken tributes and musical performances. Before four hundred guests, I expressed my gratitude to Johannes Bahr for his excellent work and the successful completion of this mammoth task. Pilar Nores cut the red ribbon at about 6pm, and Radio Diospi Suyana was officially open. The end of the festivities marked our beginning. The five-person crew aspired to a long-term goal of broadcasting Diospi Suyana programming via satellite to the far reaches of the country. For a small team, we had big plans.

16

Predicament in Poltocsa

Each journey through the mountains was an exhausting nine hours, a round trip of nearly three hundred miles. One hairpin turn followed another, churning our stomachs. We made the trip from Curahuasi to Andahuaylas five times in pursuit of the right location for our antenna. We finally found the perfect spot, atop a large hill overlooking the town. The property belonged to the Carreño family. They had been willing to rent out some of their land in the past, but had never before agreed to sell a single plot. After reading *I Have Seen God* and hearing the story from me personally when I visited their home, however, the Carreño family were willing to make an exception. More precisely, Señor Carreño, a devout Catholic and former priest, made a unilateral decision to support our work, exhorting his family, 'God is with the people of Diospi Suyana!' The ninety-one-year-old patriarch picked up his pen and signed to close the sale at the local notary's office.

The story of Diospi Suyana is full of trials and hardships, but we have always managed to persevere. We officially took possession of the property and started making plans for the erection of the transmission tower. But then, out of the blue, we were met with fierce resistance from a small village called Poltocsa, which consisted of maybe 350 mud huts about half a mile from our projected tower site. Approximately seven hundred adults and 2,300 children lived in this poor community. Ironically, there were already six aerial towers already on the mountain. They had been there for years. Why was the addition of one more causing such an uproar?

'The radio waves are changing the climate,' some said. 'Our children will be born deformed,' said others. 'The mountain makes scary noises at night!' The Quechua are a superstitious people, afraid of dark forces, including Apu, the malevolent deity of the mountain. 'Will Mother Earth, Pacha Mama, approve of a seventh tower? Why was it hailing the other day? She must be angry!' To outsiders such as ourselves, this belief system was both perplexing and extremely frustrating.

Doris Marco and I travelled to Poltocsa four more times in efforts to allay their fears. We scheduled community briefings but hardly anyone showed up. We went door to door, collecting signatures in support of our tower and proselytising anyone we met along the way. By 10pm that Saturday night we had collected 268 signatures. Would that be enough? Physically and emotionally exhausted, we collapsed into our hotel beds.

The town hall meeting was scheduled to begin at 7am on Sunday 17th February. Please excuse the military jargon, but this was *the* pivotal battle and it wasn't looking good for us. A quorum of 175 was required to proceed, so we were delayed another hour waiting for more people to arrive. We stood outside in a schoolyard where the mayor had made it virtually impossible for me to share the Diospi Suyana story. If we had been permitted to use the school auditorium, we could have easily presented our work and the community benefits of our radio in peace and quiet.

One after another, villagers took to the floor to condemn our plans. Doris, José and I had no other option but to endure the barrage of hostilities. The mayor made no effort to hide his contempt for us. He orchestrated the meeting in such a way as to assure a negative outcome. It became increasingly clear that all our efforts had been in vain. Those countless hours of driving on dark and dangerous roads, all for nought.

More villagers arrived, and we finally had the legal minimum to begin. We realised that if the vote were taken right then, we would be standing all alone. The people were afraid of their own elected officials. They feared that if they sided with Diospi Suyana, the water for their fields would be cut off. We had heard many such concerns over the previous week.

My mouth had long since gone dry. Had all our prayers for God's provision been in vain? That very morning, had I not sent out an emergency appeal to the prayer warriors of Diospi Suyana? Where were the Christians of Poltocsa who had promised to help us? Only a few people had dared to speak up on our behalf at all, and even then, did so without the bold conviction we so desperately needed.

Finally, the *Alcade* invited me to make my case. What could I possibly say?

'Doris, while I'm talking, you pray!'

Doris nodded. She had of course already been praying silently through this entire ordeal.

I didn't have much time. I jumped right in, telling the crowd about my childhood and my dream of becoming a missionary doctor to the poor. I talked about Tina, who had actually provided medical treatment to some of those in attendance.

'We are here to help you,' I called out, projecting as much as possible in the absence of a microphone. 'We aren't here to exploit you or make a profit. We want to alleviate pain and bring healing.'

I shared stories of some of the suffering I had seen since coming to Peru. 'The radio will enable people to learn more about how Diospi Suyana can help them, what services are offered and which doctors are available!'

When I was finished, a few more villagers had their say. Most were vehemently against Diospi Suyana.

Just before the vote, I was allowed to address the assembly one last time. 'Dear people of Poltocsa, the decision is entirely yours. I urge you to follow your heart and not be swayed by what others here are telling you!'

The mayor explained how voting would work. All those against our aerial tower would line up on the left. All those in favour would line up on the right. After hearing all the combativity of the last several hours, we knew how this would go. Our plans would be blocked and we would be forced to leave. But at least we would have closure. Better a sad end than endless sadness, as the saying goes – right?

As soon as the highest-ranking official raised his hand, all the people flocked to his side. The *right* side. The crowd stretched across the entire schoolyard to the opposite wall. The image was striking, the vote unmistakable. We could hardly believe what we were seeing. Nobody stood on the left – not even one of the presumed opponents who had so eloquently lambasted us just minutes before. The result: 108 votes for Diospi Suyana; seventy-two abstentions. Not a single vote against.

An overwhelming victory for reason over fear and superstition, antagonism and intimidation. Doris, José and I all wiped our eyes. All the prayers along the way had not been in vain after all.

At the conclusion of the four-hour assembly, each of the 180 participants was required to sign the meeting minutes, waiting their turn under the blazing sun. I was one of the last to sign. I have never been so thrilled to add my signature to such a beautiful document!

Back at the hotel, I drafted a quick update for our website, then the three of us hit the road, heading home to Curahuasi. Four taxing hours through the mountains, but we were riding high on our triumphant victory!

17

Exercise is good for you – get those pensioners up off the couch!

On 14th March 2014, the Diospi Suyana family formally bade farewell to Barbara and Udo Klemenz. As the couple stood on the stage of our auditorium, eight hundred guests rose to their feet to applaud their incredible contribution. Udo had voluntarily led the construction of the main hospital, the auxiliary dental and optometry clinics, the Kids' Club house and the school. In the glow of a blue spotlight, Barbara proudly held up a wooden motorbike I had just presented to them with the words, 'A motorbike for you so that you can come back quickly when we need you!' It was a joke, of course. Their retirement was well deserved and long overdue. The Klemenzes boarded their plane for the umpteenth time and headed home to Germany.

In 2015, the young engineer Johannes Bahr stepped into the breach and, as already mentioned, headed up the construction of our broadcast station. When this project was completed, he and his wife Angela relocated to Lima and resumed a normal, professional life.

A year and a half after leaving Diospi Suyana, Udo and Barbara did a radio interview with the German Christian broadcaster ERF Media. At the end of the interview, presenter Rolf-Dieter Weidemann asked the couple if they would ever undertake such a mission again? What he really meant was, if they could go back in time, would they make the same choices?

Without hesitation, Udo and Barbara answered with a resounding, 'Absolutely!'

Far away in Peru, I listened to this dialogue with delight. I saw a window of opportunity and decided to jump. While I understood the intended context of the Klemenzes' response, I confess I deliberately interpreted it a bit more freely to suit my own purposes. The hospital was about to add an additional floor and I needed a construction manager.

On 1st March 2016, I was back in Europe and decided to pay the Klemenz family a visit. Having no patience for chit-chat, I cut right to the chase. The three of us quickly reached an agreement. The compensation would be zero euros, as usual. This rate had always worked for us before. And why put things off? In order to commence construction in conjunction with the dry season, an April departure seemed prudent. The Klemenzes are always receptive to logic. In a nutshell, our plan was to have the roof down in May and back up again by November – a thoroughly ambitious undertaking. Not to mention that patient care would be continuing as usual on the ground floor. Upstairs the jackhammer, downstairs the quiet of the operating theatre. Upstairs the thick coating of dust and construction debris, downstairs the quintessential cleanliness expected in a hospital setting.

On 13th May, Udo wrote his first construction report and we were back in the groove. As far as I was concerned, that was a good thing! Why should a pensioner be stuck at home, bored on the couch? One can only feed the birds in the park so much anyway. Wouldn't we rather do a little construction work onsite and clean the rust off the joints as we climb the stairs? Eight hours a day for fifteen months in the good, clean air – who could ask for more? This was the fifth major project for the Klemenz family and it would be the 'last hurrah' of their working lives. The very last one. Word of honour!

18

A man from Baden-Württemberg surrenders in the Ecuadorian rainforest

Each new chapter at Diospi Suyana is preceded by a most remarkable series of events that can only be described as breathtaking. This was the case when Udo Klemenz miraculously came on board just as we needed a construction manager to turn our dream of a hospital into a reality. While our school was being built, senior secondary schoolmaster Christian Bigalke 'just happened' to wander into one of my presentations in the Ruhr Area of Germany. He caught the spark and ran Colégio Diospi Suyana with his wife, Verena, for eight years. The Welch Family, halfway across the world in Sydney, Australia, read a book for teens – and suddenly our modest plans for a local radio station exploded beyond our wildest imagination. Even non-Christians are amazed at these incredible happenings. But for the faithful on the front lines, they are continuous confirmation that God is in control and holds every thread in this tapestry of life. He is indeed the Master Weaver, and Master Mind, of Diospi Suyana.

This next instalment is no exception. Prepare to be blown away!

It was a Sunday evening. I was visiting with family friends in Curahuasi, sitting in the living room with a pen and paper, recording the most amazing story. As I filled my sheet of paper,

I was handed another. This too was covered with bullet points in no time at all. When I reached the end of a fifth page, I downed what remained of my lemonade, jumped in my car and drove home as fast as I could. I had to share this incredible story with the world, a bizarre family saga with a beautiful outcome.

Elba Cevallo felt the unrelenting hopelessness of her situation. Her husband had abandoned her and their six children, a fate that is repeated a thousand times a day in South America. The thirty-two-year-old Ecuadorian packed up her brood and few belongings and boarded a bus towards a new life in the colourful coastal city of Guayaquil. Perhaps she could find employment there. Sure, the pay would not be lavish for her as an unskilled woman from the countryside, but perhaps it would be just enough to enable her family to survive.

Elba found shelter in a slum, but paid work remained elusive. With no money, the family struggled for bare existence. There were no social services or rich relatives to come to their aid. Elba was drowning in a pit of despair. There was no way out.

'Mama, where are we going?' The children looked up at their mother questioningly. Elba remained silent, her eyes moist and mouth tight with resolve. Their path through the city came to an end on a busy bridge. The children, five girls and one boy, could not fathom why Elba had brought them to this place. No one had ever taught them what 'extended suicide' meant. They were far too young to understand their mother's torment and the tragic impact it was about to have on them all.

Elba's face turned ashen. She and the children peered over the bridge railing into the depths below and shuddered.

'Mama, what's wrong with you? Let's get away from here!'

Not a word escaped Elba's lips. All she had to do was jerk herself up and pin six little pairs of hands to herself with both arms. Her desperation would give her the courage needed to end this nightmare for herself and her beloved babies. One last moment, then the plunge into darkness, and the agony would finally be over.

'Go on, JUMP!' a voice in Elba's head commanded menacingly. 'That's why you're here. Get on with it!'

Elba looked at the small figures by her side, each child's face more precious than the next. Perhaps it was maternal instinct, perhaps a vague hope of a miracle, but something pulled Elba back from the brink that day. Without explanation, Elba led her children away from the bridge. They wandered aimlessly through the city streets until they reached a nearby park.

Elba suddenly heard music – a hymn. Instinctively, she turned to her left and saw a group of people singing. She wondered what they were doing – she had never encountered street evangelists before. The singing stopped and a young man stepped forward to speak.

'If you are at the end of your rope,' he entreated in a steady voice, 'call out to God in your time of need. There is no other answer to your troubles, not even suicide!'

Elba was stunned. How could it be that this stranger knew her story? Of course, he didn't. He was preaching to the small audience as the Holy Spirit led. But for the first time, Elba felt seen. Slowly, children in tow, Elba approached this group of evangelists who would likely have elicited little more than a passing smile from most Europeans.

God. Did He even exist? Elba was unsure, but the seed of hope was planted. Would this God actually care for *her*, a destitute mother of six?

On that afternoon in 1962, Elba took God's proffered hand and held tight. Many might dismiss such conversions as 'superficial', or perhaps as a 'drug' that helps people deny their misery for a little while, not as anything yielding real change, and certainly no permanent cure for pain and hunger. But this young Ecuadorian woman felt God's love all around her, holding her close. She saw that He was truly the Father of widows and orphans. God heard Elba's prayers and provided for her and her family in very tangible and practical ways – food on the table, schooling for the children, a roof over their heads. Elba never imagined she herself could experience such love and life that day on the bridge, ever grateful to the One who saved her.

Elba went on to found a church community in Guayaquil that today has more than two hundred members. Her children all became committed believers and now live in Ecuador and Europe. It was one of her grandchildren, forty-one-year-old Rebecca, who shared this incredible tale. Rebecca would not have been sitting across from me in Curahuasi that day had Elba ended her story on the bridge so many years before.

Scene change: Daniel Müller was born in Eberbach, Baden-Württemberg, in 1977. His parents were committed believers and so he was raised in a home of faith. He did not doubt that God existed, but he had a hard time swallowing the biblical claims of Him as sovereign Lord. Daniel rebelled against the idea that anyone or anything, even God, could tell him what to do. He wanted to be free to make his own decisions, without interference from the 'Almighty'.

Daniel's parents run a bookshop in Aglasterhausen; they have done so for many years. Betty Gabriel lives right next door to that bookshop. Betty is from Ecuador and is one of Elba's five daughters who came so close to being a casualty of her mother's torment on that fateful day. Betty and her German husband are Christians, and Betty had often spoken to Daniel of her home country, thousands of miles away on the equator.

Daniel had finished school and was ready to explore the world. His parents knew two men from their church circle who were travelling to Ecuador to establish a Christian care home for children. They gave Daniel permission to join these men on their mission.

Their time in the small Andean country was a fiasco. The dream project never got off the ground. One of the men had an affair, and his marriage subsequently fell apart. The other man found the task too much for one and gave up as well. Daniel was back in Germany within a month. Maybe there was a God, but Daniel had certainly had enough of 'Christians' – hypocrites, gossips and worse.

A year later, Daniel was legally an adult and decided to return to Ecuador to see more of the yellow beaches and volcanos that he had admired previously. Betty encouraged Daniel to visit her sister Noralba, who lived in Guayaquil with her husband Felix. The couple spent most of their time ministering to the Cayapa Indians in the mangrove swamps along the Pacific coast lowlands. But they were not your 'typical' missionaries. In his 'wilder' days, Felix had served time in the notorious Quito prison for robbing a bank. Overcrowded cells offered no privacy and were illuminated by a single bulb, with a filthy bathroom with one shower for the hordes of unwashed inmates. In these grim surroundings, Felix found God and was released several years later on good behaviour. He met Noralba at a church course, and the couple decided to dedicate their lives to serving God. When Daniel knocked on their door in Guayanquil in April 1995, they took the German up north to their mission post without further ado. Once they reached the city of Esmereldas, they travelled a further eight hours by bus inland then onward via canoe through thick swamps for what seemed like an eternity.

Daniel was thrilled with anticipation. He could not wait for the hammock, the jungle, the delicious and exotic dishes that awaited him. But once again, Daniel's dream adventure did not go according to plan, and in fact turned into a nightmare. A nasty gastrointestinal bug confined Daniel to a sick bed, where he was plagued by assaultive stomach cramps and boredom. Noralba and Felix were consumed by running a school and church for this Indian congregation in the jungle, so Daniel was pretty much left to himself.

One day, Daniel discovered a German book on the dresser. Maybe Betty had sent it to Noralba as a gift. Perhaps it had even come from his parents' bookshop! With little else available to engage him, Daniel began to flip through the pages. Several hours later, having read the book cover to cover, Daniel's worldview was turned upside down. He no longer felt strong and confident, a worthy master of his own destiny. He now realised how small and fragile he actually was, and in his unexpected convalescent quarters, Daniel found himself longing for true security and a life full of meaning beyond himself.

'God, I am willing to trust You and to do Your will!' Daniel was shocked to have such a desire fill his mind. 'But, God,' he prayed, 'I don't want to do this alone. Please let me talk about this with someone I can trust.'

Daniel was due to leave the rainforest the very next day. That was the plan. His hosts would take him to the bus terminal via canoe early in the morning, then send him on his way, alone. A heart to heart with Felix and Noralba simply wouldn't be possible as they paddled across the jungle rivers. Daniel was gutted, desperately wanting answers to his many questions. But it wasn't going to happen here, he thought, as he slipped into a restless sleep.

During the night, it began to rain. First, just a drizzle. Then it became a downpour. In the morning, the house stood on its high stilts in the middle of a flood of muddy water. A *force majeure*. There was no way Daniel would be able to leave as planned. Noralba and Felix weren't even able to do their normal daily tasks. The flood kept all the villagers trapped in their homes. A long day stretched ahead of them – a gift of opportunity for the conversation Daniel craved. In those hours, Daniel made a decision. 'God, be Lord of my life!' he whispered. 'And forgive me for all I have done wrong in my past!'

Back in Germany, Daniel began to understand that faith in God can be compared to an ongoing mission in life. A Christian becomes an instrument in God's hand. He wondered what he could do to show God's love to others in a practical way. 'Seek and you will find …' (Matthew 7:7).

In 1997, Daniel completed a voluntary social service year at a Palestinian children's care home on the West Bank. The initial twelve months turned into eighteen. And suddenly, Daniel found himself at the centre of resurging Arab–Israeli tensions, played out with violent protests, tear gas and police. The twenty-year-old experienced first-hand what others might only ever read about. At great personal risk, Daniel continued to serve Arab children in need and gained increasing insight into their treacherous living conditions.

Florian Sies was another young volunteer at the children's home. He and Daniel soon became friends. When their Middle East assignment came to an end, the two decided to continue travelling together, this time to 'The Sun', 'The Land of Dreams' – Ecuador. The path led them first to Guayaquil, to Elba Cevallo's home, where Daniel got to know and love the entire Cevallo clan. Ultimately more interesting than the dear, wise woman herself was her granddaughter Rebecca. The girl was exotic and beautiful, with chestnut brown eyes and a slender figure like a cedar from Lebanon. Daniel's heart was captured. It was love at first sight for both of them, and Daniel simply couldn't bear to tear himself away. After about a week, Florian had to face up to the reality of continuing the journey alone. His fickle travelling companion was about to ditch him for a pretty woman at the equator. When Cupid's arrow strikes, promises dissolve.

Daniel never intended to get married before he turned thirty, but on 29th July 2000, seven years 'too early', he and Rebecca tied the knot in Heilbronn. It was a summer day with sweltering heat not unlike the norm in Guayaquil. More than two hundred guests from Ecuador, Italy and Germany gathered in a festively decorated church hall for the happy occasion. Among them was Florian Sies. He had long since forgiven his buddy for abandoning him on their tour of the Andes. Elba Cevallo, Rebecca's grandmother, was also in attendance at the wedding.

Life was treating Daniel well. After a three-year apprenticeship as an orthopaedic technician, he was enjoying his practical work and his salary allowed for a comfortable existence. He had a wife, a house and a car. They made holiday trips to the beach. In 2007, their first daughter, Kimberley, was born. In 2009, they welcomed a second, Kylie. Both girls were sweet, just like their mother. For fourteen years, the Müller family of four enjoyed a tranquil and idyllic life in the heart of Baden-Württemberg. And yet Daniel was somehow unsettled. Surely life had to be about more than the cosiness of their own four walls?

When Daniel spotted a magazine ad for a humanitarian organisation in 2015, he instinctively knew that he and his family were in for a change. *Christliche Fachkräfte International* was seeking an orthopaedic technician to work in Albania. The Müller family welcomed this formidable challenge and moved to the land of the Shqiptars. There, what was once a job became a calling. For the first time, Daniel felt a deep sense of fulfilment. Had he finally found his place in the world? Unfortunately, no. Where there is light, there is also shadow. Despite their best efforts, Daniel and Rebecca struggled to learn the Albanian language. Their lack of proficiency limited their social contacts to a very small circle of friends. The local school system left a lot to be desired. And Rebecca, a trained hairdresser, was unable to find a job. It soon became clear to the Müllers that they would need to move on after their three-year commitment. But what then? The Müllers hadn't the faintest idea.

For Christmas 2015, Daniel's parents gifted him a book from their shop. The title was unusual: *I Have Seen God: The Miraculous Story of the Diospi Suyana Hospital in Peru.* Daniel devoured the contents in just a few days. Could this hospital way up in the Andes be the next step for Daniel and his family? He drafted a casual email inquiry to the hospital, but held off sending it. Rebecca did not love the idea and wanted to consider other alternatives. Her homeland was Ecuador, and there had been tension between her country and Peru for centuries. The isolation of the mountain Indians was a far cry – in culture as well as miles – from the lively coastal city in which she had grown up.

The Müllers pursued a multitude of options. *Christliche Fachkräfte International* had several vacancies available in Tunisia, Angola, Tanzania and even Thailand. Every single one fell through, often on what seemed to be a simple technicality. Daniel scowled, 'We are apparently not needed!' He shrugged his shoulders, frustrated. He had so firmly resolved to show God's love to others through service, yet every door seemed to shut against him.

Time was of the essence. Without another overseas opportunity, the family would need to return to Germany in 2017. Daniel suddenly remembered the email he had drafted six months prior. It was Friday 12th August 2016. He opened his laptop, pulled up the saved message and hit 'send'. His last shot.

The following afternoon, the Müllers had invited some friends over for a barbecue in the garden. Daniel's mobile rang. When he answered, there was a Klaus John from Peru on the line. Daniel's spine tingled. His eldest daughter Kimberley recalled, 'Dad suddenly had a strange expression on his face. I knew right away that something special had happened!'

We got right to business. I shared that the hospital already had a trauma unit and a physiotherapy unit, so an orthopaedic clinic would be an ideal addition. I then 'ticked the boxes' for all the points that were so dear to the Müllers: Yes, the medical and educational needs of the girls would be well taken care of. There was a hair-stylist job for Rebecca in the make-up room of the TV studio. And Spanish is spoken at Diospi Suyana – a language they already knew!

My closing remark stayed with Daniel: 'Mr Müller, we absolutely need you in Peru!'

On 22nd October, the Müllers arrived in Darmstadt for the official interview. I was pretty tired, having rushed back to Hessen after a lecture in East Frisia the previous evening. Immediately following the interview, I needed to travel to Gummerbach for still another engagement.

The Müllers were undecided. Our conversation at the restaurant was pleasant and low-key – much like the autumn day outside. But they seemed to be hoping for something more exciting, the electric thrill of a new adventure.

'Mr Müller, just come to Peru and see for yourself.' My spontaneous plea fell on open ears. The money for the flight had come as a surprise, just twenty-four hours earlier, when a friend had handed Daniel an envelope containing €1000. Daniel had never been given a donation in his life! When he asked his friend why he was conferring such a generous gift, his friend replied that he had just received an unexpected tax refund and felt led to hand it over to Daniel.

On 9th January 2017, Daniel was in Curahuasi, sitting with Udo Klemenz and me around a large black table, examining various plans for the construction of an orthopaedic clinic. Shortly afterwards, we moved outside to take some measurements.

'No problem,' declared the engineering legend of Diospi Suyana, 'There's still room for another single-storey building on site!'

'We could build the clinic, but that only makes sense if you're actually coming,' I challenged Daniel. 'Please call your wife and make a decision – preferably today!'

Daniel reached for his phone and dialled Rebecca's number. He had no idea what he could say to convince the Ecuadorian that a new life high in the thin air of the mountains was a good idea. Daniel braced himself for a tough conversation and took a deep breath as he heard Rebecca pick up the call. But before he could even begin, his wife abruptly hijacked the conversation.

'You won't believe what happened yesterday!' she gushed. 'I met a Peruvian woman from Cusco right here in the village! She raved to me about Curahuasi – she said the landscape is gorgeous and the climate is mild. It would be a wonderful home for our children!'

With this unexpected turn of events, Daniel and Rebecca both agreed that all the signs were clearly pointing to Peru.

Daniel returned to cold and rainy Albania while Udo Klemenz got to work on the newest addition to Diospi Suyana.

'But Dad, we don't want to go to Peru!' the girls argued vehemently. 'We don't have any friends there! We should move to Germany instead, near Grandpa and Grandma!'

The total opposition of his daughters didn't make the situation easy. 'Why didn't you bring us pictures?' they demanded. Daniel regarded his daughters, their normally sunny faces now looking like dark storm clouds.

That same week, Daniel received a phone call from a German aid worker posted in northern Albania. Alexandra Winter was a trained physiotherapist and was interested in visiting the orthopaedic clinic where Daniel devoted his time.

'Of course, you are welcome,' Daniel extended politely, while realising his guest would unfortunately be walking right into the middle of his current family drama.

The night before Alexandra Winter was to arrive, eight-year-old Kylie had a peculiar dream. In the dream, Kylie saw a woman wearing a crown pendant on a chain around her neck. The woman put a laptop on a table, and Kylie could see a red ball on the keyboard. She could also see a tarantula on the screen of the laptop. Kylie remembered all of these unusual details the next morning.

Alexandra showed up at the Müllers' house that afternoon. After dinner, she pulled out her computer to share some pictures of Peru. As it turned out, the physiotherapist herself had spent two years at the Diospi Suyana hospital. Life is full of surprises!

Kylie stared at the Lenovo laptop. There was a red trackball in the middle of the keyboard, just like in her dream. Kylie looked up and saw Alexandra's necklace. It had a small crown dangling from it.

'What does this mean?' asked Kylie, shyly.

'It means I am a child of the King,' was Alexandra's enigmatic reply.

Over the next few hours, Alexandra shared hundreds of photos from Curahuasi and Peru. 'You would love working at Diospi Suyana,' she encouraged. 'You will find such a beautiful environment there.' Her enthusiasm was infectious and was beginning to break through even to Daniel's resistant offspring.

Kylie continued to stare at the computer screen, completely astounded by what she now saw. Alexandra had just enlarged a photo of a tarantula so it appeared life-sized. Mistaking Kylie's reaction for an aversion to spiders, Alexandra assured her that the multitude of tarantulas and other spiders in Peru rarely caused any trouble.

Before going to bed, Kylie confided in her parents, sharing her dream from the previous night. 'Nothing like this has ever happened to me before!' Kylie stammered, overcome with emotion. 'I recognised the crown, the red button, the tarantula – all from my dream!'

Daniel and Rebecca hugged their daughter close. They understood God was at work. After all, Diospi Suyana was no ordinary hospital. When people seek the will of God, He answers. He prepares each of us, even children, for the tasks He has given – invisibly, mysteriously, but beyond a doubt and at exactly the right time.

19

Blue blood

In autumn 2016, Diospi Suyana rose to nobility, in a manner of speaking. Dr Nikolaus von Abendroth and his wife, Dr Johanna von Abendroth, joined our team in Curahuasi. In the dental clinic, Dr Nikolaus exuded the typical calmness of a northern German as he fitted the first dental implants in Diospi Suyana history and Johanna served as a physician in our outpatient clinic while they raised four children at home.

The dignified 'von' in their surname was not the only impressive aspect to this couple! On more than one occasion, I was carried away with joking comments about the name of our resident aristocrats. I really didn't care if their titled status came through birth or royal endowment; what mattered was that they were *here*.

It's easy to envy royalty. We see their holiday excursions and elaborate wardrobes displayed through countless pages of magazines. Although we don't know them personally, we crave personal details of their private affairs, and if photographic evidence of romance happens to include a castle or other impressive scenery, the story will no doubt make the front page – total tabloid fodder. Our fascination with blue blood makes for quite a lucrative media industry. I must emphasise here that I don't personally read printed matter of this kind. Only sometimes. When no one is watching.

For the honour of a doctorate degree, one must toil long hours and fight through constant fatigue. Even the stars of Hollywood pay their price for fame by learning endless scripts.

But those with a 'von' on their business card are spared all this blood, sweat and tears. From birth, they have an established – and highly respected – place in society. In today's PR world, social status is everything. It increases 'market value' and conveys prestige and attention. Who of us mere mortals wouldn't fall silent and stare if a prince or duchess walked by?

So we see pictures of a magical summer night in a palace garden, or we imagine sharing a private cruise through the South Seas or scoring the VIP box at Wimbledon, all with no worry about the cost. It sounds like a dream, but we know better. All that glitters is *not* gold. The world does not deliver all it appears to promise. And often a sparkling façade serves only to hide a frightening emptiness.

But I'll let you in on a little secret: *all* Diospi volunteers are royalty. What Alexandra Winter told little Kylie Müller is absolutely true. That is why Diospi Suyana has developed as favourably as it has. We have a 'good connection' and we rely on Him shamelessly.

As children of the King, we have clear access to the most powerful Ruler ever. If I want to speak with the Most High, I don't need a fancy invitation or diplomatic papers. God has assured me that He is available at any time of the day or night. He is happy to receive visits and prayers from His precious children. All our long-term volunteers – whether they be doctors, nurses or teachers – belong to the kingdom of God, as do my wife and I.

First thing every morning, Tina and I go to the 'throne room' to present our petitions. This is not mindless ritual but passionate dedication. We have a personal conversation with our King. We are even on a first-name basis, as you might expect with close family members. It would be foolish to behave as though we were on our own. But please understand, although we bring our requests to God, we trust in His omniscience and omnipotence. He will answer in His way, in His time and for His glory – just as He has done every step of the way with Diospi Suyana. It fills me with pride and gratitude to be a chosen child of God. Without this connection, I cannot imagine what my life would be like.

It was a Wednesday afternoon when Daniel Müller and I arrived at the Streifeneder company headquarters in Emmering, near Munich. The Bavarian company is renowned worldwide for orthopaedic equipment of the highest quality. But such quality comes with a price tag.

I looked over at Daniel and said, 'We'd better pray before we meet the managing director.' Daniel nodded in agreement. And so we appealed loudly into the four cubic metre airspace of our rental car, convinced that our words would penetrate all earthly barriers and reach the ears of our Father. So very far away and yet so close. When we were finished, I shouldered my laptop bag and together we walked expectantly through the main entrance doors.

Michael Leitmair, the managing director at that time, and two colleagues greeted us. They listened patiently as Daniel and I shared many pictures and made our request for their support. 'We are in the process of setting up a state-of-the-art orthopaedic clinic for the poorest of the poor – would you like to help us?'

The director understood our message immediately. He assured us that he would look into possible options and get back to us. Five weeks later, Mr Leitmair informed us that Streifeneder's original asking price had been reduced by 50 per cent! In exchange for a donation receipt, Diospi Suyana saved a whopping €20,000! And just like that, the outfitting of our new orthopaedic clinic with the most modern technology was sorted.

20

Rio de Janeiro *sans* samba on the Strand

You might say it was Australian Chris Welch who first put the bug in my ear about satellite transmission back in 2015. I'm no technician, but even I understood the enormous potential this mode of communication could have. Imagine someone sitting in a studio somewhere, creating audio-visual content with a program, then electronically sending the data 25,000 miles out into space. Satellites receive the signals and retransmit them literally all over the world, where they can be picked up by antennae and broadcast locally. An insanely fascinating concept! And all the more so when considering the ability to reach remote areas where even internet connections are few – places like the mountain villages of the Andes.

If it's so easy, why doesn't everyone use satellites to communicate their messages across the planet? Can you imagine how politicians might utilise this to reach the outlying areas of their constituencies? Or how a small bakery might become so well known that its rolls would fly off the shelves each morning? So why not? The answer comes down to expense. The cost is way more than would be reasonable for an individual or even a small business. But what about an organisation like Diospi Suyana, which exists off the generosity of others and therefore takes the matter of spending *anything* very seriously.

For the life of me, I cannot recall where I first heard the name ARSAT. The Argentinian telecommunications company had competitive pricing, making it broadly accessible. I needed to explore this possibility further!

On 4th May 2016, I set up my laptop in a small conference room in ARSAT's Buenos Aires headquarters. Photos from the mountains of Peru flashed on the screen in rapid succession. It was a historic event – the Diospi Suyana story told for the first time in the capital city of Argentina. Francisco Jasminoy, Sales Manager for Northern South America, said that he got goosebumps when he heard the remarkable tale. Project Manager Pablo Pérez was also visibly moved. These experts took their time illustrating and explaining the finer technical points of satellite communication, what equipment would be needed and how much it all would cost. As I stated on our website, this was 'an outrageously exciting idea' and the price was 'extremely attractive' – could this dream become a reality for Diospi Suyana?

I had a lot to think about. Before I boarded the plane for my next speaking tour in Europe, I met with an editor from ARD[9] and with Pastor Rubén Proietti, head of the Evangelical Council of Churches in Argentina. It's really quite incredible: wherever I share about Diospi Suyana, people listen. It doesn't matter if the audience is an executive media board or a group of schoolchildren, housewives or hikers, university professors or pub-goers – they all are captivated from the moment I flip up the screen and invite them to listen to our story.

Three weeks later, the Welch family arrived in Peru. Chris and I set to work finding the best deal on the satellite market. In January 2017, Chris brought the international company INTELSAT to my attention. After buying out its arch-rival PanAmSat in 2006, INTELSAT became the largest commercial satellite provider, with fifty satellites serving more than two hundred countries.

Chris reached out to the various regional offices of INTELSAT to try to negotiate a workable contract. Once we

---

[9] ARD is the first and one of the most important television channels in Germany. It is run by the state and has offices in many countries.

had a foot in the door, my plan was to share the Diospi Suyana vision to the powers that be, in the hope that they would be inspired to drop the price. The USA executives had no time or interest in hearing more about Diospi Suyana but they did offer us a link for US$1,000 per month. That wasn't a bad price, but we kept looking.

Through an unexpected turn of events, the Spanish telecommunications company Hispamar suddenly rose high on our list of options to explore. It came in with a preliminary offer of US$600. Chris and I decided to fly to Rio de Janeiro as quickly as possible to work out the details with the South American regional executives in person. Our flights were booked and our bags were packed. En route to the airport, however, we received a discouraging email from Rio. They apologetically noted an error and announced the correct price would be more than US$1,000!

Chris and I were flummoxed. We looked at each other, uncertain of our next steps. Should we cancel our trip? I had already booked my onward flight from Rio to Frankfurt. We decided to go to Rio anyway. One never knows what might be accomplished in a face-to-face meeting!

The red-eye flight landed in Rio at 4.35am. An hour later we were sitting in a small café, biding time until our 9am appointment. After freshening up quickly in the gents, we proceeded to the company conference room and the uncertainty that awaited.

Our presentation to sales director Sergio Chavez and his team clearly touched their hearts. The concerning message we had received on the way to the airport was immediately forgotten. Chavez offered a massive price reduction, but qualified that it would need to be approved by the global headquarters in Madrid.

Almost giddy with our good fortune, Chris and I spent some time getting to know the Rio-based Hispamar employees and 'talking shop' about details, should this all come to fruition. We were especially impressed with how well its satellite control centre was equipped.

Chris probably could have stayed there all day, but I was in a hurry to get to yet another meeting, this time a 2pm appointment with an ARD correspondent.

Two hours and two hundred pictures later, we headed back to the airport. It was a warm and beautiful day, with bright sunshine and blue skies. Out of one taxi window we could see Sugarloaf Mountain glistening in the distance. Out the other, Christ the Redeemer with arms still outstretched, such a poignant visual reminder of God's power and love.

'What did you see in Rio?' our taxi driver asked casually on the way to the airport.

'Nothing!' Chris and I declared. 'We are not tourists!'

Once we were past security, Chris and I opened our laptops and got to work. My Lufthansa flight was scheduled to depart for Germany at 11pm. Chris would have another seven hours to kill before his Avianca flight left for Lima. We were strictly business all the way, telling ourselves that touring without our wives probably wouldn't have been fun anyway. It was a fast and furious trip, but filled with thousands of impressions.

Two months passed and we still had heard nothing from Rio. The directors in Madrid clearly did not share Sergio Chavez's enthusiasm for Diospi Suyana. They were all about 'the bottom line'. When we did finally receive the twelve-page contract via email at the end of May, we were greatly disheartened. Some clauses were simply difficult to understand. Others seemed to severely limit the scope of our operations. It just wasn't going to work.

'Chris,' I said, 'we're going to call the INTELSAT people in Miami one last time.'

On the phone a matter of minutes later, I put our cards on the table. 'We have this formal offer from Hispamar – can you do better?'

After a year of negotiating with three major telecommunication companies in Argentina, Brazil and the US, the time had come to make a decision.

'Yes, we can!' assured the INTELSAT executive on the other end of the line.

And so it happened. On 17th June 2017, we signed a five-year contract with INTELSAT. Our personal visit to Rio had motivated Hispamar to offer a 75 per cent discount off the going market rate, and that special price was cut even further by INTELSAT. Over a period of five years, Diospi Suyana has saved more than US$30,000! For only US$515 a month, we are now making the best news available to thousands and thousands of Quechua homes in southern Peru.

21

Our tenth anniversary countdown

I prefer to concentrate my energies on a single task. When that task is complete, I can move on and focus on the next. I tackle things one at a time, in order, all the while hoping that no one will interrupt and confuse my system. My wife is completely different. The quintessential multi-tasker, she can start the washing machine, talk on the phone and check her email simultaneously, then in a heartbeat shift her attention from home to medical matters and share lab results with her team on her way to the emergency room.

My brain doesn't work that way, and yet I continually commute between Europe, the USA and South America. I change planes as frequently as others change their shirts! I have to admit that sometimes I wake up from an in-flight nap not really clear on where I'm heading. No big deal, though – my seatmates always know our destination. These constant shifts in time zone, location and language can be like poison to my sixty-plus-year-old brain.

Long before sunrise on Wednesday 7th October 2015, I got into a taxi in Curahuasi and headed for the airport. I got off the plane in Lima around 9am. Shortly after lunch, I was scheduled to share our work with the head of Bitel. Since 2013, this Vietnamese telecommunications company has supplied the Peruvian market with both broadband internet and a mobile phone network. Upgrading to broadband would solve our chronic internet issues once and for all!

I was led into a large conference room where two Vietnamese and a Peruvian were waiting for me. The general director, Hoang Quoc Quyen, gave me the floor. As the Asian men did not speak Spanish, I cheerfully presented in English. My forty-minute discourse ended with a request to provide our hospital with a fibre optic connection – free of charge, of course.

The Vietnamese was moved nearly to the point of tears. 'Of course we will help you,' he assured.

Peruvian advisor Edwin San Roman chimed in, 'We are different from the Spanish company that let you down so badly before. You can count on us!'

Success across the board! I didn't want the impressions of the day to fade. As I packed up my laptop, I urged the men to come to Curahuasi and see Diospi Suyana for themselves.

Ten days later, San Roman and the Vietnamese executives settled into their guest rooms at the back of the hospital. My wife, Dr Jens Haßfeld and school headmaster Christian Bigalke took excellent care of our guests of honour – in my absence, I might add, as I had departed Peru forty-eight hours earlier for a seven-week lecture tour.

The Vietnamese were treated like royalty. Our team showed them every detail of our hospital, the school and the broadcasting station construction. They were clearly impressed. And, of course, we pointed out the potential benefits of faster internet connection for our daily operations at every possible opportunity. On the evening of the first day, Tina whipped up a three-course meal for our guests that would have impressed any professional chef. It's true that the way to a person's heart, or wallet, is often through the stomach. The general manager smacked his lips audibly, his cultural indication of appreciation for the delicious fare. Everything was going according to plan.

And then it wasn't. As we learned later that week, the Vietnamese hadn't accepted our invitation because they wanted to make a donation; they came because they hoped to recruit us as paying customers. Emails and phone calls were exchanged, to no avail. Our hopes were beginning to crash, much like our existing internet connection so often did.

Shortly before Christmas, I met with San Roman in Lima. In this conversation, the Bitel advisor drew a hard and final line through our broadband proposal.

'Dr John,' he remarked with great regret, 'today is my last day at Bitel. I'll be moving on to another company.'

So that was it. I bowed my head and rubbed my hand over my face.

On Peru's Independence Day, 28th July 2016, Pedro Pablo Kuczynski was sworn in as Peru's new President. The venerable economist had won against Keiko Fujimori by just 41,438 votes, but the extremely narrow margin of 50.12 per cent was enough to secure his place in the Presidential Palace, as well as appointments for his most loyal supporters at all levels of government.

Kuczynski's father had practised as a doctor in Berlin but, because of his Jewish faith, had fled Nazi Germany in 1933. He ended up in Iquitos, the largest metropolis in the Peruvian Amazon. There, he established a medical clinic for lepers. His son Pedro Pablo had a formidable CV, with extensive experience in politics and international finance, as well as an exceptional education. It was precisely this man that I wanted to meet, ideally in the Palace itself.

I was not after a selfie or an autograph, but I knew from experience how critical it was to have a good relationship with the Head of State. A direct line to the President can clear mountains of red tape and even keep corrupt officials more honest in their dealings with Diospi Suyana.

Who of 33 million Peruvians wouldn't want an audience with their leader? You may recall from my first two books that our rendezvous with Presidents Alan García and Ollanta Humala were preceded by incredible events that atheists call 'dumb luck' and Christians call 'miracles from God'.

I tried everything to get close to 'PPK', as most Peruvians call him. Having no delusions about my own limitations, I prayed daily for God's guidance and direction.

A business acquaintance offered to put me in touch with a close friend of the President. On a Friday evening, I met with Arieh Rohrstock and Señor Stoll at the Lima Country Club. Señor Stoll was on a first-name basis with the President. We discussed possible courses of action and I left feeling optimistic, but unfortunately nothing came of our attempted networking.

I forwarded a formal request through the Apurímac regional office. As the weeks passed with no response, I had to accept that this effort was probably also going to be in vain.

Even the German Ambassador Jörg Ranau offered to speak to the President on my behalf when he accompanied him on a trip to southern Peru. I was so sure that, this time, the precious connection would finally be made. But once again, there was no word from the Palace.

The tenth anniversary of Diospi Suyana was coming up at the end of August. What I wouldn't give to have the President there to help commemorate the incredible day we opened our hospital doors for the first time! But such an invitation would only be accepted through channels of personal dialogue and mutual respect. Shouting from the perimeter of the Palace fence would likely only brand me as a troublemaker and perhaps even land me in jail.

And then one day, my mobile rang. I held my breath as I heard the governor's voice on the line. Señor Wilmer Venegas had an extremely encouraging message for me.

'Dr John, Kuczynski's personal advisor has offered to see you on 19th May. Please be at the Palace rear entrance at 11am. Don't be late!'

Arriving as directed, I stood with anticipation in my polished shoes and impeccably tailored suit, waiting to be granted entrance. The doors opened, I was led through another checkpoint, then finally through long corridors into an elegant office. A gentleman in his seventies sat behind a table in the middle of the room, beaming as I walked in.

'I am so glad to finally meet you, Dr John,' he declared in a deep, booming voice. 'For two years, my brother Edwin has been telling me stories of Diospi Suyana!'

He thrust his business card into my hand. Maximo San Roman was the man's name, as I read in complete astonishment. He had already served his country as Vice President in the 1990s. And his brother Edwin San Roman was the Bitel advisor we had welcomed to Diospi Suyana. He had seen our work with his own eyes and even enjoyed my wife's cooking!

I shared my Diospi Suyana presentation, but knew I had found a friend even before I began.

'It would be wonderful if the President would grant you an audience and be present for your anniversary celebrations,' San Roman said enthusiastically. 'I will make the suggestion!'

As I stepped outside the Palace, I could hardly contain my elation!

Every few years, most missionaries take what is called a furlough. During this time, they usually head home for several months to visit friends and supporters, participate in training or take care of urgent personal matters. My wife and I prefer to be in the field as much as possible, so we only take a furlough every six years. Our next was due in 2017. We planned to fly to Frankfurt via Madrid with our son Florian on 20th June, and to return to Peru in time for the August anniversary celebration.

San Roman strove to arrange an audience with PPK for us, but the President's schedule was jam-packed, with no room to squeeze us in. We stayed in close contact via phone, WhatsApp and SMS, but there was little change. The first week of June flew by and I called San Roman with an urgent appeal.

'Señor Roman, we are running out of time,' I implored. 'We fly to Germany on 20th June. The 19th would be our last possible opportunity to meet the President!'

Señor Roman could not make promises on behalf of the President, but he could advocate for us. The clock was ticking and my angst was growing. Missing out on a chance to connect would be such a shame. Tina and I prayed to God for an open door to the President and to his heart.

Finally, on Saturday 16th June, San Roman sent an email that renewed my hope and spirit: 'Monday morning ...'

Not taking any chances, we left for Lima on Sunday. Florian waited back in the mission guesthouse. Tina, Dr Haβfeld and I stood before the imposing walls of the Palace, dressed in our best. At 11.45am, we took our seats at a heavy wooden table in a distinguished meeting room.

President Kuczynski was seated at the head of the table. Maximo San Roman was directly to my left.

Our encounter was sometimes serious, sometimes humorous, and very cordial throughout. Even while I was in the midst of displaying the photos of Diospi Suyana, the President declared, 'There should be a hospital like yours everywhere in Peru!'

Everyone at the table was thrilled with such an enthusiastic endorsement.

At the end of my presentation, I felt emboldened to take the next step. 'Mr President, it would be a great honour for all of us at Diospi Suyana if you would attend our tenth anniversary celebration on 31st August!'

'Let's see if that's possible,' Kuczynski said as he stood and disappeared through double doors into an adjoining room.

While he was gone, San Roman praised our work in Curahuasi effusively.

The President returned to the table in just a few minutes with excellent news. 'That will work. I will be there and will bring some members of my cabinet as well.'

Tina, Dr Haβfeld and I all looked at each other and laughed. We could not have imagined a better outcome.

Late that evening, San Roman sent a follow-up email which read:

It was a most interesting and pertinent visit. The President was able to take a close look at your exceptional service to our country. I am so pleased that he accepted your invitation to the Diospi Suyana anniversary festivities. For a long time, I have heard about your incredible work through my brother Edwin. It will be an honour to have the opportunity to visit and see with my own eyes. Thank you for all you do for the poor and marginalised in Peru. Have a safe trip and come back soon!

The seating on the Air Europa flight was cramped and the service was minimal, but we were in high spirits as we flew above the clouds. At the eleventh hour, our dream meeting with the President had actually become a reality. On top of that, we would see him again on hospital grounds for our celebration in six short weeks! As it says in Psalm 37:5, 'Commit your way to the LORD; trust in him and he will do this.' This timeless promise of the Bible once again proved true for us.

Unlike previous building projects, we were progressing on schedule. The extension of the first floor was done and the new building that would house the orthopaedic clinic was close to being finished. The Flores company from Cusco was on track to complete installation of an elaborate tent roof over our amphitheatre. Up in his office, Udo Klemenz laboured for weeks on a wooden model of our first five antenna towers. The dignitaries, including the President, and the media would be so amazed by the extensive development of Diospi Suyana over the past ten years!

The dry season essentially guaranteed us good weather. With the expected attendance of President Kuczynski, we knew our sizable venue would be filled to capacity. Tina and I were feeling positive and looking forward to the event with joyful expectation.

I must confess, I was beginning to feel a bit of angst as the day approached. And that is why I returned to Peru the first week of August to join in the preparations.

On Friday 11th August, Doris Manco accompanied me to a meeting at the Presidential Palace. I did my best to convey the importance of our upcoming commemoration to the President's inner circle because I had concerns he might – for whatever reason – back out.

'We have become well known throughout the entire country, thanks to ample television and media coverage,' I entreated. 'A hospital serving Peru's most needy deserves special attention and public support from the national government.' I added that President Kuczynski's planned participation would also be an excellent opportunity to address the current nationwide teachers' strike that was affecting several million students. With no end in sight, Kuczynski would have a platform to offer a personal message of reconciliation to a very large live audience.

'Yes, don't worry, the President will be there!' we were assured. Relieved, Doris and I left the Palace and, once outside, took a deep breath.

'Let's go see the editor of *Caretas*,' Doris proposed abruptly. 'The main office is just on the other side of the Plaza de Armas. Maybe Marco Zileri will see us!'

Doris comes up with some ingenious ideas. *Caretas*, or 'Mask' in English, is a weekly news publication, well known for its investigative journalism since the 1950s. Politically liberal, the magazine is much like the German *Der Spiegel*. No wonder, then, that the founders of *Caretas* actually looked to the work of Rudolf Augstein, founder of *Der Spiegel*, as a model for their own periodical development. Editor in chief Marco Zileri was also a vocal and staunch atheist.

We didn't have an appointment. I checked my watch: it was just before 1pm.

'Doris, Zileri is probably out having lunch now!'

But Doris wasn't deterred by my dismissal. 'We are here. God can open any door!'

We crossed the square and rang the bell at the entrance to the five-storey building. A concierge seated behind a glass wall buzzed us in. 'Who would you like to see?' the man asked politely.

'We would like to see Mr Zileri.'

'Right. Let me ask upstairs.' The man regarded us closely as he picked up the telephone receiver.

Doris and I were not fooling ourselves. Zileri had never met us and had no idea who we were. For us to actually get a spontaneous invitation up to the executive offices? That would take a miracle.

The concierge hung up the phone. 'You can leave your written request with me. I'll send it up after lunch,' he assured.

We weren't going to be dismissed that easily. 'Please tell his secretary that we would really appreciate the opportunity to have a few words with him in person – just two minutes!' Our tone was both resolute and pleading.

The man picked up the phone one more time. We waited, a bit awkwardly, but praying silently for God to open this door.

'Alright,' the concierge acquiesced. 'You may go up, but you'll have to be quick!'

Doris and I exchanged a satisfied glance and started up the many stairs.

When we reached the executive floor, we peered into the open doorway of an office. A tall, lean man was engaged in conversation with another visitor. While he was talking, he gestured to a nearby sofa, indicating we were to take a seat and wait. We immediately complied. I took my laptop out and booted it up, just in case ...

'Who are you and what do you want?' Zileri asked as he turned his attention to his unexpected guests.

I introduced myself and immediately launched into our objective. 'We are about to celebrate the tenth anniversary of the Diospi Suyana hospital, which has treated hundreds of thousands of poor Quechua so far,' I effused. 'The President will even be there! I've got some pictures – you've got to see them!'

Zileri settled himself in an armchair and indicated with a nod of his head that he had no objection to a short PowerPoint. He had no idea what to expect.

I clicked through the first few slides of my presentation, speaking about Diospi Suyana with an increasing – and apparently infectious – passion.

'Get the photographer!' Zileri barked to his secretary. 'Get him up here right away!'

Zileri was clearly hooked by our story. I continued, bolstered by such an unforeseen enraptured audience.

'Take pictures of him and make sure you capture his eyes!' Zileri directed the photographer as he arrived. I don't think there is anything particularly special about my eyes, but maybe they flashed with my enthusiasm?

Twenty minutes later, the presentation and photo opportunity were over. I looked at the floor, waiting for Zileri's 'verdict'. We had 'slightly' exceeded our promised time limit of two minutes, but Zileri certainly could have kicked us out earlier if he had wanted to.

Zileri was visibly affected. 'I have always been an atheist,' he professed. 'I don't believe in God – this should not be possible!'

'Please come to our celebration in Curahuasi, then you can make up your own mind about Diospi Suyana.' Doris' invitation seemed to sway him.

'Where exactly is your hospital located?' asked Zileri. 'I will come!'

Time was running short to prepare for our big event, and every minute counted. The Flores company had not yet come through with the thick, UV-resistant tarpaulin we needed for the steel frame of the amphitheatre. So I was on the phone, and perhaps on their nerves, urging them to hurry up and not cause embarrassment. The President himself would be on our stage! It was not a time to be unprepared.

I bought a new overhead projector in Lima because my wife and I both wanted to share photos while we addressed the audience. On Wednesday 16th August, I dropped by the Ministry of Health to extend a personal invitation to the Minister and Vice Minister. From there, a taxi hurried me to the airport so I could catch my next flight.

Back in Germany, I continually monitored developments in the Peruvian teachers' strike. Teachers were now demanding that their salaries be doubled, and they were refusing to take the required proficiency tests. Strikes are as common in Peru as alpacas in the Andes. With a little time, heated tempers cool and order is restored. But this one was different. Emboldened by leftist unions, demonstrations escalated in streets and squares across the nation. Protesters even marched to the seat of Congress one day with the intention of storming the Legislative Palace. The police had to use force to quell the attack.

On 24th August, as Tina and I were beginning our return journey to Peru, protests in the streets had become violent. News media portrayed bleeding faces on both sides. The teachers' strike had already dragged on for two months. Students feared losing an entire year of education. The general population was losing patience with the situation and demanded government action.

Once back in Curahuasi, we unpacked and tried to realistically assess the current state of affairs. Would the presence of our high-profile guests inspire protest action on our own grounds? Would demonstrators attempt to hijack our widely publicised event for their own purposes? Tina and I had a growing sense of foreboding. What we soon heard from anonymous informants didn't help.

The teachers wanted to mobilise and greet the President 'properly' by throwing stones, burning tyres and spewing hateful rhetoric. Diospi Suyana was at risk of becoming collateral damage in the midst of all this turmoil. On Saturday morning, I received confirmation from the highest level that the threat was very real. Nine police officers, led by Apurímac Police Chief Coronel Vasquez, gathered around my desk for an emergency meeting.

'The situation is serious,' the Coronel stated grimly. 'If the protesters are determined to turn Curahuasi into a battlefield, there is no way the President can come here. None of us wants to get involved in a violent confrontation with the teachers!'

I sensed our plans for the President's visit were about to go up in smoke. I was crushed. Outwardly, I probably looked deep in thought, but in fact I was desperately praying, 'God, what can I do? Help me now!'

'Señor Coronel, thank you for coming,' I replied slowly. 'If you don't mind, I'd like to show you some pictures so you can better appreciate the significance of our celebration.'

No one at the table had any objections. The projector and screen were already in place. I walked the policemen through each chapter of our incredible story, where seemingly insurmountable obstacles are conquered by an invisible power. I showed pictures from our youth, when Tina and I first met. I explained how our dream of a modern hospital for the Quechua Indians had become a reality through the providence of God. After forty-five minutes, each of my listeners understood that we as committed Christians at Diospi Suyana did not talk about God philosophically or superficially, but experienced Him in very real terms.

The Coronel stood up and squeezed my hand. 'Thank you, Dr John,' he said earnestly. 'I see now why it is so critical that this celebration takes place. We will help you!'

The conversation turned to brainstorming options for us to proceed in as safe a way as possible.

'We will completely shut down the Panamericana Highway between Abancay and Cusco from Thursday morning,' Coronel Vasquez indicated as his chosen course of action. 'We must prevent the protesters from reaching Curahuasi!'

The Coronel then turned and urged me to talk to the local strike leaders. 'You can easily get the teachers from this community on your side,' he said. 'We can deal with any agitators coming in from other areas.'

The policemen returned to their vehicles. I waved for a long time as I watched them drive away. Perhaps there was still hope for our momentous anniversary gala after all.

The following Tuesday, Tina and I got to work on our part of the plan. Accompanied by Doris Manco, we met up with five union leaders, each of whom held an important position in SUTEP, the confederation of unions that represents most of the teachers in Peru – including about 420 in Curahuasi itself.

We convened in a Catholic rectory. A priest served us all biscuits and tea, the refreshment a welcome but fleeting distraction from the tension that filled the room.

'May I show you some pictures of Diospi Suyana before we get started?' I asked the union leaders.

'No need. We have known about Diospi Suyana for years.' The faces on the other side of the room were hardened with resolve.

'We have nothing against Diospi Suyana,' explained one of the women, 'but the current situation is intolerable for teachers. We have something to say to the President and we *will* be heard!'

Her colleague added, 'This is huge. We are expecting demonstrators to come from across southern Peru. Not only will the President have to listen, but so will the media!'

Nothing Doris, Tina or I said could dissuade them. The strike leaders could not see past their own interests to honour the work Diospi Suyana had been doing sacrificially for the people of Peru over the previous decade.

As we prepared to leave under a dark cloud of bitter disappointment, one of the union representatives bade us farewell with an unexpected comment that immediately hit home: 'May God show you the best thing to do in this situation.'

Of course. That is exactly what we would do – pray and ask God to guide our every move.

The same evening, we called an all-hands meeting in the children's house at Diospi Suyana. Olaf Böttger, chair of the Diospi Suyana organisation, his sister Annette, business manager, and Tobias Kühl, board member, had already arrived from Germany.

'Dear friends,' I began, 'no one knows how things will go on Thursday. Given the current circumstances, we have no idea if the President will make an appearance or not. Unfortunately, we cannot rule out the possibility of violent demonstrations near Diospi Suyana.'

The atmosphere was sober. Some of our team were upset that we didn't call the event off immediately. Parents were understandably fearful for their children's safety. I sympathised with their concerns.

We had no crystal ball, no way of knowing what was going to happen. But we knew what we could do. From Wednesday morning, we would begin a twenty-four-hour prayer chain. And all of our preparations would proceed as planned.

On Wednesday afternoon, we rehearsed the full programme in the festively adorned amphitheatre, as though our efforts were guaranteed to be fruitful. Our futuristic tent roof offered protection from the hot sun and the Shadow of the Almighty protection from everything else, including our worst fears. We hung on to that hope with all our might.

While all this was taking place on the hospital grounds, I welcomed a Palace security detail to my office. These ten men were tasked with making the pivotal decision whether or not President Kuczynski would be landing on our helipad the next day.

'Dr John, we will be in constant contact with the Palace tomorrow,' the President's security chief pledged brusquely. 'We certainly don't want this to turn into a dangerous publicity stunt. We will make the call around 9am if the President and his party are good to go.'

22

31st August 2017 – too much for our nerves

The cockerel had crowed, and in the east, the first golden rays of sunlight peeked over the lush, green mountains. Our festively adorned amphitheatre made a spectacular impression with its new domed roof. Through a massive team effort, we had only just been able to complete the last of the preparations late the night before – we were ready! And yet the sword of Damocles hung over our heads. How would this day go? At this point, we had more questions than answers. Tina and I joined the prayer chain at midnight. One cannot do more than work and pray. A sense of peace came over us. And yet that peace was fragile.

Shortly after 7am, Doris Manco called me. She had heard that two hundred protestors from southern Peru had arrived in Curahuasi at dawn, despite the alleged tight police controls.

The next ill-boding call came shortly afterwards. Our head of administration, Matthais Besold, rang to inform us that the teachers were already standing on the ridge above our amphitheatre, chanting and waving their banners.

This is precisely what we had been afraid of. From their advantageous position, the protesters could easily throw stones, rotten eggs and whatever else they might like straight into the arena. There was no way the President would be able to attend under such volatile conditions.

The President's security team shared our concerns. They were communicating constantly with the Palace in Lima and with the police, very aware that more protestors were on their way. The small police detachment near the hospital would be hopelessly overwhelmed.

Neither Tina nor I had been able to sleep for all our trepidation. We rose early and began to walk the hospital grounds. We ran into a group of about fifteen Peruvians holding vigil in the broadcast centre. We joined hands and fervently entreated, 'God, please intervene!'

Perhaps fifteen minutes later, several large coaches made their way up the road to the hospital. Rugged guys in full combat gear disembarked. To my astonishment, Comandante-general Max Reynaldo Iglesias Arévalo, the top brass of law enforcement in Cusco and Apurímac, was among them.

'We have 550 troops moving into place to secure the perimeter of the hospital,' the police commander informed me. 'As far as we are concerned, we are ready!'

A long wall of protesters and police squared off along the slopes.

'Will the President be able to come?' I asked the Palace security coordinator. He shrugged his shoulders and gazed soberly towards the mountains. In the distance, the rising clamour of the protestors was unmistakable.

As planned, the police had closed the Panamericana. Within a matter of hours, hundreds of cars were backed up in both directions. This strategy was supposed to keep the protestors away by impeding their travel, but unfortunately it didn't work. Whole crowds of angry activists appeared on the hills surrounding Diospi Suyana. They came bearing banners, megaphones and a palpable determination to wreak utter havoc.

From the gates of the hospital, one could view an immense police force, a strikingly empty amphitheatre and more rioters on the way. If helicopters were to arrive with the Presidential party now, it would be a complete travesty.

Disquietude was manifest across every face. Why was my mouth so dry? I paced nervously across the expanse of the hospital. There was nothing we could do, no alternative course of action to take. We had underestimated the external threat and now we were stuck. Should we call everything off while there was still time?

Again, I found myself at the entrance to the broadcast centre. This time, about twenty staff members were gathered, with eyes closed. Doris Manco led the group in prayer. When all hope appears lost, the only thing left to do is cry out to heaven.

It was not yet 8am, but it wasn't looking good. Dr Jens Haβfeld, Chris Welch, Oebele de Haan, my wife and I were walking back and forth across the helipad. The waiting was torture. Would the helicopters land as we had planned? At this point, it was completely out of our control.

Our eyes suddenly became irritated, and we rubbed at them in attempts to find some relief. It was tear gas, carried on the wind from where the clashes between police and protestors were clearly escalating.

Phones started ringing. The highway closure was apparently affecting our invited guests possibly more than the protestors, and many found themselves stuck and in need of advice.

But when you feel lost yourself, it is nearly impossible to give direction to others. Nobody could get here. State of emergency. Our big event was ruined. It was all over and we had lost.

I looked into the weary eyes of Doris Manco. 'The work of Diospi Suyana will continue,' I affirmed, then added sadly, 'even without the festival.'

Just after 8am, I received an update from the head of security, who informed me that the President had departed Lima, despite all the chaos. A final decision would be made once he reached the popular tourist destination of Cusco. As the safety of the President was undeniably the top priority, the Palace delegation would only transfer to the helicopters if the Comandante-general himself gave the go-ahead.

A female police officer attempted to encourage me by showing a news video of the President on her phone. Just that morning, he had announced on camera, 'I'm going to Curahuasi now, where German missionaries have built a modern hospital for the poorest of our poor!'

I felt a glimmer of hope, but there was still the mayhem on the hills around our grounds.

Oebele de Haan drove up to the amphitheatre with 4,500 packed meals in tow. Countless hands had toiled together to provide a drink, sandwich, chocolate bar and biro into a plastic bag as a gift for each of our anniversary guests. But would there actually be any? The venue was still largely deserted. The police were only just beginning to allow a slow trickle of locals past the last checkpoint.

'Dr John,' bellowed the head of security, 'the President can't fly all the way out here to an empty theatre! Get your people together!'

I swallowed hard. If wishes could fill our amphitheatre, it would be overflowing, but I had no power to conjure up an audience. I had previously told the Palace that we were expecting about four thousand spectators on the day. Now the roads were closed. Anyone interested in attending our event would need to be able to walk up the three-hundred-metre driveway. If they didn't have suitable identification, the police would turn them away. I felt so sorry for the mountain church communities that had hired trucks to bring their members down to the valley. Never an easy or quick journey, the closure of the Panamericana brought their plans to a grinding halt.

Displayed on the stage was an impressive diorama created by Udo Klemenz, containing five TV towers and the orthopaedic clinic in miniature. A large picture showed the hospital with its first-floor extension. It was surrounded by a red ribbon that Kuczynski was supposed to cut as part of the ceremony that was now perilously close to not happening.

A cacophony of propellers overhead signalled the presence of a military helicopter doing a 'practice run' on the landing approach before the President's chopper arrived. If this pilot could not land on our helipad, for whatever reason, the only alternative would be for the President to land at the stadium in town. Not a safe or viable option on this day, the danger of the furious mob packing the streets was all too real. The helicopter touched down with a deafening roar. Success! It was a good thing that Oebele de Haan had taken a chainsaw to the tops of the tall trees the night before! A seed of hope began to grow.

I received another directive from the head of security: 'Dr John, speak to the people in the amphitheatre. Be clear with them that this is a religious event, not a political one!'

There was a band on stage playing beautiful songs to entertain our early arrivals. When they took a break, I took the opportunity to address the audience, emphatically reminding them of our purpose. I could not help but notice that the crowd had grown to about a thousand. Or maybe even fifteen hundred? Perhaps the day would not be so humiliating after all.

Then Carlos Franco showed up out of the blue! The former manager of Alianza Lima, a Peruvian football club comparable to Germany's Bayern Munich, brought one of his star players along. Our master of ceremonies, Agustin Landeras, didn't miss the opportunity to conduct a celebrity interview on stage.

My mobile vibrated in my pocket. Dr Schmidt, delegate from the German Embassy, and Maria Jürgens, Honorary Consul of Germany in Cusco, were being denied entry to the Diospi Suyana grounds by police. I ran to the gate and spoke to the officers myself. Eventually, the gate was opened and the faces of our honoured guests relaxed.

'Get ready and get your wife,' a familiar voice barked. 'The helicopters are on their way. You'll be able to receive the President and his entourage shortly!'

I hardly dared to believe my ears. 'Tina!' I called. 'Where's Jens? It's about to start!'

As the helicopter came into view, I retreated into the orthopaedic clinic for a moment alone. The clinic was still completely empty inside. Through the windows, I could clearly see the helipad eighty metres below. I burst into tears – tears of relief.

'God, thank You!' My short prayer burst from my soul in the midst of this vacant space.

Pulling myself together, I ran to find Tina and Jens so we could greet our distinguished guests.

The hospital tour with the President and visiting dignitaries took about half an hour. In the infirmary, I pointed out a distinctive painting illuminated on the wall. Pastor Bruno Spießwinkel from Schleswig-Holstein had painted it especially for Diospi Suyana. It depicted Jesus' feeding of the five thousand with only five loaves and two fish.

'Mr President, the story of Diospi Suyana is much like this,' I explained. 'We had no money, no equipment, no staff. But God created something huge from the little we shared.'

The President visited two of our wards, chatting with patients as he passed through. Several had travelled no small distance to get here, coming from three different Peruvian states. Each expressed satisfaction in and gratitude for the exceptional treatment provided by our medical staff.

By this time, we were beginning to feel more comfortable and confident. It was a beautiful, sunny day. Our audience had grown in number and enthusiasm. We had moving music being played live on stage. It was time for the official programme to begin.

The students of the Diospi Suyana school paraded onto the stage. All Peruvians joined in singing the national anthem. An astonishing number of people also joined in singing the German national anthem, the words to which were projected on the back wall of the stage. Happy faces were everywhere, the President's included. We marvelled that they had made it – the Head of State himself, his ministers, deputy ministers, other dignitaries representing a wide cross section of Peruvian society, and a rather contented chief advisor Maximo San Roman.

'Our guest list today reads like a Wikipedia article,' I joked in my opening remarks.

The first sixty minutes of the programme were broadcast live on TV Perú, the national public television network, throughout all twenty-five Peruvian states. We will never know how many tens of thousands tuned in that day to hear about the Hospital of Faith. Martina explained how the love of God and resurrection of Christ were behind all our work. Everyone who listened could not miss the fact that God alone is our strength and our hope – in both this life and eternity.

In his speech, President Kuczynski referred to Diospi Suyana as a work with both 'heart and expertise'. This was high praise, commensurate with being knighted! At the age of seventy-eight,

Kuczynski understood the scope and impact of our work with the rural poor. In addition to his broad professional and political achievements, he had studied economics and political science at the elite international universities of Oxford and Princeton in his youth. He knew the harsh reality of life in the Peruvian mountains, and he discerned that Diospi Suyana had done something extraordinary to make a difference in his country and the rest of the world. This recognition is what drove the President and his ministers to invest an entire day in order to be present at our anniversary celebration, despite all of the challenges and unrest. Addressing my wife and me, along with the entire Diospi Suyana team, the President spoke earnestly into the microphone: 'Thank you, thank you, thank you for all you have done and are doing for our Peru!'

Our anniversary celebration lasted two and a half hours without incident. Outside our gates, the situation remained tense, but fortunately no one was injured and no blood was shed. An estimated 3,500 guests and an entire nation of television viewers got to witness the benefit of trusting God, even in the twenty-first century.

That night I wrote on our website, 'With this encouragement, we enter our second decade with confidence. Faith in God, not just in words but in action, won the respect of the government, the media and the entire population today!'

23
Afterglow

If you've ever been to a football match in a packed stadium, perhaps you've experienced this phenomenon: the electric energy and excitement of the crowd, and then half an hour after the final whistle blows, all is quiet and still, as if nothing has really ever happened. That was the feeling I had after our gala ended, despite having been on pins and needles every minute of the actual production. I must admit, the experience certainly aged me.

Not all of our guests hurried off the premises. A group of perhaps thirty people, mainly members of the press, business owners and guests from abroad, remained in Curahuasi overnight. I took the opportunity to offer these dear friends a detailed tour of Diospi Suyana. Marco Zileri and his photographer were among those who lingered. The events of the day clearly touched the *Caretas* editor in chief, and he struggled to maintain his composure. A seasoned journalist with a keen eye, he had picked up on peripheral details that others might likely have missed. He was astonished to see that when a Quechua woman standing next to him in the crowd greeted my wife, Tina gave her a friendly wave back.

Curious, Zileri asked the woman if she had ever actually met my wife.

'Of course!' the woman affirmed. 'I know Doctora Martina well. She has been treating my children for many years!'

Her response made an impression on Zileri. Although we rubbed shoulders with the highest levels of government and wealthy CEOs, we lived out our faith in God by loving all people. We are all equal before the Most High, with or without a suit and tie.

Over the next few days, several television channels continued to broadcast extensive coverage and commentary on our grand celebration, which was viewed in private homes and public venues across the country. For better or worse, many South Americans can be a bit over the top when it comes to praise. Channels 4, 5, 9, and 24 portrayed us in such a gilded light, we were certain to have queues for days! Channel 9 (ATV) went all out in its eleven-minute news segment, declaring, 'Diospi Suyana is one of the best hospitals in Peru!'

On 21st September, exactly three weeks after the big event, Marco Zileri himself penned a six-page expository piece in his magazine *Caretas*. His target audience was the educated middle class, the intellectuals of Lima. He chose an unusual headline, given that he was a professed atheist: 'Here They Believe God Is Visible!' This was a nod to the Spanish title of my first book, *Dios Es Visible*, but also a true statement of the conviction held by all Diospi Suyana staff.

Zileri, a prolific writer as well as editor, summed up his impressions of Diospi Suyana as follows: 'In Curahuasi, God can clearly be seen at work, while the state is virtually invisible. Catholics and Protestants, Jews and atheists are all striving together to support this mission hospital, with no thought of personal gain!' And then he quoted a remark I had made almost in passing: 'We have struggled with doubt. It is not enough for us to say that we believe in God; we want to live out our faith. That is why we work here day after day, year after year. We will not give up!'

Unfortunately, one day we would be tested in a whole new way. Our greatest challenges would no longer be the poverty of our patients or our own lack of funds, but the malicious envy of other institutions and hostile indifference of state authorities. But we still had a year of grace before all that started.

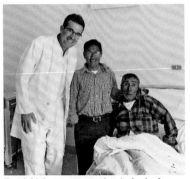

Daniel Ticona recovering in bed after his operation. Beside him, his nephew Constantino with Dr David Brady. The journey from Cusco to Curahuasi itself was an incredible challenge for the eighty-two-year-old.

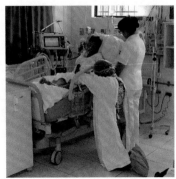

Gladys Illesca knelt at the bedside of the injured boy and prayed for his healing on 1st December 2018.

Dr Jens Haßfeld (right) removed a huge cyst from the patient's right ovary.

Anyeli (class 5) and Gino (class 1) have been attending Colegío Diospi Suyana since March 2019. Their family had heard about our school on the radio.

Social worker Debora Centner (to the right of the post) entertains a group of girls at a school camp.

Principal Christian Bigalke (right) in conversation with Vice-Principal Nikolas Sierras (left) and psychologist Esther Castillo (centre).

Matthias and Jennifer Rehder with their children, Janne and Lina.

Hard-working bakers showing off cakes they prepared for the school festival in June 2019.

Campesinos listen as Pastor Marco Acuña preaches at the funeral of a young woman.

Dr Georg Steinfurth and his wife Kerstin (third and fourth from the left) on the front page of the *ÄrzteZeitung* (German medical journal) on 17 February 2016.

The Welch family in their former home in Sydney. They had used their own money to purchase the many boxes full of electronic equipment at an auction.

My first lecture in Romania. Around six hundred people attended the presentation at the Biscrica Poarta Cerului church in Timisoara.

Dutchman Oebele de Haan constructed a crane to hoist the roofing panels upwards.

Surveyor Jürgen Waltersbacher under the eaves of the mission hospital. The roofing panel project was essentially his doing.

Civil engineer Johannes Bahr built the lowest two floors of the media centre. He also supervised the renovation of our guesthouse in Lima and helped Udo Klemenz build our school.

Six missionaries gather in the dining room of our guesthouse. (From left to right) Susan Kirchhoff, Annerose Müller, Annette Goss, Dana Hennig, Stefanie Heese and Mechthild Pochert.

The Diospi Suyana guesthouse in the Surco neighbourhood of Lima. Although it looks small and modest from the outside, inside, it has more than 420 square metres of living space.

Doris Marco holds the issue of the Peruvian news circular *Chaski* in her hands. The August 2016 inauguration of our media centre is featured on the front page.

180 participants sign the minutes of a Poltocsa town hall meeting on 17th February 2017. After an intense debate, Diospi Suyana was given the green light to build a radio tower on the nearby hill.

Dentist Dr Nikolaus von Abendroth and his wife Dr Johanna von Abendroth with their children Salomé, Linnéa, Jonathan and Leonard.

Under the direction of civil engineer Udo Klemenz, the Diospi Suyana Hospital was extended upward by one floor, doubling bed capacity.

On 19th May 2017, the Peruvian head of state Pedro Pablo Kuczynski granted us an audience in the Presidential Palace. (From left to right) Advisor Maximo San Roman, Dr Klaus-Dieter John, President Kuczynski, Dr Martina John and Dr Jens Haßfeld.

View of the full amphitheatre during our tenth anniversary celebration. The tent roof had been completed just a few days earlier.

Heavily armed police officers at roll call at the hospital entrance. In total, the Peruvian government mobilised a force of 550 to protect our anniversary celebrations on 31st August 2017.

Press photo on the amphitheatre stage during the anniversary celebration. The President of Peru and Dr Schmidt from the German Embassy holding a picture of the hospital.

My wife and I share a brief history of Diospi Suyana. Our presentation in the packed amphitheatre was broadcast live on public television to all twenty-five states of Peru.

Daniel Müller fits four-year-old Nehemias Huaiman with a prosthesis. The boy was born with an underdeveloped left leg.

Occupational therapist Susi Rottler helps Britney with her new prosthetic arm.

Past and present Diospi Suyana missionaries gathered in Wiesbaden for a mission festival and shared a song in Spanish during the church service on 8th October 2017.

On behalf of the German President, Ambassador Jörg Ranau presented us with the Order of Merit of the Federal Republic of Germany. The ceremony took place at his residence in Lima on 25th April 2018.

A relaxed evening at the private home of Albert Lee (left) on 3rd May 2018. Mariano Blázquez (right) of the Federation of Evangelical Religious Entities in Spain shares his testimony.

Professor Irvin Moblin and his staff posed for a photo after my presentation. The professor emeritus (grey hair and grey jacket in the middle) was my mentor at Yale University from 1991 to 1993.

The Diospi Suyana media station next to the mission hospital. The programmes are broadcast via a satellite provided by INTELSAT.

Australian Chris Welch connects our broadcasting facility in Puerto Maldonado to the satellite in space.

Teacher Mandy Rosenkranz was one of the many staff members who donated blood for the treatment of the severely injured Abraham K. On the right, Dr Martina John draws the needed blood.

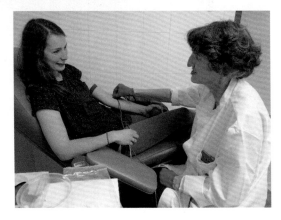

On 18th September 2018, my wife addressed the citizens of Curahuasi. The demonstrators gathered to express their support for the work of our mission.

On 7th July 2018, four of our doctors were honoured by the Peruvian medical authorities: urologist Dr David Brady, paediatrician Dr Dorothea Brady, gynaecologist Dr Miriam Boeker and traumatologist Dr Tim Boeker. In the middle of the picture is the head of the Cusco Medical Association, Dr Héctor Paucar Sotomayor.

The golden wedding anniversary of Udo and Barbara Klemenz on 15th September was one of the highlights of 2018. In total, the couple has poured an entire decade of their lives into the development of Diospi Suyana.

Jewish Health Minister Silvia Pessar helped Diospi Suyana Hospital to regain its operating licence.

On 24th June 2018, we presented our work to the Prime Minister Salvador del Solar at the Government Palace. That same evening, he arranged a meeting for us with the Minister of Health, Doctora Garcia Zulema.

The day after the birth of their fifth child, urologist Benjamin Zeier and his wife, physiotherapist Lena, made the decision to go to Peru. The children are named Kaila Deborah, Mila Grace, Elias Fabian, Lucas Benjamin and Jonas Kilian.

Meeting of the department heads in my office on 11th June 2019: (from left to right) Deputy Director Dr Jens Haßfeld, Head of Nursing Damaris Haßfeld, Dr Martina John, Dr Klaus-Dieter John, Dr Thomas Thielmann, Head of Administration Steven de Jager, and workshop manager Oebele de Haan.

Dental technician Elisabeth Franke worked in our clinic for almost five years. The CAD/CAM machine in the picture can make a dental crown in twenty minutes.

Group photo at the Plaza de Armas of Curahuasi. Many hospital employees took part in the Independence Day parade on 28th July 2019.

Markus and Christiane Klatt returned to Peru with their sons Johannes and Emanuel in January 2019. The Klatt family had to interrupt their mission service for a year while Christiane underwent cancer treatment.

Every year, more and more patients come to Curahuasi and queue up for an opportunity to receive medical treatment at the mission hospital.

Johannes B Kerner interviewed us at the fundraising gala 'Ein Herz für Kinder' ('A Heart for Children') on 7th December 2019. The televised programme was viewed by an estimated 3.7 million people.

On 5th February 2018, the Kessler, Kügler and Tielmann families all arrived together at Lima Airport. Our missionaries make personal sacrifices to serve at Diospi Suyana for at least three years.

Our chairman Olaf Böttger interviews master optician Dorothea Töws in a restaurant in Darmstadt. Olaf Böttger has been the backbone of Diospi Suyana in Germany since he first volunteered back in 2002.

A patient with a suspected coronavirus infection is resuscitated during a CT scan.

Dr Ollie O'Neill with his wife Zoe and their children Isobel and James, from Sheffield. Ollie is a pediatrician and Zoe is a physiotherapist. They are our first long-term missionaries from England.

24

The mission festival

It is common for international mission organisations to support 'festivals' during which missionaries return to their home countries in order to publicly give an account of their work. Largely celebratory, these are also a time for those who serve to share challenges and invite prayer. Friends and supporters get to hear a first-hand account of the missionaries' life 'in the field', often far removed from their own in both distance and detail. We thought that the tenth anniversary of Diospi Suyana was a perfect, if not overdue, opportunity to host such an event.

The three-day festival was held from 6th to 8th October 2017 at the Baptist Christuskirche in Wiesbaden, Germany. On the Friday evening, we invited former Diospi Suyana missionaries to share their experiences at the hospital. Neither traffic nor stormy weather could deter the ninety guests who made the long journey to the capital of Hesse. A happy reunion for adults and children alike, the opening scene was full of hugs, how-have-you-beens and glances towards the door to see who might pop in next. A mission abroad brings people together, and gratitude was a common theme in the conversations that took place that evening. The opportunity to serve in Curahuasi was a life-changing experience!

On the Saturday evening, more than four hundred people were in attendance at the church hall for our main event. Tina, our daughter Natalie and I reviewed the highlights of the last ten years via a multimedia presentation. Pastor Marco Acuña and his assistant Nohemi Quispe shared their perspective as

Peruvian colleagues. It was a multifarious programme, replete with stories and testimonies from South America. Time flew, but no one was watching the clock. Protestants and Catholics came together in harmony to hear what God can do when people trust Him.

As the evening drew to a close, Nick Howard, the American pastor of the church's English-speaking congregation, took the floor. 'Let's be honest,' he declared in his soft Texas drawl, 'Diospi Suyana can only be explained by God's grace!' Of course, he was right.

I bade the crowd goodnight, inviting them to return at ten o'clock the next morning for more. The guests all waved to the video camera on their way out and headed home. Certainly, they could not help but wonder, 'If God works like this in Peru, couldn't He do the same here in Europe?'

On the Sunday morning, cars with foreign licence plates lined the streets around the church. Finding a parking space was a real challenge! The Christuskirche hall was jam-packed with five hundred guests, sitting in close quarters, not unlike a Ryanair flight. The celebration service flowed smoothly from start to finish for more than two hours.

We opened with inspirational music led by Carolina Jochum and Dr Jens Haßfeld. When Markus Köhler, Managing Director of United German Mission Aid (Vereinigte Deutsche Missionshilfe), addressed the audience, he dropped an astonishing statistic: the organisation had already sent a total of ninety-five missionaries to Diospi Suyana!

The motto of the mission festival was 'Changed Lives'. Tina and I referred back to this continuously as we shared our presentation with fifty photos representing the dramatic way in which Diospi Suyana has made a positive impact on the lives of countless patients and staff. Even beyond our gates, the rest of Curahuasi and even the whole region of Apurímac has been blessed. The formerly desolate mountain village has developed into a booming town with more than five hundred new jobs created as a direct or indirect result of Diospi Suyana. Our staff have been the catalyst for enormous improvement in the areas of health, education and media. Every single resident of Curahuasi could bear witness to these changes.

Pastor Ulrich Parzany delivered a gripping thirty-minute sermon on Jesus' healing of the paralysed man. Surely no one could have dozed off during this talk! He reminded the audience that Christians are called to be the hands and feet of Jesus, to share the gospel through love and service to others.

Six missionaries were commissioned towards the end of the service, their departure to Peru imminent. Before the offering was taken, I encouraged everyone to give only what God had laid on their hearts. No one should give 'too much', I said. That day, what people gave in support of Diospi Suyana totalled nearly €5,000. It was the most generous collection anyone could remember in the history of the church.

'Please don't wait another ten years to do this again!' 'Your stories have really renewed my faith in God!' The feedback we received from our departing guests was so uplifting.

But one comment in particular from Pastor Parzany stuck with Tina and me. 'Diospi Suyana has grown incredibly,' he said thoughtfully, 'but God always finds a way to keep His workers humble.' We both winced imperceptibly. Should we take his words prophetically? Should we be preparing for a rough ride?

Time would tell.

25

From one lot of bad news to the next

The Diospi Suyana mission festival ended on Sunday afternoon. The enthusiasm of the guests from Germany and abroad was infectious, and I expect some would say that the effect went both ways. In any case, we were flying high and looking forward to a few good nights of sleep to wind down.

Not forty-eight hours had passed when we received a disturbing email. The Hamburg law firm Harte-Bavendamm contacted us on behalf of its client, the German Red Cross (DRK – Deutsches Rotes Kreuz), accusing us of trademark infringement and demanding that we immediately remove the Diospi Suyana logo from all public displays within and beyond German borders. Failure to do so, the message warned, would result in legal action against us.

I remember exactly how I felt as I skimmed the ominous directive displayed on my screen. Anxious and despondent. I shook my head in disbelief and let out a long sigh.

With around three million members, the DRK is one of the largest humanitarian aid organisations in Germany, with close ties to many influential political and financial entities. According to Wikipedia, this charitable powerhouse generates a staggering 4.5 billion euros in revenue each year. A legal battle between Diospi Suyana and the German Red Cross would look a lot like David confronting Goliath. Nobody wanted to play that game.

Of course, we also had good lawyers and high-profile contacts, but the subsequent feedback we received was even more discouraging. The president of a large corporation with direct connections in the federal government cautioned me strongly over the phone: 'Dr John, the DRK is untouchable. There is no way you can win this!' Woe is us!

With God's help, we had spent the last decade building Diospi Suyana into an established and respected entity. Through a multitude of presentations and media coverage, we could prove that twenty million people in Germany alone had heard our name at some point. Since 2005, the Diospi logo had adorned every one of our publications. By autumn 2017, we had presented the story of Diospi Suyana in twenty-three countries. Millions of people all over the world have come to associate the Diospi Suyana logo with our work in Peru. The allegation made on behalf of the DRK could not have created a bigger predicament for us.

We nervously speculated what the fallout would be if the DRK prevailed. Would we be forced to destroy all our brochures, change our website and letterheads, paint over the sign at the entrance to the hospital and remove the appliqués from our uniforms? What about our books? Tens of thousands of copies printed with the logo on the back had been stocked or already sold.

One week later, we sent an eleven-page justification statement to DRK Secretary General Christian Reuter and requested an urgent meeting in Berlin. We pointed out that ou logo had been registered as a protected trademark in Germany for thirteen years, and a concern had never been raised in all that time. Our logo was also protected under trademark law in Peru.

We concluded our statement as follows: 'We appeal to the DRK to consider the facts and leave our logo intact. As we have clearly illustrated in the preceding pages, the Diospi Suyana logo has a completely different form, symbolism and history. There is absolutely no risk of confusion with the DRK logo.'

Although our two organisational logos may differ, we do share a passion for serving the sick, the broken and the outcast.

Henry Dunant, founder of the Red Cross movement and committed Christian, confessed near the end of his life, 'I was merely an instrument in God's hand!' My wife and I would say the same about ourselves.

On 11th November, Tina and I travelled to Berlin to present our stance to the DRK in person. We attempted to maintain utmost cordiality while holding firm to our determination to defend the Diospi Suyana logo with all means available. Earlier that autumn, the DRK had found itself under fire, with various media outlets reporting doubts about the integrity of the organisation, citing the incongruity of high executive salaries with simultaneous public appeals for donations. In addition, blood drives tended to produce very lucrative results, calling into question the DRK's non-profit status.

The *BILD* newspaper was quick to take an interest in our dilemma. After our meeting at the DRK's main office, we went straight to the Axel Springer headquarters to speak with one of the editors at *BILD*. Europe's most widely circulated newspaper would end up backing us publicly.

Professor Ludwig Georg Braun, Honorary President of the Association of German Chambers of Industry and Commerce, intervened on our behalf several times with DRK leadership.

And finally, Armin Dörr, attorney and long-time friend of Diospi Suyana, succeeded in engaging the support of Clifford Chance LLP, one of the world's largest and most pre-eminent international law firms. On 4th December, I visited its Düsseldorf office and shared my usual presentation with two lawyers there. Afterwards, they prepared and filed a lengthy protective letter to prevent the court from granting a preliminary injunction against the use of the Diospi Suyana logo.

The dispute with the DRK continued until the end of the year. Finally, we re-registered our logo – slightly modified with a shadow effect – as a text and image trademark. The statute of limitations would end on 11th June 2018. If the DRK continued to challenge our logo, a court battle would ensue, and we were prepared to fight. All of these activities just described, and countless others behind the scenes, clearly illustrate our unwillingness to give up. And, of course, we prayed fervently for God's help. The outcome remained uncertain, and the lack of resolution weighed on our nerves.

And then there was a second predicament to keep us up at night. In October and November, we discovered some seriously shady dealings in our optometry clinic. Almost by chance, some employees had become suspicious and voiced their concerns, leading to an immediate investigation. Americo V, who had been trusted to provide exemplary service in the clinic for more than eight years, was suspected of extorting money from patients for his own personal gain. When confronted, he denied everything with wide eyes of innocence. I gave the order to interview all five thousand patients Americo had dealt with during his time at the hospital. The findings were devastating. Americo had defrauded more than three hundred patients and done lasting damage to the reputation of Diospi Suyana.

I immediately consulted with our lawyers at Estudio Olaechea. In a cross-examination in my office, we managed to record Americo's full confession on video. He promised to pay back all the money he had stolen and to personally apologise to each of his victims. We were so distressed by such unexpected deceitful and malicious behaviour in our midst, it was months before we could mentally move on.

At the turn of the year, we went from the frying pan straight into the fire. The Klatt family had to leave the language school in Cusco and rush back to Germany after Christiane was diagnosed with cancer. Why would God allow this to happen to such a young missionary when she and her husband were so desperately needed at the hospital? Christiane, a surgical assistant, and Markus, an electronics technician, were so clear that they had been called by God to the mission field. Their rigorous language studies were nearly complete. They and their children had adjusted to the Peruvian culture and overcome so many hurdles. Now their service in Peru was at risk of being over before it had really even begun. A bitter pill for the Klatts to swallow, and also for our team.

The surge of bad news didn't let up. In 2016, we had purchased a VHF radio frequency in Puno through public tender. But more than a year later, we were still awaiting permission from the Ministry of Transport and Communications to start building our antenna tower. As the weeks continued to drag on, we became increasingly concerned that we had become a victim of Peruvian bureaucracy or, worse, of covert government corruption.

Things got worse and worse. A private clinic in the city of Andahuaylas misused our logo to attract clients. We learned that the doctors there were falsely claiming that the clinic was affiliated with Diospi Suyana. This particular clinic was profit-based and charged exorbitant fees for its services. With our logo plastered all over the building, the private clinic's misrepresentation caused significant damage to our reputation.

The exhilaration of our tenth-anniversary celebrations in Peru and the mission festival in Germany was abruptly eclipsed as more and more crises demanded our urgent attention simultaneously. We couldn't help but remember Pastor Parzany's prescient remark on the final day of the festival: 'God always knows how to keep people modest and humble!'

26

The German President sends his regards

There's only so much bad news a person can take. Maybe we can withstand a single blow that would fell others, but when it's just one thing after another, there inevitably comes a moment when it is all just too much. There is a saying in English that illustrates this phenomenon perfectly: the straw that broke the camel's back.

At Diospi Suyana, we want to honour God and serve our neighbour. In the early years of our work, the media in particular encouraged us to downplay our beliefs. Since we rely on donations and only a very small minority in Western Europe claim to be Christian, we were strongly cautioned to not alienate potential supporters by advertising our faith. Well-intentioned advice that my wife and I never heeded. We knew that Diospi Suyana would never succeed without God, our strongest ally. And the Bible affirms throughout that the God of Abraham, Isaac and Jacob helps those who go forth in His name. When our world came crashing down in the spring of 2018, we ached for consolation and encouragement. And God heard the cry of our hearts.

Years ago, my son Florian and I went shopping at Karstadt for a few small items. At the checkout, the cashier handed us two scratch cards, promising that if we were winners, she would give us the money right away. Florian scratched the foil off his card to find he had won! Brilliant! If I remember correctly, he got about €10. We smiled and laughed. When it was my turn, I scratched with my fingernail and looked closely at the card. I too had won! We were delighted with our unexpected good fortune. Days later, we were still telling people about our experience. Prizes are definitely a mood booster, no question about it. Who hasn't looked around the table with glee after drawing the 'You've won second prize in a beauty contest' card from the Community Chest in a game of Monopoly? The emotional impact is even stronger when someone presents you with an award for an actual achievement – something you've *earned*. Hang a medal around the neck of a young scout after a successful scavenger hunt, and they will keep that round piece of tin in their desk drawer for the rest of their life!

From time to time, my wife and I receive recognition for our work. Our accolades have included Peruvian citizenship *honoris causa*, an honorary diploma from the Peruvian Congress and a sparkling Medal of Merit from the Presidential Palace. No one deserves these honours more than my wife. Tina works so hard; I easily downshift in order to counterbalance. Sometimes she does too much of a good thing, though. She is usually the last one to leave the hospital each evening. She continues her efforts at home, spending hours on the internet researching therapies her patients so desperately need. She is incomparable in her dedication as a doctor and team leader, and God is using her to write an incredible modern mission story. Unfortunately, this means we don't get to spend a lot of time together. I occasionally joke that I need to join the queue outside the hospital to get an appointment with her. Perhaps that is stretching it just a bit, but it is certainly not an exaggeration to say that, along with my late parents, Tina is my greatest inspiration.

In 2006, Albrecht Einbock from the Saxony Ministry of Social Affairs nominated us for a special honour. This was before the Diospi Suyana hospital had even opened! About five years later, we received a similar nomination from Baden-Württemberg, and in autumn 2017, another was initiated by a certain Helmut Steitz from the Baptist Christuskirche in Wiesbaden. Whether or not these submissions were read by the relevant departments in Berlin, I cannot say. What I do know, however, is that in early 2018, the German Ambassador rather cryptically summoned me to Lima for 'an important matter'. He offered no further explanation.

The morale booster that occurred several months later was exactly what Tina and I needed after all the recent turmoil at Diospi Suyana.

On the evening of 25th April 2018, the lights of Lima shone brightly in the clear night sky, visible for miles. Ambassador Jörg Ranau and his wife had invited forty distinguished guests from key political, business and church circles to their official residence. After generous words of praise and appreciation, the Ambassador, on behalf of German President Frank-Walter Steinmeier, presented us with the Order of Merit of the Federal Republic of Germany. The cross, suspended from a ribbon boasting the colours of the German flag, is the only federal decoration in Germany, awarded for extraordinary achievement in political, socio-economic and intellectual fields. A very high honour indeed.

We very gratefully accepted the medals on behalf of all the staff and friends of Diospi Suyana. We pointed out that by that time, more than 160 long-term missionaries, 230 businesses and more than 100,000 donors had contributed to the success of Diospi Suyana. But from start to finish, it was God who willed and worked for His good purpose. He alone deserves the glory.

The three-hour cocktail reception that followed brought together many of our supporters. Unfortunately, one of the invited guests was unable to make it owing to a business trip. But Dr Roger Albormoz, former president of the Peruvian Society of Anaesthesia, wrote from abroad, 'It is my wish that the God of heaven, whom Dr John always talks about in his speeches, may continue to bless the work of Diospi Suyana in the future!'

27

Yale, Harvard, and Clie

The next morning, Tina and I flew back to Cusco along with the Haßfelds and Doris Manco, then drove the usual three hours to Curahuasi. We would probably never wear our Order of Merit medals again but would secure them in a safe deposit box at a bank in Wiesbaden at the next opportunity. But at that moment, I had other things on my mind besides medals and speeches. Albert Lee had just sent me an itinerary for my upcoming tour along the east coast of the United States. I almost called the whole thing off.

'Albert,' I had grumbled at him sometime back in March, 'I'm not coming to America to go sightseeing! If there aren't enough scheduled presentation opportunities, I'd rather stay in Peru!' My tone on the telephone that day had been quite brusque. The Korean entrepreneur, who owned the largest laundry business in the New York City borough of Queens, informed me he wanted to take me to one or two tourist attractions between my presentations.

'Klaus, don't say that,' he entreated. 'You should definitely come. There's someone important I'd like you to meet as well.' Well, that piqued my interest …

On the afternoon of 3rd May, my United flight landed at Newark Airport and memories came flooding back to me. In October 1985, I had set foot on US soil for the first time, right here, to undergo almost eighteen months of top-notch training at six universities. Thirty-three years had passed since then.

Many of my supervisors from that period were now either enjoying their retirement or had passed away.

Via WhatsApp, Albert directed me from baggage claim to the proper exit. As I got into his car, I saw a somewhat stocky man sitting up front. 'Klaus, I'd like you to meet Mariano Blázquez,' Albert called out. 'He is the Executive Secretary of the Federation of Evangelical Religious Entities in Spain (FEREDE), and he will be accompanying us for the next few days!'

Ah, so this was the mystery celebrity Albert had mentioned on the phone! The drive through the evening rush hour traffic was gruelling, and it was late when we finally reached the Lee family's stately home in Englewood.

Three men at a table. Some snacks and drinks. I was in the company of two remarkable conversationalists. On my left was Albert Lee, an American of Korean descent who had spent years living in Argentina. He spoke Spanish more fluently than English. Although he had grown up as a Buddhist, he had come to the Christian faith through a series of hard times following the death of his mother. On my right was Mariano Blázquez Burgo. This Spaniard, who had served with FEDERE for more than two decades, began to share his story.

'I was a staunch atheist,' Mariano began, 'but then in 1971, I met some people in Madrid who claimed the power of God had set them free from the drug scene!'

Probably just a load of rubbish, the young Mariano thought to himself. And yet he was intrigued. He met a whole group of young believers. It was the era of the 'Jesus People'. In many countries, drug addicts were turning from mood-altering substances to life-altering faith. A few days later, Mariano returned to the site of his initial encounter. 'How are you today?' a young Christian woman greeted him. Mariano answered bluntly, 'If you really want to know, things are terrible!'

'If you want, I can pray for you!' the new convert responded. Mariano really didn't care if someone prayed for him or not. It's not like God existed anyway, he reasoned cynically. She was free to babble on as much as she wanted.

The ex-addict knelt down on the floor next to Mariano and asked for God's blessing, His intervention and His presence.

'I felt like I had been struck by lightning – I had an encounter with God that turned my life around immediately!' Mariano professed with a youthful exuberance. 'To this day, almost fifty years later, I know God keeps me safe in His hands!'

I regarded Albert and Mariano with gratitude. Although I had only been in the US for a few hours, my trip had already proved worthwhile. I live for stories like Mariano's. They remind me that the same God who guides my own life is also working in the lives of others. Everywhere and always.

Ten days and ten lectures. Not every event leaves its mark on me, but there are others I will remember and treasure forever. Not one, but two such highlights took place on 10th May 2018.

We set off just before half past ten to make our way up the east coast. Traffic was heavy on the I-95, but we were grateful that our satnav guided us around the worst traffic jams. We zipped along, Albert Lee at the wheel and, behind me, Korean pastor Jim Park dozing in the back.

Two hours later, in Branford, Connecticut, I was reunited with Dr Irvin Modlin for the first time in twenty-five years. The professor had been my mentor at Yale University from 1991 to 1993, guiding me in the research lab and in lectures. Dr Modlin and his research team have published hundreds of articles in the world's most prominent medical journals. At that time, Dr Modlin was even a member of the assembly that selects the Nobel Prize laureates in the field of medicine.

Dr Modlin had officially retired years earlier, but instead of spending his time enjoying the arts, he remained committed to science, working tirelessly with a team of cancer researchers.

We arrived right on time, and I connected my laptop to a large projection screen. Ten minutes later, the grey eminence himself arrived, and we shared a long-awaited handshake. Like so many scientists at Harvard and Yale, Dr Modlin is Jewish. Decades earlier, his father had taught the Talmud in Cape Town, South Africa.

After some refreshment, I began my presentation. There were ten people in the room besides me, an excellent international mix including several Koreans, a South African, women from Poland and Ecuador, and even a native Palestinian woman.

For a solid hour, no one took their eyes off the screen. Dr Modlin was clearly captivated throughout. When I was finished, Dr Modlin shared his reaction, speaking very deliberately: 'Many of my medical residents from back in the day now work as senior physicians at major US hospitals. They have achieved a great deal and have much to be proud of. But this, what has been created in Peru, is much better!'

It was my turn to address the esteemed scholar and 'crème de la crème' of the medical world. 'Professor Modlin, may I ask if you believe in God?'

'Of course,' my former mentor replied, 'There is absolutely no question about that for me!'

'And do you believe this God cares for us as people?' I followed up.

'Of course,' he said again. 'Without a doubt!'

And then we were back on the road, this time on the way to Boston. At 7pm, I would be speaking to a group of students and professors at Harvard University, where I myself had studied for several months back in 1987.

A private room in a Japanese restaurant had been booked for the occasion. More than twenty students and faculty from Harvard, MIT and Boston University lined the sides of a long table, eager to hear the story of Diospi Suyana. Before my presentation began, I struck up a conversation with Kwan-Soo Kim, Professor of Psychiatry and Neuroscience at Harvard Medical School. One of the most gifted minds in his field, this man too professed a solid Christian faith.

It was quite late when we left Boston, heading south on the interstate. I managed to get three hours of sleep before Albert Lee dropped me at New York City's JFK airport at 4am so I could catch a 6:15am flight to Grand Rapids, Michigan.

There I was met in Arrivals by David Coyotl, a Zondervan Publishing marketing director from Mexico. I was there with a very specific goal in mind: for Zondervan to publish my second book in Spanish. The first book, with the Spanish title *Dios Es Visible*, sold 10,000 copies. I felt it was time to take the next logical step. The initial conversation didn't go badly; however, Zondervan had undergone significant reorganisation and had eventually become a subsidiary of the publishing giant Harper Collins in 2011. I had no idea if the new executives in New York and Nashville would have the slightest interest in a story like ours. Diospi Suyana was far away with a foreign cast of characters.

When I returned to New York the next morning, I couldn't shake the thought that I should get in touch with the Spanish publisher Clie in Barcelona. I knew that Clie was well connected and had a successful market in South America. But I didn't actually know anyone who worked there, nor did I have a clue if the miracle of Diospi Suyana, trusting in God, would be received with enthusiasm.

But God had provided me with an unexpected ace to play, so to speak: Mariano Blázquez, the FEREDE Executive Secretary. A few emails were exchanged and a door was opened. Tina and I met with Clie Director Alfonso Triviño and Editorial Advisor Silvia Martínez in person at the Barcelona headquarters on 21st June 2018. They were hooked.

'If Zondervan turns you down, for whatever reason, we will publish your book!' Alfonso gave us his verbal commitment on the spot and backed it up in writing soon after.

The waiting game with Zondervan continued. When the response finally arrived weeks later in August, I rolled my eyes in irritation.

Yes, they would publish my second book, but the conditions stipulated in the remainder of the lengthy email were unacceptable. Zondervan had the audacity to require not only that we provide the Spanish translation, but also that we purchase nine thousand copies of the book up front! Zero risk for Zondervan; all liability fell squarely on Diospi Suyana.

Three days later, after consultation with Diospi Suyana Chair Olaf Böttger, we gratefully accepted the offer from Clie instead. The Clie team negotiated a favourable deal, translating my book into Spanish at its own expense. It also arranged for several thousand copies to be printed on site in Lima, an ingenious idea which saved us the high overseas shipping costs.

Back in Lima sometime later, I was able to hold the printed books at last, pleased with the quality product in my hands. I heard the words of Albert Lee, replaying in my memory: 'Come to New Jersey! There is someone important I want you to meet!' Unbeknown to either of us, he was exactly right. Mariano Blázquez, this passenger in airport pick-up cars, teller of incredible personal stories and opener of elusive Spanish doors, had indeed become a life-changing figure for me.

28

The lame can walk

The lame could walk! Nothing like this had ever been heard of before! Tales of Jesus' supernatural healing spread like wildfire around the Mediterranean coast, drawing the desperate seeking a similar story. In one case, four men even removed a section of a roof so they could lower their paralysed friend through to lie at the feet of Jesus as He preached inside. Without care for legal consequences or the ire of the homeowner, they focused on what mattered – helping their friend regain the use of his legs.

To lie crippled and helpless on the floor, completely dependent on others, feeling worthless, stigmatised and shunned – most of us can only imagine the horror of such an existence.

When my wife and I visited Ghana in 1983, we were shocked by the number of disfigured children and adults we came across. I will never forget the time we were literally surrounded by a sea of miserable faces and broken bodies dragging themselves along the ground as best they could.

At the end of February 2018, Daniel Müller arrived in Curahuasi with his wife and three darling daughters. The small town in the Andes would become their home for the next five years. To be fair, the girls would have preferred to stay in Germany, but they understood that their dad had an important job to do. Big and small, male and female, all were to stand on their own two feet again.

Before long, the shipping container full of orthopaedic supplies completed its journey and was unloaded behind the hospital. Daniel immediately began to set up the clinic. At that time, we had no idea how the locals might react to his prostheses!

Nehemias Huaiman was born with a congenital limb defect and was missing a large part of his left leg. Unable to walk, he was a sorrowful sight. Other children played and ran around, but he could only crouch in the corner and look on with bitter resignation. There was no cure, no hope of recovery. Nehemias endured this tragic state until 19th September 2018, when Daniel fitted the boy with a prosthetic leg. A photo taken before the fitting shows a small four-year-old boy with a sad expression on his face. Once the leg was securely in place, Daniel took his young patient outside for some fresh air. For the first time in his life, Nehemias could learn to walk – he mastered the new challenge in just two hours. Nehemias' face was completely transformed by his joy, and my audiences are always moved when they see his beaming face in the 'after' photo I've included in my presentation slides. Nehemias' parents paid just US$200 to completely turn their son's life around, a mere 2 per cent of the actual cost of more than US$10,000.

Victor was another patient seen at our new orthopaedic clinic. Victor was a father and a farmer in the small town of Izcuchaca. Like many Quechua farmers, Victor got up with the sun to tend his fields. One morning, he stopped to remove some stones in front of the running combine harvester. His left leg got caught in the rotating blades. Blood sprayed across the golden field, and Victor was left with a mangled stump. Even three operations at a hospital in Cusco could not ease his suffering. Following a recommendation, Victor's relatives brought him to see Daniel Müller. Today, Victor has a new leg and has even been able to resume working in his fields independently.

Britney's mother was completely stunned. When she breastfed her newborn daughter for the first time, her eyes locked on the baby's left arm. It barely reached where the elbow should be, and ended in a thick club shape. The single mother put all her hopes into a foreign aid organisation that promised a solution for the missing left hand, making several long journeys from Cusco to Lima with her young daughter. Two years later, she finally received a prosthesis for Britney – but it was the wrong hand! A crushing disappointment. When Britney first started school, the other students reduced her to tears with their cruel teasing. But all that is in the past now, as Daniel Müller has 3D-printed a perfect prosthesis for Britney, and occupational therapist Susi Rottler has been helping her get used to it. The highlight of our Christmas 2019 newsletter was a photo of an exuberant Britney enjoying a delicious jelly dessert – from a cup she held in her prosthetic hand.

During a mobile medical outreach to the remote village of Kishuara, a good four hours away from the Diospi Suyana hospital, it became apparent what a ripple effect a single prosthesis could have on an entire community.

Brad Vasquez, one of six children in a single-parent family, had received a prosthetic leg from us two months prior. Now he stood before two hundred people, microphone in hand, publicly welcoming Diospi Suyana staff to his village where he was clearly something of a celebrity and hero. The Quechua of Kishuara first learned of Diospi Suyana through Brad's ordeal.

The orthopaedic clinic is the latest addition to the Diospi Suyana hospital. Daniel Müller was the missing piece of the puzzle, now a member of a highly motivated team consisting of both physical and occupational therapists as well as a trauma specialist. The man from Baden-Württemberg regularly sends me photos of his happy patients, many of which I post online the very same evening. The reaction is sensational every time. The thousands of views and 'likes' on our Facebook page prove that people still rejoice when the lame walk, just as they did back in Jesus' day.

29

Udo's last encore (really!)

'It's all your fault,' I have often said in jest to Udo Klemenz. 'If only you had had the foresight to build the hospital with all these extensions upfront, then you and Barbara wouldn't need to keep coming back!' Admittedly, there may be different opinions about this question of 'guilt', but the fact remains that the growth of Diospi Suyana has exceeded our wildest expectations.

The brand-new broadcast station had already outgrown its walls. One Sunday afternoon, our Dutch workshop manager Oebele de Haan suggested we add a third floor for additional office space. Structural engineer Jürgen Engel from Mettingen ran checks to see if this would even be feasible.

Our surgery department was also bursting at the seams. With eight skilled surgeons on board, the four existing operating theatres were simply insufficient. During a walk through the hospital, I found myself in our recovery room, gazing at the external wall. This wall would have to go, I concluded. That solution would give us room to construct two additional operating theatres in the inner courtyard, still connected to the main building via a wide corridor.

Even Christian Bigalke sent out an 'SOS' on behalf of the Diospi Suyana school. At least three additional kindergarten classrooms were needed to accommodate all the students. We had no choice but to construct another building.

Architects Tina and Kornelius Linder, who had drawn up the initial plans for the school pro bono back in 2012, weren't waiting long for my call. Maybe because it was getting close to Christmas and, in the spirit of the season, they couldn't refuse my request? They created the blueprints for all three projects and somehow 'forgot' to ever send us an invoice.

It just so happened – and Christians don't really believe in coincidences – that the Klemenzes sold their house in Niederbiel and became owners of a ground-floor flat just outside the village. Such a process normally takes months, if not years, never mind the stress of it all, but this had miraculously gone off without a hitch.

On 11th April 2018, they sat in their newly renovated flat, enjoying slices of the delicious Black Forest gateau Barbara had made to share with their 'distinguished visitor' from South America. Their guest held dual citizenship and had come to ask a special favour. His keen eyes searched the Klemenzes' bookshelf until he spied what he was looking for. With satisfaction, he opened a large atlas and pointed to a country on the Pacific Coast of South America. Sharp as they ever were through sudokus and whatnot, they understood immediately.

Barbara paused for a sip of coffee before remarking insightfully, 'People might say we're crazy, but we've got to do what we've got to do!'

On 21st June 2018, I posted the following headline on our website: 'No Fake News – the Klemenzes are back in Peru!' With all his expertise and experience, I had no doubt this seventy-five-year-old engineer was up for the triple challenge at Diospi Suyana. And the readers of our website had faith in him too.

30
Life and death

Many months of hard work go into starting a media broadcast. The first step is to acquire a frequency, or channel. Next, a suitable location for the station must be found. When the construction workers come in, they have quite a job to create the passive infrastructure, including the concrete foundation pad, perimeter fencing and equipment storage. All of this must happen before the aerial technicians can commence the building of the actual radio tower. Then there is the matter of the power supply. Usually, the cables need to run from the valley, uphill to the elevated station. Permission must be granted by the owners of every property the cables cross, and that can be a hard sell. With all the tricky little details and frustrations, giving up sometimes seems an attractive option. But if we persevere, somehow, on one fine day, the last hurdle is cleared, the technicians go home and our real work begins.

Our broadcast waves span an area as large as Great Britain. There are no motorways outside the capital city of Lima, which means travel to anywhere else is arduous and slow. For the last few miles, our pick-up and a fully laden truck make their way carefully over treacherous dirt roads, steeply uphill, or down into the hot, humid furnace of the rainforest. The whole ordeal feels like an expedition into the unknown. When Chris Welch and his team unload the transistors, antennas, cables and satellite dishes, they often come to a distressing realisation: 'We've forgotten one of the parts!' There is no point complaining. Someone needs to head into the next town and hope they can source what is needed there. Even without such complications, installation work normally takes between four and six days.

I myself am usually home in Curahuasi or abroad on a speaking tour while all of this is going on. I look forward to regular updates from Doris Manco. Whenever she calls, I say a prayer of thanksgiving and post news of the positive developments on our website.

At noon on Sunday 1st July 2018, our team had been successful, and the satellite connection was working. Radio Diospi Suyana was broadcasting in Puerto Maldonado, a city in south-eastern Peru. One last photo opportunity and then they jumped back in their vehicle for the fifteen-hour drive home to Curahuasi, leaving behind the newest addition to the growing number of Diospi Suyana radio towers cropping up across the country to fill homes and lives with the best news ever.

At 5.49am just two days later, Reynaldo was hosting our morning show when his phone rang. The caller was distraught, desperate. The Peruvian security guard – let's call him Pedro Huaman – had been pushed to the brink of total despair when his wife ran off with another man. He had his service revolver at the ready and had been fully intending to end his misery with a bullet through his brain when he heard words of hope on Radio Diospi Suyana 107.7FM. He paused and wondered, 'Can God even help me in this hopeless situation?'

Reynaldo and Pedro dove deep during their long phone conversation. Pedro's revolver remained holstered. No shot was fired. At home in the Puerto Maldonado suburbs, Pedro stood strong for the first time in weeks.

The very next day, 4th July, a call came in from the pit of Puerto Maldonado – the city prison. Hell on earth for those who have made life hell for others. 'Thank you for your programme,' the inmate on the line gushed, 'Thank you, thank you, thank you!'

Radio Diospi Suyana had only been on air in Puerto Maldonado for two days, and yet our broadcasting had already saved the life of one heartbroken young man and given comfort to another serving time in the desolation of a South American prison. When our technicians heard this news, they understood that every drop of sweat the previous week had served a holy purpose.

On Saturday 18th August 2018, Radio Diospi Suyana began broadcasting in the Andahuaylas province. From the radio mast site, we could see the entire valley, the sprawling city and the surrounding foothills. All 100,000 inhabitants within would be able to tune in to 96.1FM from that moment on.

Doris Manco, the manager of our broadcast centre, announced this most recent accomplishment to many friends and family, including her own father in Lima who was bedridden in the last stages of cancer. Although his body was failing, his senses were not. His daughter's enthusiasm, coming through loud and clear over WhatsApp, was contagious and he rejoiced with her. For three years, he had encouraged Doris to join Diospi Suyana. 'The work there is perfect for you!' he had always said. Sharing her joy at this moment was a gift to both of them. Armando Manco passed away early the next morning.

Diospi Suyana strives to spread the best news in the world via satellite and radio towers. We bring good music, educational programmes and health tips for the entire family. But we are about so much more than entertainment and education. Jesus promised, 'The one who believes in me will live, even though they die.' This statement from John 11:25 takes on special meaning in light of Armando Manco's death. A devout Christian, he and his daughter will see each other again one day. There is no greater assurance than the words of Christ Himself.

Although the Jews worshipped on Saturdays, the first Christians met on Sundays, the first day of the new week, the day Jesus rose triumphantly from the tomb. Their encounter with the Risen One changed everything – how they lived their lives here on earth as well as their perspective about the life that is to come. With this revelation, Jesus' disciples were willing to die as martyrs while sharing His story. Thomas gave his life in India, Peter in Italy and James in Jerusalem.

Over the last two thousand years, millions upon millions of people have placed their hope in the resurrection of our Lord. By the time the initial German manuscript of this book was completed, Radio Diospi Suyana had a broadcasting area with a population of one million people. Hopefully, the day will come when we can reach *ten* million, as I am sure you will agree!

Everyone knows that media success and even longevity all comes down to ratings. How many listeners or viewers are actually tuning in? To get high ratings, programming must appeal to the masses.

'Bad news is good news,' the news industry claims. What does that mean? Bad news makes headlines. Bad news *sells*. Everyone loves to hear about a scandal, whether reported by a tabloid or a more 'reputable' source. But good news? This explains why mass media rolls their eyes at Christian broadcasting. If it doesn't get the listeners, it doesn't get the ratings. If it doesn't get the ratings, it doesn't generate the advertising revenue. But the Christian faith is not for sale. It cannot be marketed. Those who view our efforts as 'unprofitable', and therefore a waste of time, are completely missing the point.

The music video for Hillsong's 'What a Beautiful Name' has been viewed on YouTube approximately half a billion times. It would take some time to find a secular tune that can boast such a result. Grand Prix races and such may be thrilling, but at the end of the day, when the adrenaline rush has subsided and we lie awake, pondering the meaning of life and beyond, they offer no answers. Only faith provides a response of value, hitting the heart of humanity. That is why Christian programming will always find an audience. Regardless, our mission remains to share the message of Jesus Christ, and we will not give up.

31

A hot potato

It's never easy to take a public stand on controversial issues. When emotions run high, it's easy to make a lot of enemies in a very short time. Nevertheless, I will speak openly here. What I am about to write is at the core of the worst crisis we have ever experienced at Diospi Suyana. While I am a free citizen with the right to state my own opinion, please know that I respect the right of others to do the same as well, even if we see things differently.

During the autumn of 1988, my wife was working as a junior doctor at a large hospital in Cardiff. She was working the night shift and grabbed a bite to eat in the hospital cafeteria around 7pm. A young English gynaecologist joined her, and they began to discuss their respective cases.

'In the NICU, we are fighting for the life of a premature baby born at just twenty-four weeks – hopefully, it will survive,' Tina shared.

The gynaecologist countered, 'I'm supposed to induce the abortion of a twenty-three-week-old baby now. I think that's horrible!'

In the spring of 2016, I had a long conversation with Trevor Sampson in Johannesburg. The gifted musician has been helping disadvantaged youth in South Africa for many years. He has such a heart for these kids, having grown up with similar challenges himself.

It is truly a miracle he is even alive. His single mother wanted to terminate the pregnancy. It wouldn't have cost her anything because her own mother, Trevor's grandmother, was the person responsible for performing abortions in their town. She did her deed with long knitting needles, efficiently and impassively. Years later, as the old woman lay dying, she screamed in anguish, 'The children I aborted are all here accusing me!' Her death was horrific, and this scene was forever burned into Trevor's memory.

At Diospi Suyana hospital, our aim is to help those most in need, from the disenfranchised Quechua to the vulnerable farmers. Who is more helpless than an unborn child?

Abortions are prohibited at our hospital for four reasons.

The first reason is the medical ethics of Hellenism. The Hippocratic Oath to 'do no harm' dates back to around 400 BC and is still the foundational guide for medical professionals today. Even two thousand years later, young doctors take this oath at the start of their careers, vowing to facilitate neither euthanasia nor abortion, and to preserve both their lives and their art.

The second is the Bible itself. All volunteers at Diospi Suyana are committed Christians. The Bible is clear that God, not humanity, is Lord over life and death. God loves every human being, even the unborn. The first chapter of Jeremiah states that God told him, 'Before I formed you in the womb I knew you, before you were born I set you apart' (Jeremiah 1:5). And David declares in the 139th Psalm, 'Your eyes saw my unformed body; all the days ordained for me were written in your book before one of them came to be' (Psalm 139:16).

Third, Post-Abortion Stress Syndrome (PASS). The psychological impact of an abortion can have profound short- and long-term effects on the mother. Symptoms can range from pervasive guilt and depression to nightmares and thoughts of suicide. An analysis by the Elliot Institute found that of 260 respondents, only 5.1 per cent reported no adverse mental health issues following their abortion. While actual percentages vary from study to study, it is clear that countless women suffer traumatic stress after an abortion.

And finally, Peruvian law. Abortions are illegal here, with a few exceptions, such as if the mother's life is in danger.

Here in the 'Christian' West, we go to more trouble to protect animals than unborn humans. We treat embryos as objects, masses of protein with some DNA. Did you know that 97 per cent of babies are completely healthy at birth?

Unfortunately, pro-life advocates are often labelled as religious fanatics in the media, condemned for beliefs that are considered archaic, intolerant and oppressive. Conversely, pro-choice supporters are portrayed as more progressive, understanding and respectful of women. I follow this development of tribalistic thinking with great concern.

32
A life hanging by a thread

It was Tuesday 21st August 2018. As usual, our waiting area was overflowing with patients. One woman of about thirty-five years – we will call her Maria Quispe – was called back to our assistant gynaecologist's office. On her intake form, she had indicated a primary complaint of vaginal bleeding. The young doctor began prepping for an ultrasound to take a closer look at the uterus. At that moment, Maria collapsed and lost consciousness, a large pool of blood spreading around her at an alarming rate.

Dr Antonio Carrion did what any junior doctor would have done in such a situation – he called his supervisor, Dr Miriam Boeker. The two doctors rushed Maria into one of our operating theatres, where during the emergency procedure, it became clear that Maria was suffering a miscarriage. She was immediately given an IV drip and blood transfusion. A D&C procedure helped stop the acute bleeding. An hour later, Maria was lying in a white bed on the ward, her life no longer in danger.

Maria was feeling much better the next day. She had some breakfast and shared her story with one of our midwives.

A few days earlier, Maria had visited a well-known *farmacia*. Already mother to several children, Maria requested some tablets to induce an abortion. 'Come back tonight,' the woman behind the counter told her. 'Bring 195 *soles* [approximately a week's wages], and I'll give you what you need to get rid of the baby.'

Maria did as she was told. She received four tablets and two suppositories with the active ingredient misoprostol, as well as instructions how to use them. Maria is only alive today because she was here at Diospi Suyana hospital when the heavy bleeding started. If she had been at home, no doubt she would have bled out before anyone could help her.

What the pharmacist did was illegal on several counts. First of all, aiding and abetting an abortion in Peru carries a prison sentence of several years. Second, misoprostol is a controlled substance and should never be sold without a prescription. As if this wasn't bad enough, the price the pharmacist charged was downright extortionate. Misoprostol is very cheap to produce, only one *sol*, or about 25pence, per pill. But the desperation of women with unwanted pregnancies drives the price way up, sometimes even one hundredfold. In this case, the pharmacist probably pocketed 190 of the 195 *soles* Maria paid her. Black market abortions are a highly lucrative business in Peru.

Maria wrote up her experience in an affidavit. That afternoon, I contacted the local prosecutor's office and requested an appointment, stating my intention to press charges in my official capacity as hospital director. I was invited to appear at 11am the next day.

On Thursday 23rd August, I arrived right on time with three Peruvian colleagues. After the usual exchange of pleasantries, I explained the incident and proceeded to lodge my complaint: 'Madam Prosecutor, this pharmacy has shamelessly exploited my patient's distress, and in a manner that nearly killed her. This butchery must be stopped!'

The Public Prosecutor was unmoved. She refused to accept the case, stating dismissively, 'There is a police protocol, and that is sufficient.'

By law, suspected abortions must be reported to the police. There *is* a police protocol, but more often than not, it seems a mere formality here in Peru. Cases are misfiled, archived or even discarded, with zero accountability for those involved.

'Madam Prosecutor,' I tried again, 'our patient almost died. It is my right and my duty to report this incident, if for no other reason than to protect other women in the future!'

I tried to be as friendly and convincing as possible, but she refused to hear. We appealed on behalf of our patient for a good forty-five minutes, but to no avail. We finally left the office, disgruntled but unwilling to accept defeat.

Back at the hospital, I immediately got on the phone to the Ministry of Justice and Human Rights. Dr Maria Adrianzén, Director of Interfaith Affairs, did not mince her words. 'Tell the prosecutor that it is her duty to accept your complaint. If she refuses, I will personally put the case on the desk of the Minister of Justice tomorrow.' That was quite a proclamation!

So I returned to the Public Prosecutor's office that afternoon, three Peruvian witnesses again in tow. 'Madam, I am sorry to bother you again, but I would like to file my complaint now!'

The prosecutor responded brusquely, 'I already told you this morning that I am not accepting your charges.' She turned to Edgard Montalvo, a local national general accountant at Diospi Suyana, and said, 'Explain to him,' pointing her finger and regarding me with scorn, 'that the case is closed as far as I am concerned.'

Her contempt was palpable. She noted my German accent and shamelessly implied that, as a foreigner, I was a bit slow to comprehend.

I looked her straight in the eye and showed my hand. 'Madam Prosecutor, I have already spoken with a senior official at the Ministry of Justice and Human Rights. She assured me that if you fail to execute your duties in this case, she will elevate it to the Minister himself tomorrow.'

You could have heard a pin drop. The prosecutor had not expected this.

She broke the silence in an icy tone. 'You take a seat outside in the waiting room. My secretary will process your complaint.'

After about fifty minutes, I was finally able to accomplish what I had set out to that morning. It was an odd situation. Why on earth had the prosecutor behaved in such a bizarre manner?

Sooner or later, everything hidden comes to light. That very evening, we gained a clear understanding of an unexpected connection. The prosecutor lived in the same building as the pharmacist and was even a friend of the family. Regardless of whether or not a crime had been committed, the prosecutor would always have her friend's back. She was in a position of power and knew how to use it to protect and deflect – at the expense of frightened women, desperate for a way out of their situation, at the mercy of criminals who care more for profit than the lives of their customers. She was aware of all this, and still chose to put her personal interests first.

I shared this story at our next staff meeting and a sober discussion ensued. Every Peruvian schoolchild knows that South America is rife with corruption. No one is shocked to hear about drugs, smuggling or illegal abortions – until they hear about them happening in their own communities.

At the end of our meeting, we prayed together for God's protection. We had tangled with a dark coven that was well connected throughout Curahuasi. There was bound to be a backlash, but no one could foresee what would happen next.

33

The birthday party that never was

'Such a day, as wonderful as today…' So goes a German folk song. Dr Tim Boeker was celebrating his thirty-eighth birthday – his second trip around the sun in Peru. In front of their house, the birthday boy was working the barbecue. As soon as the charcoal was ready, he would start grilling the sausages, their spicy aroma already causing his mouth to water. The Boekers had invited some friends to come over after work with their children to celebrate. There would still be time to enjoy the last warm rays of sunshine outside. It was 28th August, the middle of winter in South America. After dusk in the Andes, the temperature drops quickly, so the Boekers would then usher their guests into their warm, cosy lounge for a pleasant end to a busy day of service. Tim looked over at the snow-covered mountains and shook his head. It was hard to believe that he and his family had found their home here in Curahuasi. But sometimes life is full of surprises …

Professor Dr Hans Grüber, Tim's maternal grandfather, had been a missionary doctor himself. Dedicated to this calling 'without compromise', he had served on the Indian subcontinent an entire decade, toiling long hours that kept him away from his wife and children. Not exactly a great family life, as Tim's mother recalled. Many look back on childhood with a sense of warm nostalgia, but Tim could sense his mother's ambivalence whenever her famous father's name came up in conversation.

Young Tim swore the last thing he wanted to do when he grew up was to become a missionary doctor. All his aunts and uncles nodded their heads, confirming the wisdom of this decision.

But perhaps it was just in his blood? In any case, Tim began studying medicine in 2001. Two years later, he married fellow student Miriam Schulte. The two shared a deep faith in God, a common profession and an idealistic outlook. Moving to Freiburg im Breisgau to pursue further study and medical training, Tim, who was practical by nature, found himself drawn to the field of traumatology. His wife, no less skilled with her hands, chose gynaecology.

One October day in 2005, Miriam had to retreat to the WC. As in many homes, this 'Warm Clubroom' was stocked with a variety of reading material. Miriam was leafing through an MLP financial magazine when she came across a four-page article titled 'Life Project Peru' about a doctor couple from Wiesbaden who were planning to build a modern hospital in Peru. Back at that early stage, Diospi Suyana was more dream than substance, but something about the bold intent of these Christians from Hesse resonated with Miriam. 'Tim, read this!' she insisted, after finishing her important business.

Strapped for cash like most young academics, the Boekers made the 'dangerous' – and ultimately life-changing – decision to support Diospi Suyana financially. Having been added to our mailing list, they received five newsletters each year detailing the progress towards this insanely ambitious project. As far as they were concerned, their regular donation was the extent of their involvement with Diospi Suyana. Tim was still staunchly against the idea of practising medicine on the mission field.

In October 2006, Miriam wrote a short email to the Diospi Suyana office in Germany. It read, 'As my husband and I will be finishing our medical studies next year, we wanted to find out what level of training and experience doctors must have to be considered for a post at your hospital, or if you only accept specialists. We would be grateful to hear from you!'

The world will never know if she wrote this message secretly by candlelight, or perhaps Tim was out working the night shift. What is clear, however, is that despite Tim's notorious hard-headedness, Miriam's email set a course in motion, with an outcome no one close to them would have ever expected.

In March 2012, Drs Miriam and Tim Boeker attended a Diospi Suyana informational meeting to learn more about the details of a prospective mission to Peru without obligation. Their many questions at the end of the event gave the impression that the couple was toying with the possibility, if not playing with fire.

The Boekers took the plunge and announced to their dumbfounded relatives, friends and colleagues that they would be moving to Peru the following year with their young sons, five-year-old Sem and one-year-old Joah.

Senior physician Dr Wagner tried to appeal to Tim's ego, praising his skill and indirectly suggesting that medical missions were for the less capable, a developing world 'escape route' to some halfway meaningful activity. Not to mention that it was hardly a stepping stone for career advancement.

Professor Schlickewei also felt compelled to caution the talented young doctor in private. The former chair of the German Society for Paediatric Traumatology and Orthopaedics sought to dispel any romantic notions Tim might have. 'Best to leave that one alone. Living in Peru would be quite a shock to your system!' He continued gravely, 'There, you would have neither the equipment nor the quality prostheses to do a proper job!'

Their words fell on deaf ears. In September 2016, the Boekers packed up their worldly goods and boarded a plane. With them in a small Moses basket was four-month-old Liah, their third child.

… At last, a wisp of smoke rose up from the grill, and the first licks of flame appeared between the charcoal briquettes. Tim looked on with satisfaction, ready for his guests to arrive. And then his mobile rang. 'Dr Tim, we need you in the emergency room right away!'

34

Drunk and without a driving licence

Franziscus C downed one last beer and glanced over at the car on the side of the road. It belonged to his family and was somehow still roadworthy, despite its age. The seventy-eight-year-old didn't have a driving licence, but his blood alcohol level was such that he didn't care. There was no harm in going for a short drive through Curahuasi. It wouldn't be the first time he had done so. Up until now, the police always seemed to look the other way. 'Ah, here comes Franziscus again,' they would laugh. 'Let's leave him alone!'

There's a common saying in Peru: *'No pasa nada!'* In English, this means simply, 'Nothing will go wrong!' If everything has gone well so far, why would anything bad happen the next time? Señor C approached the car unsteadily, opened the driver's door and plopped himself clumsily down on the upholstered seat. He turned the key in the ignition and steered onto the Panamericana, accelerating west towards the setting sun.

A shadow suddenly sped towards him. Faster and faster. What was that? Franziscus squinted and tried to clear his head. But it was too late. He collided head-on with a taxi, totalling both cars in a split second. Franziscus hit his head against the windscreen, but was very fortunate to have no broken bones.

In the taxi, the driver and passenger in the front were spared the worst by their seatbelts and airbags. But in the back seat, it was a completely different story. One of the two passengers there was a man in his thirties named Abraham K. Fast asleep and without any protection at the moment of impact, he was flung violently inside the vehicle. The force of the collision caused extensive trauma to both legs; his right femur shattered into four pieces. Blood poured from his mouth as his teeth had bored deep into his tongue.

Within ten minutes, the fire and rescue service took the five injured victims to the emergency room of the Diospi Suyana hospital. Doctors and nurses immediately attended to the patients. While our staff are naturally efficient, they come together to function as smoothly as Swiss clockwork in emergencies. The doctors quickly assess the extent of the injuries as the nurses start an IV. The lab technicians obtain the appropriate blood samples. If the patient needs a breathing tube, gastric tube and/or urine catheter, it is expeditiously provided.

X-rays and CT scans confirmed that Abraham's injuries were the most serious. The call to our traumatologist was purely routine. Minutes later, Dr Boeker rushed through the long corridors into the emergency room. His birthday party would have to take place without him.

The plan was to stabilise the patient and surgically reconstruct the femur the next morning.

Abraham was an employee at *Posta Medica,* a local state-run health facility. This entitled him to free medical treatment at the *EsSalud* Hospital in the state capital of Abancay.

At 8.30am, Victor V, director of *Posta,* arrived at the hospital with Abraham's relatives to request a speedy transfer to the state hospital. Dr Boeker filled out the necessary forms, wrote a summary of the key findings and lab results, and included a copy of the X-rays in the file. All seemed good to go for a smooth transfer over the mountains to Abancay.

Three-quarters of an hour later, Victor V was back. 'I just called *EsSalud,*' he reported. 'Because of the Santa Rosa de Lima holiday, they aren't doing any operations this week!' He turned to Dr Boeker. 'Please do the operation here. His relatives want this and so do I!'

Tim consulted with his team, including anaesthetist Dr Leslie Ichocan. Everyone was in agreement to help the injured *Posta* employee as soon as possible and push back the other seven operations scheduled for Wednesday 29th August. The pre-op consultation with the anaesthetist revealed a number of critical factors that had not been brought up the night before – Abraham suffered from chronic asthma and frequent urinary tract infections.

The operation lasted more than five hours. Dr Boeker managed to stabilise the bone fragments via intramedullary nailing and cerclage wiring. As the right thigh muscle had increased pressure owing to the trauma, Dr Boeker had to make a deep incision through the surrounding fascia to prevent acute compartment syndrome, an excruciatingly painful condition that interferes with blood flow and can potentially necessitate amputation of the limb or even cause death of the patient if not addressed quickly. Once the swelling subsides, the wound can be closed without further risk.

Later that evening, we were all feeling positive about the patient's post-op prognosis. But as the saying goes, one should not praise the day before the evening, or in this case, the weekend.

The next day, Abraham had developed compartment syndrome in his left leg, and the pressure in his right remained elevated. Dr Boeker performed emergency fasciotomies on both legs. Abraham's heart stopped while in theatre but was immediately restarted by the surgical team.

Friday, Saturday and Sunday were characterised by severe haemorrhaging owing to disrupted coagulation. Our staff, including our traumatologist himself, donated most of the twenty-one units of blood and plasma required to stabilise Abraham's fragile haemoglobin levels. Despite acute kidney failure, we were able to maintain normal potassium levels with frequent adjustments. His blood pressure remained stable, and a ventilator kept his oxygen saturation levels in the upper range. However, Abraham still had significant oedema throughout his body and was losing enormous amounts of fluid through his wounds. Tim continually changed the soaked dressings and cleaned around the wounds. He spent much of the first week of his thirty-ninth year of life at his patient's bedside. As a fellow surgeon, I could empathise. After endless and exhausting hours in the operating theatre, a bond had been formed, and he did not want to take his eyes off the patient for a minute.

Meanwhile, Abraham's precarious hold on life was beginning to slip. The extent of his injuries from the accident, his pre-existing conditions and unforeseen complications combined to make a positive outcome increasingly unlikely. Deeply concerned, we discussed every minute detail and even consulted with two intensive care centres in Germany. Tim and Miriam informed the Diospi Suyana prayer chain. Most of the missionaries joined in, asking for God's blessing and healing. Abraham's condition continued to decline. God would have the final word.

35

Defamation, intrigue and hate

On Sunday morning, Ricardo C, a dentist at the Curahuasi clinic, called in to the national radio and television station *Exitosa* to launch some outrageous accusations against Diospi Suyana. He claimed that the hospital had no anaesthetist and, therefore, a nurse had administered the anaesthesia for the case in question. On this widely public platform, the dentist demanded to know why our patient had even been placed in the ICU after a simple injury, insinuating it was a move to keep relatives and health workers away from the patient. Surely this must be indicative of malpractice, the man alleged indignantly. He appealed for the Peruvian Medical Association and even the Ministry of Health to take immediate action. It is possible that most Peruvians were asleep when the programme first aired, but it was repeated on Monday morning, 3rd September, piped at full volume through offices, buses and a slew of public spaces.

We, the staff at Diospi Suyana, were utterly stunned. For five days we had struggled day and night to save Abraham's life. We had donated our own blood, administered the most expensive medicines and done absolutely everything in our power for him. And our thanks was to be publicly vilified by a misinformed whistle-blower?! You may have heard the expression, 'There's no smoke without fire.' Those listening to the radio programme had no idea what had actually happened but seemed willing enough to believe that something unethical must have. Malpractice is not uncommon in Peru's hospitals, so why would Diospi Suyana be any different?

As directors of the hospital, Tina and I had to take action. In difficult situations, I always pray that God will tell me what to do. Two ideas came to mind. I remembered that a small camera was mounted in the back corner of the ICU, recording continuously for security purposes.

'Benjamin Azuero, I need your help!'

The head of our IT department understood what I needed right away and pledged his assistance. 'We'll review the footage from the entire week in detail and make a note of who entered the ICU, when and how often!'

A massive undertaking, for sure!

Second, I concluded that it would be advantageous to invite the head of *Posta Medica,* along with other leadership members, to an emergency meeting in my office. The first meeting led to a second, recorded via mobile phone with everyone's consent. The director of *Posta* apologised for the accusations made by his odontologist. He said that he could confirm that both the patient's family and relevant medical staff had received regular updates regarding Abraham's progress. He assured us that it was apparent how much our staff cared for the well-being of their colleague.

Abraham's condition deteriorated rapidly during the night of 4th September, so we decided as a team to transfer him to the *EsSalud* Hospital in Cusco, where he could receive dialysis treatment. Oebele de Haan, anaesthetist Dr Leslie Ichocan, Dr Julian Swanson and nurse Maribel kept him alive during the risky journey through the mountains. It was a last-ditch effort to save our critically ill patient.

At 2.15am, Tina and I were in the ICU, collapsed into our chairs and completely exhausted. All around us, it looked like a battlefield. That is precisely how it felt too. We realised bitterly that our patient was about to lose his fight against death. Everything Tim, Tina and the other staff had done over the last six days and nights would be for nothing. And to be treated with such hostility on top of all that! With a wearied and anguished expression on her face, Tina fretted, 'They're going to finish us off now!'

The Bible tells how, when Peter was walking on water, he saw the high waves and was gripped by raw fear. 'Lord, save me!' (Matthew 14:30). To this day, that desperate cry for help echoes through the ages. Woe to us if our faith in the omnipotence of God is deluded. Nothing would be worse than finding no firm hand to take hold of our outstretched arm.

Four hours after arriving in Cusco, Abraham died. We were informed that the hospital there did not have a ventilator available, so a nurse had to manually provide oxygen via a resuscitation bag the entire time. Not a good situation at all.

Of course, it was clear to us that the *Posta* dentist who so vehemently denounced us was not acting alone. The great success of Diospi Suyana had long been a bitter pill for some in the medical field. Hundreds of thousands of patients treated, onsite visits by two presidents and eight ministers, as well as forty-one positive TV reports about the 'hospital of faith' had only fuelled the envy. Since the beginning of our work in 2007, we had dealt with caustic remarks from private hospitals across the country. We were a thorn in the side of many doctors in the profit-orientated market. A medical facility receiving widespread acclaim for treating the poor with such a high standard of care was an anomaly and a huge nuisance. We are also staffed by foreigners, easy to frame as a common enemy.

On Thursday 6th September, a delegation from the Apurímac regional health directorate (DIRESA) in Abancay showed up on our doorstep unannounced. 'We have heard serious allegations and need to get to the bottom of the matter,' we were informed accusingly. The meeting in my office resembled a tribunal, the tension palpable. A DIRESA official stood in the centre of the room with his camera pointed directly at me, as if I were a serious criminal about to be sentenced. But when Tina and I presented a detailed chronological development of the case, the atmosphere in the room changed abruptly.

'We didn't know all that!' exclaimed the doctors from Abancay. We had obviously become the target of malicious defamation initiated by our opponents at *Posta* and others. After a guided tour of the hospital, the damage was undone – at least with our DIRESA visitors. The head even said in farewell, 'Soon, I too will come to you as a patient!'

On Friday 7th September, the employees of *Posta* organised a demonstration, publicly blaming Diospi Suyana for the death of their colleague. Victor V was out front, frenziedly waving his arms and inciting the crowd. How could this be, after he had pleaded with us to treat Abraham in the first place? Day after day he had witnessed our hard work and ethos with his own eyes. Now he was trying to turn the entire community against us. Another demonstration was planned for Saturday, immediately after the funeral, to be held at the gates of Diospi Suyana. They wanted to mobilise eighty cars and create complete chaos. There was even a call to burn down one of our buildings. The tone and content of their signs left no doubt regarding their willingness to use violence. 'Gringo, we will make you pay!' was scrawled in angry letters across a large banner. Rumours ran wild through Curahuasi. It would be easy to inflame *campesinos*, mountain farmers with little schooling, particularly when they were under the influence of alcohol. In any case, nobody seemed to care about the facts, only about stirring up strong emotions.

Early in the morning, I flew to Lima and apprised the lawyers of Estudio Olaechea of the situation. The oldest law firm in Peru has supported Diospi Suyana with free legal advice since 2008. No fewer than four lawyers were activated that weekend to draw up a formal complaint of Grave Defamation. Two of them accompanied me to the *Exitosa* TV studio, where I explained the events of the past week in a live broadcast. The well-known investigative journalist Nicolás Lúcar interviewed me, granting sufficient time for me to refute the dentist's unfounded accusations.

I presented on camera the signed affidavit of our anaesthetist, which had been corroborated by fourteen staff witnesses. Dr Leslie Ichocan alone had administered the anaesthesia for Abraham's operations. The evaluation of our security video feed in the ICU was highly enlightening. Several of our IT specialists had spent a long night analysing the recordings. The results were indisputable: Abraham's relatives had been allowed in to see him twenty-eight times over the six days. Medical staff – including nurses, doctors and laboratory staff – had come to the patient's bedside to provide care 267 times. I looked directly into the camera lens and emphasised that there was probably no other patient in Peru receiving that degree and quality of care.

I then explained the severity of the initial accident and the complications that followed. I included a twelve-page list of the 532 services performed for the patient at our hospital: lab tests, X-rays, CT scans, ultrasounds, infusions, dressing changes, blood transfusions, medicines and, of course, the operations previously mentioned. The astronomical bill had – as expected – not been paid by anyone.

An additional 'service' provided by Diospi Suyana sounded totally unique. Throughout the ordeal, thirty missionaries had taken part in a prayer chain, interceding around the clock for the life of our patient. It became obvious to every viewer that the dentist's third allegation – that the patient had been neglected – was absolutely ludicrous. Twenty minutes of airtime illuminated the smear campaign initiated by the *Posta* contingent, to whose motives we were now fully wise.

Elsewhere, efforts to shield the hospital continued. Dr José Olaechea called me from his bed at home. The head of the sixty-lawyer firm had the flu and could hardly talk. 'Klaus, I know you need our support in Curahuasi right away,' he croaked. 'I will get in touch with my government contacts and the head of the police. The state must protect you!'

Other friends of Diospi Suyana also took action. Even the state governor intervened on our behalf. Forty-five policemen arrived in Curahuasi the next morning to buttress the local force in keeping the hospital, our patients and staff safe from harm.

As I provided brief updates on our website, Christians around the world joined hands in prayer for Diospi Suyana. We received letters of encouragement and solidarity from Australia, Paraguay, Germany, Switzerland and, of course, Peru. A group of Curahuasinos even organised a special intention Mass at the local Catholic church, offering prayers for Diospi Suyana and even specifically for Tina and me.

The opposition continued to turn up the heat. Pictures of Abraham's lifeless body appeared on social media with the caption, 'Killed by Diospi Suyana!' More and more Facebook users jumped on the bandwagon of denigrating our mission, among them the pharmacist I had recently reported for her criminal abortion activity.

Franziscus C was the one who, in his drunken and unlicensed state, caused the horrible accident, setting off an unfortunate series of events that culminated in Abraham's death. And yet, as a member of one of the wealthiest and most powerful families in town, with relatives in just about every civil organisation, nepotism ensured his crime was wholly swept under the rug and forgotten. In fact, the focus on Diospi Suyana sadly appeared to be a smokescreen, a perfectly staged distraction.

Trouble seldom comes alone. Amid all the turmoil, we received a letter from the council demanding the payment of property tax for the hospital. The amount was high and the letter itself was an outrage. We had been granted a formal exemption to this tax by the mayor's office back in 2003. After all, the hospital was the most tremendous boon to the community in living memory. Two hundred families were employed with us. Another hundred taxi drivers made their living shuttling patients to and from the neighbouring towns. More than fifty hotels and restaurants profited from the thousands of people who flocked to Curahuasi for medical treatment from all over Peru. And to date, hadn't we already provided more than 60,000 medical services for Curahuasinos? It appeared that the 'cash cow' of Diospi Suyana was not only to be milked but now also slaughtered. Bon appétit!

Tina and I were fed up. On Sunday 9th September, I visited *Radio Horizonte* and delivered an ultimatum to the local community. 'If people continue to malign us and devalue our service here, we might as well shut down the hospital and go home!' I was adamant that ungrateful patients and a double-crossing town council were no motivation to stay in Curahuasi!

My words hit their mark. Families tuned in to the radio broadcast across the region stopped and held their breath. It was beginning to dawn on the Curahuasinos that their economic prosperity and physical well-being were closely entwined with the presence of Diospi Suyana. The departure of our hospital would set the community back at least fifty years.

Bringing my rhetoric to a close, I spoke calmly and firmly into the microphone for emphasis: 'My wife Martina and I are fifty-seven years old. We have given everything for this hospital since 2004. Perhaps now it is time for us to say goodbye!'

The following Monday, the winds of change began to blow through Curahuasi. A few women took to the streets and collected more than three thousand signatures on a petition to save Diospi Suyana – a welcome encouragement. Taxi drivers announced a rally in favour of our mission. Overnight, posters appeared on cars and motorbikes declaring support for our cause. And then, the pièce de résistance, Mayor Danilo Valenza himself led a march through the town, all the way to the gates of our hospital. The message was unmistakable: 'We need Diospi Suyana and will stand by it at all costs!'

While all this was going on, I was hosting a delegation from the Instituto Superior, an institution dependent on our hospital for nursing student internship placements. I was in the middle of explaining the mission and history of Diospi Suyana to my guests when we were interrupted by the crescendo of the crowd, chanting unbridled solidarity with the work we had created with hands from all over the world, trusting in God.

Outside, Tina grabbed a megaphone and climbed onto a chair to address the throng. 'Dear fellow citizens,' she began, 'for eleven years we have been here, helping and healing you in our hospital. You know us well. We did everything we could to save Abraham's life, but he died as a result of his tragic accident. We would never wilfully endanger the life of another human being!'

She paused as warm applause erupted from her audience. But Tina wasn't finished. 'But we are very concerned about these personal attacks, this smear campaign. On top of that, the council now wants to collect property tax from us, going back on an official exemption that was granted years ago, even though we make no profit and all our living expenses are covered by the generous donations of others!'

The mayor was visibly uncomfortable. It was his move.

He reached to take the megaphone from Tina and publicly vowed to honour all valid contracts for his entire term of office. Diospi Suyana could rest assured in its tax-exempt status.

By Monday, we were confident that we had regained the support of our village with integrity. Elsewhere, though, this unspeakable circus was still bouncing wildly from ring to ring. But we continued to pray with anxious hearts for God's intervention and justice.

36

The wedding celebration of the year

The Abraham K case was the most aggressive attack on our good reputation to date. We understood that our opponents were not concerned with law and order but with causing Diospi Suyana real harm. We were under pressure and on edge.

In the middle of all this madness, we had a very welcome diversion – we hosted the wedding celebration of the year. Sure, some would claim that the wedding of Prince Harry and Meghan Markle was the social highlight of 2018, but I would beg to differ. The sacred oaths of the aristocracy are often short-lived, and tabloid tales of sordid affairs and discontent often quickly replace the fairy-tale coverage of the ceremony itself.

The golden wedding anniversary of Udo and Barbara Klemenz had much more significance in my eyes. More than a hundred guests turned out on 15th September to mark this momentous occasion, looking on as the Klemenzes solemnly walked down the aisle of our festively decorated hospital chapel. The magnificent musical programme by Christian van Rensen and Debora Centner was a fitting tribute to two people who have become such shining examples of faith for many, including myself.

I began my speech by describing the career of this extraordinary couple. Referencing a verse from Galatians (5:1), I spoke about the freedom to which Christ has called us. Through His power, we are no longer slaves to manmade religious constraints and no longer have any reason to fear death. In closing, I posed a rhetorical question: Is it possible for a person to live a genuinely selfless life? Udo and Barbara Klemenz immediately come to mind as two who have done just that.

On 14th February 2005, Barbara and Udo Klemenz attended their weekly church home group. The topic of discussion that evening was the sending of the seventy-two disciples, as recorded in chapter 10 of the gospel of Luke. As everyone said their farewells at the door, a friend challenged them all to think of what God might want to send them out to do.

The next morning, as Barbara and Udo sat at the breakfast table, Barbara brought the conversation around to the subject of God's will. 'Udo, we really need to pray about this!' And so they did.

On Wednesday 16th February, the two pensioners were still searching for an answer. Suddenly inspired to fervent prayer, they entreated, 'God, show us the way. We are ready to go. We want to do Your will, no matter what it is!'

At the exact same time, I was sitting with a lawyer in my home town of Wiesbaden. During our conversation, he mentioned that he knew a construction expert with extensive international experience.

That statement immediately grabbed my attention. After all, my wife and I intended to build a hospital for the poor in rural Peru, but we were still seeking a skilled engineer and consultant who was willing to work for free in order to make that happen.

Two minutes later, I picked up the phone and dialled the Klemenzes' number. Udo and Barbara were still in their kitchen, praying. No sooner had they said 'Amen' than their phone rang.

I have told the story of what followed more than 2,800 times during my presentation tours around the world. Hundreds of thousands have heard it from my mouth, and millions more have read it in the press.

Udo and Barbara Klemenz travelled to Peru on 3rd August 2005 to head up our hospital construction project. But they didn't stop there. Udo built not only the Diospi Suyana main hospital but the eye and dental clinics too. Then he constructed the children's house and an impressive 8,500m² school. Finally, he completed multiple hospital extensions over time, doubling the bed capacity, and took on whatever projects we threw at him – large or small – along the way. In Paul's letter to the Romans, he urged Christians to offer their bodies 'as a living sacrifice, holy and pleasing to God' (Romans 12:1). That is precisely what Barbara and Udo Klemenz have done. They prayed, 'God, our money, our time and our ambitions are Yours. Do with us what You will!'

There are countless stories about the Klemenzes I could share off the top of my head at any time. One of the most memorable involves Udo's crossing of the Sahara Desert in January 1977. After several years of working for the Philipp Holzmann construction company in Libya, Udo and three friends were ready to go on the ultimate adventure. The group set off from the Mediterranean port city of Marsa el Brega in two fully loaded ATVs and headed south. They covered more than twelve hundred miles in four weeks before being captured by Chadian soldiers in Ounianga Serir – not exactly one of their planned stops! After five weeks under military guard and a load of diplomatic red tape, the adventurers were finally set free.

You can trust a 'desert fox' like Udo with just about anything. Without a doubt, this veteran engineer was just the right person to give Diospi Suyana shape in concrete and stone. The man from Niederbiel is fearless and confident, in contrast to his wife who lost her mother when she was three and was raised by a stepmother who was quick to find fault. Barbara's childhood memories are filled with pain, and her self-esteem stunted to this day by the trauma she endured years ago. But what God has done in her is nothing short of fantastic. In 1987, during a period of personal crisis, she wondered if her life was worth anything. A line from the film *The Captain of Köpenick* came to mind and made her wonder what she would say to God one day. That day, she finally grasped that God loved her, just as she was, giving her a hope and a future.

Between 2005 and 2019, the Klemenzes spent a total of ten years in Peru. Their willingness to sacrifice knew no bounds. During their first few days in Curahuasi, they helped my wife and me remove pigeon droppings from our house. As decent housing was scarce, they stayed in a cheap hotel for four months with no privacy but plenty of noise as other guests came and went. Barbara and Udo have been by our side through all the trials we've endured at Diospi Suyana. They have encouraged us, prayed for us and worked unbelievably hard. Without them, Diospi Suyana simply would not have happened. They were and continue to be instruments in God's hand, living out their earlier prayer with purpose and faith: 'God, here we are. Do with us what You will!'

37

Did Diospi Suyana kill the patient?

Queues of patients stretched along the hospital driveway once again. The street vendors set up their stalls to sell biscuits, sandwiches and drinks to the crowds. Life was back to normal. At the back of our complex, Udo Klemenz's men were building the second floor of our broadcast centre. Udo was going full steam ahead because he wanted to finish the roof before the rainy season started. Outside the surgical wing, masons were laying layers upon layers of bricks. After breaking through the existing wall, their efforts would increase the number of operating theatres to six.

Time heals wounds and turbulent feelings eventually calm. Usually. Every now and then, we picked up on vague threats from the medical community, but by now we were quite distracted by our hectic daily routine and the endless bureaucratic demands of government authorities.

I myself was travelling through the Netherlands on yet another presentation tour, fully occupied with getting to each venue on time. On 31st October, I packed my things and jumped in my rental car to head home to Wiesbaden. The news I received from Tina on the phone that evening knocked me flat.

Around noon, the Public Prosecutor's office had hand-delivered a subpoena for all the files related to the Abraham K case. The girlfriend of the deceased was charging us with 'negligent homicide', and it was up to the same prosecutor we had tangled with only two months before to decide whether or not to take the case. Likely still stinging from the Ministry of Justice's intervention on our behalf to hold her accountable for charging her friend with aiding and abetting illegal abortions, this current situation provided the perfect opportunity for revenge.

The girlfriend arrived at the Public Prosecutor's office, the *Fiscalia*, for the oral deposition. She was accompanied by a man who had only a layman's understanding of compartment syndrome, coagulation disorder and renal failure. A dentist by trade, he had gained recent notoriety through his very public and vicious attacks on Diospi Suyana. His name: Ricardo C.

The main defendants were Tim Boeker, our traumatologist, and Tina and myself, as directors of the hospital. We had been notified in writing that ten of our staff would be questioned by *Fiscalia* lawyers. Reasonable enough. However, the interrogations dragged on for hours, pushing our people to the point of exhaustion in an already tense situation. Tim entered the interrogation room with our lawyer Dr Maria Gutierrez at 3pm on 5th December. Six hours later, around 9pm, I drove my car to the front of the building, hoping to pick them up. It turned out to be a very long night for all of us. I could make out their silhouettes in the office window, but there were no signs of wrapping up any time soon. It was 1am before they let Tim go. Ten brutal hours of questioning were falsely logged as three in the deposition notes. It was even worse for Tina – the question-and-answer game lasted a gruelling eleven hours, leaving her physically and emotionally spent by the time she was allowed to go late that evening.

The investigating authorities aimed to find contradictions in the witness reports that could be used as incriminating evidence against Diospi Suyana. The Public Prosecutor overshared her annoyance with the tremendous influence of Diospi Suyana in off-the-record conversations with our lawyer. She felt we needed to be put in our place and was happy to oblige.

What crime had we actually committed to warrant such weeks of harassment? Car accident victims can succumb to their injuries at any hospital in the world. During a thorough literature review, we came across an article in the renowned British medical journal *Lancet,* which indicated a 47 per cent mortality rate for patients who develop compartment syndrome in the thigh (usually only the lower leg is affected). Abraham K had developed it in not one but both thighs owing to the tremendous force of impact. The fact that he had remained alive for another six days could really only be explained by the exemplary care provided by our team.

Tina and I consulted with the Director of the National Blood Bank in Lima regarding our blood transfusion protocols, which were under scrutiny by the *Fiscalía* owing to their ignorance. Dr Celada, the preeminent national authority in this field, submitted a detailed written statement validating our procedure.

The two ICU doctors in Germany with whom we had consulted throughout Abraham's ordeal also prepared written testimonies which were translated into Spanish for the *Fiscalía*, but likely never received the attention they deserved.

Tim and his wife Miriam felt a deep sense of betrayal. The two doctors were working so hard as unpaid missionaries at Diospi Suyana. The operations were carried out at the express wishes of the patient's family. The traumatologists at *EsSalud* had taken the day off for the holiday. Tim wasn't bothered about missing his birthday party or donating his blood. He had endured the endless hours spent in the operating theatre and ICU. But he was deeply wounded by the ingratitude and malice of our accusers.

The *Fiscalía* stalled on their decision to proceed with a formal investigation of Diospi Suyana. They let all the deadlines pass and yet still pretended that the allegations had a kernel of merit.

Franziscus C spent Christmas comfortably with his relatives. Although his drunken actions had caused the fatal accident, he was solidly protected against any investigation by his influential family name.

Even in the twenty-first century, Peru's judicial system is still rife with corruption. While we were in the firing line, the national news outlets reported the acquittal of a rapist by one of Lima's top judges – for a substantial bribe, of course. Why should we assume people will behave any differently at the local level in Curahuasi?

I once asked a seasoned lawyer from Cusco to estimate how many trials took place in Peru without outside interference, coercion, mudslinging or bribery.

The lawyer thought for a while and shook his head. 'Maybe 10 per cent,' he admitted soberly.

When we lit the candles on Christmas Eve, the scandalous threat of legal action still hung over our heads. But the peace that God gives is not dependent on external circumstances. 'The peace of God … transcends all understanding' (Philippians 4:7), Paul wrote long ago while a prisoner in Rome. It was to be his last letter, for soon after he was executed. Did a similar fate await us, figuratively speaking? We certainly had no shortage of enemies.

38
Only just legal

A hospital in Peru requires a licence to operate, just as it would in any other country on the planet. Without such a licence, no medical care may be legally provided. And rightly so. Imagine being operated on in some flophouse by shady individuals without proper training. As the anaesthesia takes effect, you catch someone writing out a massive bill which you would be required to pay – in cash – in full before leaving the establishment. It likely would not take long to realise that you had been duped by a bunch of con artists.

On 16th May 2018, I was sitting in a waiting room in Lima, listening to the TV. I was shocked to hear the head of the Peruvian dental authority declare that, in Peru, six thousand individuals claiming to be dentists were actually not dentists at all. Of course, scammers do this not because they are concerned about the population's oral hygiene but because they want to make money. For a European, this complete lack of accountability and regulation is mind-blowing. The former CEO of the Adifan Group, a conglomeration of seventeen Peruvian pharmaceutical companies, once told my wife and me that 30 per cent of the medicines available on the Peruvian market contain no active ingredient. Buyers essentially throw their money away on deceptively packaged sugar pills!

I think we can all agree that the regulatory process is absolutely essential. In Peru, licences must be renewed every three years. Following a successful onsite inspection, the hospital management will receive a new certificate in the post. Doesn't sound too difficult, really.

Our licence was due to expire on 22nd May 2018. Since the wheels of bureaucracy in Peru turn extremely slowly, our eager ladies in administration had completed the renewal application online on 17th December 2017 and then followed up with an extensive written application in January 2018. As a mission hospital, we could not risk something going wrong and wanted this taken care of sooner rather than later.

If you think our efficiency triggered a similar response from the officials, you would be sorely mistaken. Nothing happened. Our assistants, Yessica Herreras and Claudia Hugo, sent regular inquiries over the mountains to the state capital. But the only response to the multitude of emails and phone calls was a vexing silence.

On 6th July, six weeks after our licence had expired, three inspectors showed up at our door. They walked through every department in our facility and took copious notes. A good ten days later, we received their summary report. We were completely blindsided by the four pages of alleged discrepancies. Anyone reading it would have mentally pictured some ramshackle hut rather than our twenty-first-century hospital. Bizarre. Didn't President Ollanta Humala publicly praise Diospi Suyana as the best hospital in southern Peru during his visit with the Minister of Health in 2014? And what about all the accolades our institution has received in the media? Our hospital has been described as clean and friendly, with modern and innovative equipment, and our standard of care has been held up as the benchmark for the rest of the country.

I phoned one of the managers at the health authority to vent my bitter frustration. 'You are trying to destroy us!' I shouted angrily into the receiver. 'Hundreds of thousands of people are travelling here and waiting in long queues because they have such confidence in the quality of our work!'

'Your big numbers mean nothing,' Dr A interrupted my rant. 'You won't get a new licence from us until you correct all the deficiencies!' And with that, the conversation was abruptly over.

He was wrong, of course. Big numbers mean a great deal. Patients vote with their feet, passing by countless other clinics on their way to Curahuasi. They trust those who treat them with skill and compassion, so they queue up here at our doors, searching for a cure.

It really wasn't about the condition of our hospital, we knew that. The impressive infrastructure of Diospi Suyana drew the ire of many state doctors in Abancay. On top of that, we represented a more humanitarian mindset, where the practice of medicine is love in action, not just a means to make money and certainly not an opportunity to exploit the vulnerable for personal gain. In other words, we made them look bad – on more than one level.

But the health authority had the upper hand and knew it. They could nitpick, change the rules or stall us in a myriad of ways that would cause us to lose our legitimacy. Per government order, we had until 31st December 2018 to 'fix' the issues cited in the inspection report. Nearly three-quarters of a year had passed since our initial application. There were only three months left until the deadline, a very short period of time considering the snail's pace of Peruvian bureaucracy.

We were clearly at an impasse. I would need to get the Minister of Health involved somehow. A new minister, Dr Silvia Pessah, had been appointed in April 2018, and I had yet to be able to make personal contact.

So we called Lima and requested an appointment. We wrote to her, recounting the gravity of our situation. A business tycoon once told me, 'Persistence pays!' I think there is some truth to that, and I have followed this recommendation for years.

I was offered a brief audience with Vice Minister Dr Diego Rolando on 17th August. Another official whom I did not know also attended the meeting. No sooner had we sat down than the

Vice Minister's phone rang, and away he went. What a disappointment!

We made some headway in our regional capital of Abancay. Governor Dr Wilmer Venegas was willing to hear us out. The DIRESA Director, Dr Diaz, was also present during our meeting. The governor could see immediately what was happening and turned to the director. 'Dr Diaz, how many hospitals in Apurímac fully meet all the government's requirements?'

'None,' Diaz admitted.

'Then why are you making things so difficult for Diospi Suyana?' the governor demanded. 'Everyone knows that this hospital has been a blessing for thousands of people in need of help.'

The awkward silence that followed ironically spoke volumes. Governor Venegas urged Dr Diaz to expedite our licence. We were encouraged, but Health Department bureaucrats continued to stonewall us.

I renewed my efforts in Lima. Dr José Olaechea, head of the law firm that often supported us pro bono, happened to be a personal acquaintance of Roger Valencia, Minister of Foreign Trade and Tourism. On 18th September, one of the Olaechea lawyers accompanied me to a meeting with Minister Valencia. The Minister was on his way to the Presidential Palace, so I had just a few minutes to share my photos and make my request.

'Minister Valencia, I urgently need an audience with the Minister of Health, but I don't know how to make that happen!' I pleaded.

As it turns out, Roger Valencia had heard positive comments about Diospi Suyana for years. 'Dr John, I am going to meet with Silvia Pessah at Congress tomorrow,' he shared. 'I think you will have an invitation from her by the end of the week!'

Before we assembled for a group photo, Minster Valencia gave me a piece of advice: 'Don't talk to the Minister of Health about faith or God. She is a liberal Jew and probably an atheist. Just stick to the issue of your licence!'

Unfortunately, that just wasn't going to work for me. I end each of my presentations with a crystal-clear profession of my faith. I am a committed Christian, plain and simple. Not a humanist, not a politician. Jesus Christ, crucified and risen, is my only hope. There is no other.

I returned to the Diospi Suyana guesthouse to await further news.

Roger Valencia was a man of his word. Minister Pessah's secretary soon contacted me with an invitation to her office on 20th September, just two days later.

Around noon, the guards at the main gate allowed me to enter. I was escorted to a large meeting room on the fourth floor and began to set up my laptop right away. I was ready.

At 12:30pm, the panelled door opened. The Minister of Health stormed into the room with the Vice Minister at her side. I immediately stood up out of courtesy and took a step forward. Silvia Pessah scorned my greeting and launched an admonishment, 'That was pretty bold of you to tell Minister Valencia that I haven't had time for you yet!' Her dark eyes flashed accusingly at me. 'The Vice Minister received you just the other day,' she said, gesturing towards Diego Rolando. He nodded. 'What more do you want?' Minister Pessah demanded. 'Dr John, I am really rather annoyed with you!'

I felt like I had been slapped in the face. I had been hoping for Minister Pessah's empathy and support, not castigation.

'Say what you have to say but make it quick. I have little time!'

I managed to find my voice. 'Madam Minister,' I began shakily, 'I have prepared some slides to help explain our dilemma.'

'I don't want to see a presentation,' the minister huffed.

'Just a few pictures!' I quickly reassured her.

She allowed me to place my laptop on the table before her. I clicked the first slide. 'This is my family, and the little one there in the middle is me. I was just three in this picture. My family were bakers in Wiesbaden!'

The minister was still scowling at me. Everything about her body language told me I'd better get to the point – fast.

Here we all were. The Vice Minister on the left, Minister Pessah in the middle and me on the right. A Jewish scientist and a German missionary doctor. Who knew to what extent this particular constellation might influence our conversation? I sent up one arrow prayer after another as I nervously worked my way through the first thirty pictures.

And then something unprecedented happened. I can't remember when – maybe five or six minutes in? Silvia Pessah's face took on a kind, almost loving expression. Her eyes conveyed what she did not say, 'Dr John, I understand you now. I am sorry.'

I relaxed my pace and went into a bit more detail. At the end, I showed her the four-page report from DIRESA and said, 'Madam Minister, as you can see, we have reached the end of our rope!'

The highly educated Jewish woman with dual citizenship was wise. She was familiar with the ways of the world and also of the Peruvian medical profession. 'This is pure outrage!' Silvia Pessah's heart had evidently warmed to our cause. 'I am on it. Next week, I will send a team to Curahuasi to help sort this out!'

The Vice Minister's phone rang again, and he stepped outside to take the call.

'Madam Minister,' I inquired gently when we were alone, 'people say you don't believe in God at all. Is that true?'

'Is that really what they say?' Silvia Pessah appeared thoughtful. 'Dr John, God means a great deal to me. Just yesterday, I celebrated Yom Kippur with my husband!'

Only forty minutes had passed, but in that time we had managed to move from the 'chilly' reception to the warmth of unanimity.

I received two more personal emails from Minister Pessah that week. In the second, written just before she boarded a flight to Washington DC, she assured me of her full support, promising to sort everything out in the coming week so our good work could continue. And then she made a request that brought me even more joy: 'Pray for me!'

The next day, Tina, our assistants Claudia and Yessica, and I drove to Abancay to pay a visit to DIRESA. With Minister Pessah's support, the tables were beginning to turn.

On 24th September, a delegation sent by Minister Pessah arrived from Lima with the sole mission of resolving our licensing issue.

Over the next eight weeks, many meetings were held, and eventually, all our 'deficiencies' were cleared. On 28th November, I notified Minister Pessah that we had fulfilled all of the DIRESA requirements, yet still had not been granted our licence renewal. We were on tenterhooks but received only radio silence from Abancay.

At midnight on 31st December, time would run out. Our licence would expire and we would no longer be authorised to provide medical services to the people of Peru.

On that Wednesday evening, 26th December, I reached out one last time, feeling more than a little desperate. I addressed the minister with a copy to the Vice Minister.

> *I wish you a very Merry Christmas and God's blessings for the coming year. Despite all our joint efforts, we still do not have a positive resolution from DIRESA regarding our licence ... As a result, I regret to announce that Diospi Suyana hospital will close next Tuesday to avoid any legal ramifications for our institution. The timing is particularly bad, as in January there are long queues of patients seeking care from our hospital.*
> *Awaiting your reply, with best regards, Klaus-Dieter John*

At 10.20pm I received a response from the Vice Minister. Nothing from the Minister herself, but she worked her magic behind the scenes during the night. The very next morning, DIRESA called us. 'You can pick up the licence – it was issued a long time ago!'

On 27th December, we had won the final battle in a thirteen-month-long war with the regulatory authorities.

The woman who made our victory possible, Silvia Pessah, resigned from her post a week later, citing 'personal reasons'.

In my life, I have spoken to many ministers. For none of them do I feel more love and gratitude than for Silvia Pessah, the Jewish woman from Israel.

39
An unprecedented corporate tour and what really matters

Since January 2004, someone somewhere has held a private fundraiser for Diospi Suyana about every four days. Housewives, scouts, schoolchildren and pensioners have gone above and beyond to support our work in Peru. Three-quarters of the donations we receive come from private individuals rather than large corporations, a fact I cannot stress enough.

Nevertheless, I would like to tell you about a unique week in January 2019. In the middle of the icy winter, I personally visited eight companies over the course of five days, travelling a total of 2,500 miles through Switzerland and Germany. It was remarkable to be able to talk to so many insightful executives in such a short period. My tour began at MVV in Mannheim and ended at Lautenschläger in Cologne.

MVV-Energie AG, with Fred Jung, former CEO of JUWI AG renewable energy, upgraded our photovoltaic system, which was necessary after ten years of operation. The Swiss aid organisation Job International helped us to fit out our media station with furniture. On 29th January, I raced six hundred miles north, only to get caught in a massive traffic jam on the A5 just before midnight. Fortunately, I still made it to my appointment at Dräger-Werke in Lübeck on time. I had the rare opportunity to present Diospi Suyana in all its glory directly to the company's CEO, Stefan Dräger. Mr Dräger allowed ample time for our meeting and, in the end, agreed to donate new anaesthesia equipment, operating theatre lamps and ICU monitors.

From there, it was straight on to Berlin. Dr Donner from the Friedrichs lift manufacturing company shared that she was so impressed by what had been done in Peru that she had enlisted the help of Community Lift Technology eG (*GAT*), a cooperative of seventy medium-sized lift companies, to finance an external lift for our eye clinic!

Schmitz & Sons in Wickende donated two new operating tables and a wide variety of related accessories. Lautenschläger helped with a large Hospital Sterilisation and Disinfection Unit (HSDU) for our surgical materials. The total value of donations received was about €650,000. I still get overwhelmed from time to time thinking about this spectacular result, and do not doubt that God Himself arranged each and every meeting.

But when I think back to that mad week, one encounter in particular sticks with me, reminding me, and perhaps you too, of what really matters.

It was just before 1pm. Fred Jung and I were on the fifteenth floor of the MVV building, waiting for two executives to arrive. The sky was low with dark clouds. Far below us, the Neckar River snaked along like a grey ribbon alongside the skyscraper. 'Over there, you can see Mannheim University Hospital,' Fred said, pointing into the distance with his right hand, 'where the doctors fought so hard to save Joshua's life.'

I met Fred's gaze and nodded. I was well aware of the events that had transpired five years earlier, both the unspeakable tragedy and the miraculous glimpse beyond the veil.

Fred Jung is a businessman with an impeccable sense of timing. He co-founded the renewable energy company JUWI, which generated one billion euros of revenue in 2012. Figuratively speaking, he was a footballer who had made it to the top of the Premier League. And yet he remained virtually unaffected by his success. As a Christian, he had a different set of priorities: first God, then family, and *then* his company.

On 1st March 2014, Fred was doing some work at home in the garden with a forklift, believing that his children were a safe distance away. But that is when the unthinkable happened. Fred reversed the forklift, and two-year-old Joshua, who had appeared out of nowhere, was suddenly caught under the wheels.

The accident happened at 11.15am. Fred raced to the emergency room at Kirchheimbolanden with the limp body of his blond-headed child. His wife Claudia arrived at the same time and, as a doctor, immediately recognised the gravity of the situation. The hospital's trauma centre filled with medical staff who did everything in their power to save this young life. Claudia and Fred paced anxiously up and down the hospital corridor. After a few minutes, the believing Christians reached out to friends and acquaintances, asking them to pray for Joshua. 'Lord Jesus,' Fred cried silently, 'please take control!'

Dr Horst Fleck was the head of the trauma centre at the hospital where Joshua's parents had taken him, but he wasn't at work that fateful day. He had taken some time off and was on a retreat at a monastery in Gnadenthal, Hesse.

Around noon, Horst went to check the time and saw he had a voicemail from his friend Fred. 'Joshi has had an accident – please pray with us!' Horst, whose wife Christine has been supporting Diospi Suyana for years through the sale of her homemade muesli, heard the alarm in Fred's voice. He had no idea where Joshua was or any details of what had occurred, but he knew it must have been something terrible. Horst slid to his knees at the edge of his bed and began to pray.

And suddenly, although he was miles away, Horst could see what was happening in the operating room of his hospital. He saw little Joshua on the operating table, surrounded by an army of doctors and nurses attempting to do the impossible; a battle made all the more urgent because the life of a child was involved.

In his fifty-five years, this trauma specialist had never before experienced a vision. Crystal-clear images passed before his inner eye. The tension was palpable, and Horst knew the outcome would be fatal. He gazed at the lifeless body as the doctors continued to work from all sides. Two angels materialised as brilliant figures of light on either side of Joshua. In an instant, they disappeared with him upwards into another world, Joshua's face shining like the sun as they went, his body an empty shell left behind on the hospital table.

A helicopter was dispatched to transfer Joshua to the university hospital in Mannheim as an emergency case. When Fred and his wife caught up forty-five minutes later, the grim countenance of the doctor on duty communicated the devastating news without words.

That night, Joshua appeared to his father in a dream that seemed completely real. His face was full of joy, and he said, 'Dad, don't worry – I'm with Jesus now!'

Such dreams can be a source of comfort, even if the sceptic shakes his head in disbelief. It's impossible to verify dreams. Dr Fleck, however, was able to verify what he saw during his vision. He had seen an anaesthetist scheduled to be off duty that day, but as he learned the following Monday, the anaesthetist had been called in specifically to assist with the emergency situation. The series of events reported to Horst matched precisely what he had seen from afar.

Joshua's funeral was held in Kirchheimbolanden on 7th March. In front of eight hundred mourners, Fred and Claudia Jung, as well as Horst Fleck, shared their other-worldly experiences, where death has lost its sting. It is the place where God's presence reigns supreme and we are wrapped securely in His care.

In preparation for the service, Fred had memorised some verses from Paul's epistle to the Romans. These words of the apostle Paul became an anchor for him and his wife, keeping them steady in the midst of this fateful storm:

> For I am convinced that neither death nor life, neither angels nor demons, neither the present nor the future, nor any powers, neither height nor depth, nor anything

else in all creation, will be able to separate us from the love of God that is in Christ Jesus our Lord. (Romans 8:38-39)

40
Decision to set out

In the packed auditorium of the Aglasterhausen community centre, one hundred listeners applauded as I left the podium and made my way to a vacant seat in the front row. Our orthopaedic technician Daniel Müller and his parents had arranged this presentation opportunity. Daniel stepped forward to thank the audience for coming.

'Do you also need urologists?' asked the young man beside me. Normally, I'm very keen on such inquiries, but this time I had to dissuade the man. 'Not really,' I answered automatically, 'we already have an excellent urologist by the name of David Brady.' I wrote down the man's contact information anyway, just in case. This conversation happened on 19th April 2017.

Two weeks later, I emailed the man to let him know that I was in the process of talking to David to find out how long he and his wife intended to work with Diospi Suyana. I hoped there would be some overlap between David's departure and the arrival of a new urologist. One never knows, and missionary doctors can be quite hard to find. After this exchange, the young man faded into the fog of countless people I briefly chat with before or after my presentations. Some faces I remember, but most unfortunately not.

It was midday on 6th March 2018 when I suddenly turned to our urologist and blurted out, 'David, hand on your heart, how long do you plan on staying here?' I have no idea why this came out of my mouth right at that time or with such urgency.

'Until the summer of 2020,' came the resolute reply. 'Then we will return to Germany so our eldest can attend high school.' It almost seemed that the Austrian had been anticipating my question.

Summer of 2020 … the wheels started to turn in my head. I would have to do everything I could to find a replacement for David within the next two years. It would be a shame if we had to suspend the operations of our urology department for any length of time. From somewhere in the depths of my brain, the name Benjamin Zeier surfaced – the man I had spoken to in Aglasterhausen nearly a year earlier. Never one to leave any stone unturned, I went straight to my office and searched for the email address of the erstwhile interested young urologist from Baden-Württemberg. Since our initial encounter, I had bought a new laptop, and not all of my previous emails had been saved. I had a sinking feeling I had lost his details.

I nodded with satisfaction as my search proved successful, and the email address appeared on my screen. I immediately sent off a quick note, short and to the point: 'Dear Mr Zeier, what telephone number can I reach you on? Best regards from Peru, Klaus John!'

Thousands of miles away in Mosbach, Lena Zeier was in labour in the hospital delivery room, hoping for an uncomplicated birth of their fifth child. It was just after midnight on 6th March, and Benjamin was trembling right along with every painful contraction his wife endured. Some claim that childbirth is more stressful for the father than the mother. The mother is *in* it, is actively participating, and has some sense of agency, whereas the father can only watch, powerless to help. I'm inclined to agree, having been through this agonising process three times myself.

A small head of hair popped out of the birth canal, and Jonas Kilian Zeier announced his arrival with a loud cry. A collective sigh of relief went through the room. His father, who works in the emergency department as well as urology, did a quick visual scan, and was delighted to conclude that his youngest was a perfectly healthy baby boy with a rosy complexion. The midwife did her usual thing, and one more successful birth was logged with the German authorities.

Around 1.15am, Benjamin said goodbye to his wife and newborn. He got into his car and drove uphill through the darkness. In a few minutes he reached his destination, turned off the engine and opened the car door. On the hilltop, hidden among the evergreen trees, was a cross. After the birth of each of his children, Benjamin had come here to offer a prayer of thanksgiving, and tonight was no exception.

Benjamin knelt reverently in the damp grass and listened for God's still, small voice. His deep gratitude erupted and he extolled God for the gift of his wife and Jonas Kilian, for all his children and for his fulfilled life. He found himself spontaneously adding two more sentences, the content of which quite surprised him: 'Dear Father, I know that the chapter of bearing children is now behind us. Please show me what comes next in our family's story!' He opened his eyes in wonder. That prayer certainly had not gone how he had planned. He made his way through the night chill back to his vehicle as the Mosbach tower clock struck half past one – time for bed.

Lena was discharged from the hospital at about nine o'clock the next morning. She was no doubt a tough woman! Ben went into town to run a few errands. When he returned, Lena inched carefully down the wooden steps to greet him. Ben was exhausted, but excited to share his strange experience of the night before.

Lena listened to Ben's story, then abruptly asked, 'Benjamin, have you looked at your email yet? Klaus has just written to you. Klaus-Dieter John, from Peru!' And in that moment, Benjamin's world stood still.

I hadn't said anything in my email about why I wanted to get in touch with the Zeiers. But the young couple understood the implication straightaway. Lena had long since made up her mind. Turning to Benjamin, she asked, 'So when are we leaving?'

Benjamin has since written a book about his family's calling to Peru. He presented his work, *Decision to Set Out*,[10] at the Leipzig Book Fair in the spring of 2019. In it, he writes, 'Since that moment in March 2018, most things in our lives have changed. Every decision has a new target coordinate, and for us as a family, a new era has dawned!'[11] Paper is patient, accepting whatever we might want to scribe upon it. But ultimately, it is only the follow-through that is of consequence.

The Zeiers applied for a long-term assignment at Diospi Suyana and were accepted with open arms. Benjamin quit his partnership in a flourishing urology practice. The couple sold their home, complete with a pool and a garden. They began to build a network of financial supporters and shared their story in the local newspapers. On 23rd April 2019, during an interview with an SWR4 reporter, Lena and Benjamin talked about their faith that inspired this decision. My impulsive email was received by a doctor who had just prayed for clarity and purpose while kneeling before a cross one night. A timely answer to prayer, the Zeiers unequivocally accepted the invitation to Peru and never looked back.

Most people would probably shy away from such a bold prayer, as Benjamin called it. Many of us do pray the Lord's Prayer, which speaks of God's will being done on earth as it is in heaven, but deep down, if we're honest, we'd really prefer to make our own plans. As soon as a Christian starts making personal sacrifices as a result of their convictions, people take notice – even the media. I think this is what Jesus meant when He talked about the cross and the price of discipleship. 'Feel-good' Christianity or timid faith will simply not bring about the change God desires in our dark world. Ernst Jakob Christoffel, early twentieth-century pastor and founder of the Christian Blind Mission, once declared, 'Nothing shouts louder than action.' And we all know he was exactly right.

---

[10] Benjamin Zeier, *Entscheidung zum Aufbruch* (Mosbach, 2019).

[11] Zeier, *Entscheidung zum Aufbruch*, p 23.

41
Mysterious flight LA2061

Unresolved legal disputes cause a great deal of stress, sometimes manifesting somatically as stomach ulcers and the like. Shattering nerves and sleep, they can drive people to the brink of despair. It was no different for us in regard to the Abraham K case. Public Prosecutor Rene C intentionally disregarded all timelines and kept us dangling from a very long string. Weeks of uncertainty turned into months.

Eventually, our lawyers appealed to the State Supreme Court in Abancay and asked for a ruling. Dr Maria Gutierrez and Dr Luis Velarde from Olaechea law firm travelled to Abancay on Wednesday 3rd April, to attend. It started with a bang! Our *Fiscal*, the prosecutor from Curahuasi, was notably absent. It just so happened that she had been removed from office owing to corruption and incompetence. Good move, although, in our opinion, long overdue. It was her successor's first day of work, and he was not yet familiar with the Abraham K case. The judge gave him one week to review the file and determine whether there was any merit at all to the allegations of negligent homicide.

Talk about a baptism by fire for a new *Fiscal!* To further complicate matters, the dentist Ricardo C appeared in his office a few days later. 'If you dismiss the case,' he brazenly threatened, 'we will turn the population against you!' There seemed to be no end to this man's deceitful manipulations. 'Diospi Suyana has been deserted,' he lied. 'Hardly anyone from Curahuasi goes there any more!' Those who get caught up in such delusions completely lose touch with reality. The truth was that in 2019 we were approaching an all-time high of 58,000 patients treated – almost 25 per cent more than in the preceding year. And nine thousand of them were Curahuasinos, many of whom literally ran to us for care.

Dr Arcangel remained calm and level-headed. He objectively scrutinised all the evidence submitted by both sides and, finding absolutely no indication of wrongdoing on the part of Diospi Suyana, he dismissed the case without further comment. He, too, could ascertain that these allegations had more to do with a shameless vendetta against Diospi Suyana than what had actually transpired with the patient. Tina and I, as well as the Boekers, sighed a heartfelt prayer of deep gratitude.

But we rejoiced too soon. Five days later, the lawyer for the other side appealed, and updated documents were sent to Abancay for review. It was apparent that our opponents were not to be underestimated. Realising that everyone familiar with the case was clear on how hard our doctors had worked to save Abraham's life, Ricardo C and his friends changed their tactics. Instead of absurd charges of negligence, they were now questioning whether it was even legal for our hospital to perform such operations. In addition, they went after Dr Boeker personally, asserting that this ten-year traumatology veteran lacked sufficient credentials for his current role.

The propagation of the charge presented some serious concerns. Licensing matters are incredibly complicated in Peru; anyone in the medical profession can tell you that. I deemed it an appropriate time to reach out to the new Minister of Health, Dr Zulema Tomas, and the head of the Peruvian Medical Association. We called and sent letters, to no avail. We tried working through established contacts, but the doors remained firmly shut.

Finally we received a very brief – and dismissive – email from the Ministry of Health. The Peruvian Medical Association also brushed us off. No one at the national level wanted to get sucked into our affairs. We were all alone – except for God. He heard our prayers and saw our silent tears.

We didn't want to go to Lima in May, but it was a necessary evil. Tina, Tim, our anaesthetist Leslie and I all gave our statements in court. I had filed a charge of aggravated defamation against the dentist. Olaechea's eloquent indictment sought heavy damages as well as a two-year prison sentence for the scoundrel, who failed to appear in court. He evidently tried to dodge the noose by simply ignoring the summons. Considered an additional offence in many other countries, we had no idea if such a strategy might work here in Peru.

On 22nd May, the four of us waited at Jorge Chavez Airport for our return flight to Cusco. Lima is a major hub, with more than 12 million travellers passing through each year. The structure has long been inadequate for such a mass influx, so huge crowds and long lines are the norm.

We were just about to board when Leslie ran up excitedly. 'Guess what! The Prime Minister, Salvador del Solar, is sitting on a bench right over there! I just took a selfie with him!' Full of pride, she showed us the picture taken less than two minutes earlier.

I studied the Prime Minister's face on the small mobile display. There was something familiar about it. He had only recently been appointed to this high-level post. How odd, I thought to myself, that in Peru, you could have your picture taken with the president of the Council of Ministers in the middle of a crowd!

Tina and I found our seats at the very back of the plane. The flight to Cusco took an hour, as usual. It was dark when we landed and taxied to the gate. I wanted to rush off the plane and head to the baggage carousel to grab my two suitcases containing the endoscopes I'd just had repaired in Lima. Several thousand dollars in value, it would be a significant loss if someone were to steal my luggage! However, my efforts to hurry were thwarted when the flight attendant announced that the 170 passengers should exit from both the rear and the front of the aeroplane. My hand luggage, unfortunately, was several metres in front of my seat, and now there was a solid wall of passengers pushing towards the rear exit. There was no way to go against that tide. We had no choice but to be patient. When everyone else had finally disembarked, I grabbed our hand luggage and followed, with some annoyance.

As I entered the terminal, I saw that familiar face again, recognising him from Leslie's selfie. The Prime Minister of Peru stood just to the side of the aisle and was deep in conversation. He must have been on the same flight, LA2061! Probably up in first class or maybe even in the cockpit with the pilots. It was the opportunity of a lifetime and one I was not going to let pass by. I strode over quickly to introduce myself as the director of the Diospi Suyana Hospital and to request permission to share more about our work with him at the Presidential Palace.

Salvador del Solar was initially taken aback but then noticed Tina standing next to me. His face brightened. 'I know you!' he exclaimed. 'I accompanied President Kuczynski to your anniversary celebration in 2017. I was the Minister of Culture back then. You really do have a fantastic hospital!'

He turned to his advisor and affirmed, 'Yes, they should definitely be invited to my office. They are doing incredible work!'

We were giddy with excitement on the ride home, mentally replaying the events of the last several hours. What were the chances of running into the Prime Minister at Lima Airport? Zero. And Leslie even got a selfie with him! Because of our inconveniently stowed luggage, we were held up on the plane for an extra ten minutes or so. As a result of this aggravation, our paths crossed, and we had a very encouraging conversation. On top of all that, he knew us and our work, and had even been to Diospi Suyana! It felt like we had just won the lottery.

On Monday evening, 24th June, Prime Minister del Solar greeted us at the Presidential Palace. Early that day, the Minister of Defence had died of an unexpected heart attack. Even up until the last moment, Tina and I were not sure that the Prime

Minister would be able to meet with us after all, despite his good intentions. But he came through. His name, Salvador del Solar, can be loosely translated as 'Saviour of the Sun'. This is a bit pompous, even for a prime minister, but he became our saviour. During our forty-five-minute meeting, he called the Minister of Health and arranged an appointment for us with the head of the Peruvian Health Service. As a parting gift, he handed us a business card with his personal mobile phone number.

Two days later, a distinguished audience gathered at the Ministry of Health to hear the story of Diospi Suyana, brought to life through words and pictures. Dr Jens Haβfeld was seated next to me, still in awe that this was actually happening.

In mid-June, I had been told that a personal audience with the new Minister of Health would be impossible owing to her tight schedule. Now she was waving at me from the head of the long conference table, encouraging me to begin my presentation. Also present were several vice ministers and a slew of directors from other departments.

We were here in this stately conference room, displaying photos of Diospi Suyana to a bunch of dignitaries, because the Prime Minister had opened the door. His support for us was evident to all, and they listened attentively. When I reached the end, I said, 'Madam Minister, we have a remarkable story, and that was the bright side of it. But now I must share the rest.' I opened a second PowerPoint and began to describe the opposition we faced from DIRESA regarding our hospital licence renewal, then concluded with the malicious defamation, threats and foul play we continued to endure as a result of the Abraham K case.

'We provide quality healthcare that people can actually afford. Many come to see us from all over the country. We are a thorn in the side of the private hospitals in south Peru. We have many enemies!' I repeated this fact, which hung in the air until my meaning was understood. It was an accusation but also a plea for help. I looked expectantly at the Minister of Health.

'Yes, you are absolutely right,' Dr Zulema Garcia affirmed. 'Unfortunately, that is the way it is in Peru. I will come to visit you in Curahuasi the week after next.'

Back in the Diospi Suyana guesthouse, Jens and I sat down in the lounge and gave thanks to God for what we saw as a week of liberation. In Psalm 42, David cries out:

> My foes taunt me,
> saying to me all day long,
> 'Where is your God?'
> Why, my soul, are you downcast?
> Why so disturbed within me?
> Put your hope in God,
> for I will yet praise him,
> my Saviour and my God.
> (Psalm 42:10-11)

The city of Lima was asleep, save for a few policemen, nurses and taxi drivers. In the silent darkness of the wee hours of 9th July, a woman arose from her bed and prepared to go out. A few minutes later, she was being chauffeured to the airport. The Minister of Health intended to keep her promise to Jens and me. She and a delegation boarded a jet to Cusco and arrived at Diospi Suyana around 9:45am. She had summoned the DIRESA officials for the purpose of conducting a joint walkthrough of our facilities.

At 10am, I welcomed Dr Zulema Garcia and her contingent into my office. Before offering refreshments, I picked up my pocket Bible. I read a passage from Isaiah 61, the same words I opened with during our ground-breaking ceremony on 24 May 2005:

> The Spirit of the Sovereign LORD is on me,
> because the LORD has anointed me
> to proclaim good news to the poor.
> He has sent me to bind up the broken-hearted,
> to proclaim freedom for the captives

> and release from darkness for the prisoners,
> to proclaim the year of the LORD's favour.
> (Isaiah 61:1-2)

Dr Garcia listened intently as I continued: 'Dear Minister, missionaries from all over the world volunteer to work at Diospi Suyana because their deepest desire is reflected in the words of Isaiah I just read. We want to help and to heal!'

Tina and I personally led the Minister and our other guests on a thorough tour of Diospi Suyana that lasted more than two and a half hours. Dr Garcia introduced herself to the masses of people filling our waiting rooms. They had come from all over the country. Some of those waiting bemoaned the general state of healthcare in Peru, some expressing their frustration with bitterness and tears. They told her, 'Madam Minister, every hospital in Peru should function like Diospi Suyana. Here they treat us with love and respect!'

In the dental clinic, Elisabeth Franke shared the advantages of our state-of-the-art CAD/CAM machine for restorative dentistry. Our small crowd looked on in wonder as a little ceramic block was transformed into a perfect dental crown via the computer-aided technology. 'Madam Minister, there are tens of thousands of dollars of equipment in this clinic,' I shared with my astonished audience, 'but our most valuable asset is not the expensive machines, but our missionary dentist from Germany, who has already dedicated four years of her life to the people of Peru.'

We made our way over to the media station. During a broadcast interview, Dr Garcia expressed her commendation of Diospi Suyana and promised us her full support. At lunch, she called across the table to the DIRESA director: 'You must always support Diospi Suyana – in everything!' A very clear charge.

The Minister had taken a seat on the minibus, but the driver waited idly at the wheel. What was going on? 'We're going to do some more filming with our drone,' one of the journalists explained to me. I looked up in disbelief. Sure enough, I could make out what looked like a tiny helicopter flying high above our grounds, a dark whirl against the bright blue sky. I had never seen anything like it in Peru. After a few more minutes of recording, the drone was retrieved, the driver closed the minibus door and they all pulled away towards the Diospi Suyana gates. We waved our goodbyes, feeling good about the potential impact of the last few hours.

'Let's give thanks to God!' Tina, Doris Manco, Daniel Müller and I gathered together in the small waiting room of the orthopaedic clinic and bowed our heads. The Minister of Health had set aside an entire day to do us the honour of visiting in person. It was no less than a miracle, and our hearts overflowed with genuine gratitude to God.

On Wednesday, Doris, head of our broadcast centre, received a link to the official video from the Minister's visit. It was only seventy-five seconds long, but the drone footage showed our hospital in all its glory through a series of breathtaking aerial shots. The Minister herself narrated the video and spoke highly of Diospi Suyana throughout. After listing the various departments composing Diospi Suyana, Dr Garcia summed up her impressions. 'I must say that what is being done here is admirable. The staff treat people with so much love, so much humanity. You see patients here from many different states – Puno, Cusco, Huánuco, Lima and Tacna. They come from all over, trusting they will find the help they need here.' We could not have hoped for a greater appreciation for our work than that.

During his nasty tirade on the radio, dentist Ricardo C had publicly demanded that the Minister of Health take a closer look at Diospi Suyana. He got what he asked for – but not the outcome he expected.

In the same week, we submitted the Minister's video to the *Fiscalia*. We also sent it, with profound thanks, to Prime Minister Salvador del Solar. Our paths had only crossed because of the inaccessible placement of our luggage, but since we had met, we had come a good deal closer to clearing our name in the Abraham K case.

42

Diospi Suyana in numbers

There is never a shortage of visitors at Diospi Suyana. When they return to their home countries, they enthusiastically share their experiences in person and online. People are moved by our story, motivated by our work, stirred to give financially and sometimes even to join us. But this chapter is not about 'bragging rights' – it's just the facts.

From October 2007 to March 2024, our doctors and nurses treated more than 530,000 patients. Over the years, the number of patients has increased slowly but surely. In our first year of operation, we provided medical care to approximately 18,000 patients. In 2019, that number had jumped to 58,000! Most of those seeking our help were Quechua Indians or other rural mountain folk.

Our total budget in the spring of 2023 was approximately US$460,000 per month – a seemingly astronomical figure. So where does all this money come from?

Since the start of our work in Curahuasi, about 220 long-term missionaries have served in our hospital, school and broadcast station. Most of them invest three years of their lives and raise their own financial support via friends and other donors before arriving in Peru. These donations never come close to the salaries our missionaries had been receiving in their home countries. The financial sacrifices people choose to make in order to come and work with us cannot be overestimated in terms of magnitude or importance. The home support received by our missionaries accounts for about 22 per cent of our operating costs.

More than a thousand individuals support Diospi Suyana through monthly bank transfers. These regular supporters and the one-offs who donate after hearing one of my talks cover about 31 per cent of our monthly expenses. These people are the backbone of our financial security. We also receive corporate support. To date, 250 different companies have provided us with necessary equipment and other materials free of charge. Considering the actual market value, these contributions make up about 19 per cent of our budget.

The patients who queue up to see us pay only four *soles*, about £1. Any additional charges for treatment are made on a sliding scale. Patient fees cover only about 28 per cent of our actual expenses. There is probably no other mission hospital in the world that provides such a high standard of care with so little financial return from the patients themselves. We are grateful to our faithful friends and supporters, and of course to God, who has made this amazing work possible.

As of March 2024, Diospi Suyana had received more than US$45 million worth of cash and in-kind contributions. Support from private individuals accounted for a whopping 75 per cent of that total, with the remainder provided by companies and other organisations. In addition to helping the Diospi Suyana Hospital, some of these financial gifts have funded our school and broadcast station.

Approximately 130,000 books about Diospi Suyana have now been printed by various publishers. More than 600 media reports through television, radio and print outlets have allowed more than 100 million people to hear about us – and that is a conservative estimate! We have compiled a database to keep track of every presentation and media feature of note.

Naturally, we value feedback from our clients. Since 2012, we have been asking men and women receiving at least one night of inpatient care from us to complete the following survey at discharge:

- Would you say that the doctors treated you kindly?

- Are you satisfied with the care you received from our nursing staff?

- Are you satisfied with the overall quality of your treatment?

- The hospital wants to share the love of Jesus with others. In your opinion, have we lived up to this goal?

- Would you want to visit our hospital again, should you become ill in the future?

- How likely are you to recommend Diospi Suyana to your family and friends?

Completion of the survey is completely voluntary. Quite a few are just in a hurry to get home and so decline to provide input. Nobody needs to fear any kind of reprisal or impact on their care since they are on their way out the door. We don't watch them fill out the survey, and they are free to submit an anonymous response if they so choose.

Our administration evaluated the first 4,037 responses received. A staggering 91.2 per cent of patients answered in the affirmative to all six questions. They were completely satisfied with their experience at our hospital. Six questions times 4,037 surveys equals 24,222 total questions asked. Of those, only 469 questions, or 1.9 per cent, received a negative response. Doing the maths, that means 23,753 questions, or 98.1 per cent, received a positive response. A 98.1 per cent approval rating would be a result not even a European or US hospital would achieve. It would never happen in Peru. Except it did.

43

A life's work that saves lives

A PR representative of a German company once told me, 'Dr John, I am amazed how easily you get Diospi Suyana featured in the media. It is usually quite difficult to get so much attention, but for you, it seems mere child's play!'

I believe our media success comes down to two factors. First, radical transparency. What you see is what you get. We give the same presentation to both Christian and secular audiences without changing our appearance or our message. I am confident that our passion for God and for justice and our hope will influence others, whether they know it or not. Journalists who profess to be atheists have written excellent articles about us without censoring our profession of faith. While they personally did not wish to accept God as the reason behind the countless miracles we have experienced, they really had no other explanation to offer.

'I just don't know,' one reporter admitted to me when I asked what he made of all the 'coincidences' that have occurred. He continued, 'It doesn't matter – it's still a good story!'

And I would add, 'What is good prevails.'

On 19th February 2013, I participated in a forty-minute interview with *1° de Marzo*, a popular radio station in Asunción, Paraguay. During this 5pm 'prime-time' broadcast, the show host asked me about my faith in God. *1° de Marzo* is a secular station and has never shown any affinity for religious topics, but here we were. While I shared some of my many experiences of God's faithfulness, I could envision the thousands of

Paraguayan commuters, heading home in their cars and packed buses, listening to what I had to say.

The second reason for our success is God's intervention. Before I ever speak to the media, I pray for God's blessing. I rely on Him to guide the encounter and to open doors for me to share. I am clear that it is not about me – I see myself only as an ambassador of God. I routinely ask the media not to reduce our ministry to a married couple's dream. 'This does no one any good,' I assert. 'But if you write that the Johns are confident that this is God's work, that He is working in our lives, that can have relevance for the reader, viewer or listener!' We all need guidance and assurance.

Over the past few years, I have witnessed incredible outcomes from my dealings with the media. On 8th September 2014, I spoke to seventy employees of B. Braun Medical in Sheffield, England. My sense of humour was well received by the audience, and there was a great deal of laughter. In February 2015, I received an email out of the blue from Patrick Horstmann. Horstmann was a professional basketball player with the Sheffield Sharks and was also involved with the Social Responsibility department at B. Braun. He had attended my talk back in September and was keen to meet me and to find ways to promote Diospi Suyana in the British media.

Two weeks later, during a short stay in the UK, we were able to meet up over pizza. 'Why don't you come to Curahuasi and bring a TV crew with you?' I suggested. 'We would drum up public interest very quickly! Long story short, nothing came of these plans, and I never heard from the athlete again. But this encounter did take a wonderful and unexpected turn that Patrick Horstmann knows nothing about. In the B. Braun guesthouse, he had chatted with Hanna Boucsein-Jäger, an eighteen-year-old Braun family member who was in Sheffield for a six-month internship. She was so enthralled by what Horstmann shared about Diospi Suyana, she ended up writing to me herself in May.

Hanna told me that she had read my first book and wanted to visit us in Peru. She wanted to bring her friend Maya who worked as an editor for a Nuremberg newspaper. The two young ladies arrived, and on 23rd October 2015, an article about Diospi Suyana filled the entire third page of the Nuremberg paper! The headline read, 'A Life's Work that Saves Lives'.

My next example is no less extraordinary. Anaesthetist Tobias Malisi arranged for me to meet the editor in chief of the leading newspaper in Saxony. On 13th May 2016, I walked punctually into the Dresden office and approached reception to introduce myself. But the receptionist immediately took all the wind out of my sails by informing me that Mr Vetterick had been unexpectedly called to a meeting with senior management and was unavailable. I returned to my rental car feeling a bit sorry for myself. 'If I were Brad Pitt with a new girlfriend, I'd have the reporters' attention for that nonsense,' I bemoaned internally. 'But I'm just a missionary doctor, and even though we have experienced the most amazing things at Diospi Suyana, nobody cares!' I looked despondently out the window at the grey sky. Then suddenly, I got a grip and began to pray, 'God, You can turn everything around – please do something!'

I was overcome with a strange sense of assurance that God would indeed intervene. Instead of driving away, I got out of my car and walked to a nearby Ukrainian restaurant. I ordered a cappuccino, got out my laptop and worked while I waited. Waited for what, you might ask. I wasn't exactly sure, but I knew He was going to do something.

My mobile rang. It was the editor in chief himself. 'Dr John, is there any chance that you are still around?'

'Yes,' I answered truthfully.

'Then come up to my office right away!'

Uwe Vetterick sat in an armchair while I told the Diospi Suyana story before a screen. At the end, he paused thoughtfully and said, 'Diospi Suyana is one more example of the old truth that it's the crazy who change the world!'

On 11th June, the Diospi Suyana article appeared in an expanded edition of the Saxon newspaper with the striking headline: 'God, the Master Builder'. The subheading was just as bold: 'There are no coincidences for Klaus John. He considers God to be the architect of the clinic.' Around 500,000 readers had the opportunity to learn about us through this three-quarter-page feature written by Christina Wittig-Tausch.

'Mr John, this is quite an experiment for us,' she confided in me, 'because most of our readers don't believe in God!'

Regardless of the readers' religious convictions – or lack thereof – the journalist had written in great detail about our matters of faith. One paragraph read:

> *Klaus John spends six months each year travelling in Europe, America, and Australia to raise support for the hospital and recruit new staff. But he also wants to talk about God, and he asks nearly everyone he meets what they believe. He has had such conversations with Christians of all denominations, with Buddhists, Muslims, atheists, with farmers from the Andes as well as Volkswagen line workers and various CEOs. Recently, he has been asking the question in Dresden, Schneeberg, and Pima. Here in Saxony, many people support the Diospi Suyana project. The name comes from the Quechua Indios language and means 'Trust in God'.*

In my first book, I shared an incident that occurred in Kleinmachnow, a posh suburb of Berlin, back in April 2004. My wife and I had told a group of fine people in the capital city about our dream of founding a hospital for the poor Indios of the Peruvian Andes. We were warned, 'If you talk about God so much, you'll never reach a mainstream audience. So you'd better put a lid on it!' The advice we received that evening was well intentioned – and deliberately ignored. Fast forward to the present: Diospi Suyana has been featured on more than a hundred television programmes, most of which have been secular.

Tina and I were invited by Germany's national public television station (ZDF) to participate in a fundraising gala for one of the country's largest children's charities, *Ein Herz für Kinder* ('A Heart for Children'). The event was held in Berlin on 7th December 2019. Before a live audience of seventy celebrities in the auditorium and a television audience of 3.7 million in their living rooms, we were interviewed by host Johannes B. Kerner.

'Do you ever reach your limit?' he asked Tina.

'Of course. All the time,' my wife replied, beaming. 'But with God's help, we bravely keep going!'

In the short documentary about Diospi Suyana shown just before our interview and later posted on the ZDF website, our faith in God was given its rightful place, beyond any shadow of doubt.

We never want to adorn our hats with the feathers of others. When God does something great, He deserves the honour, not us. Tina and I see ourselves merely as tools in the Master's hand.

44

The fight against coronavirus

On Friday 13th March 2020, I struggled out of bed at around 10am, still exhausted from the demands of the day before. After an engaging presentation to Swiss bankers and intellectuals in Zurich, I raced against the clock and traffic to make it to Konstanz in time for a second presentation. Despite the emerging threat of coronavirus, a hundred people turned up at the cultural centre to listen. But it was obvious that the mood in Germany and Switzerland had changed, and fear was spreading. Sometime between 2 and 3am, I made it back home to Wiesbaden and collapsed into bed, dead tired. My Friday plans included recovery and unhurried preparation for the next leg of my trip – I still had four more lectures scheduled. Karin Straβheim from our home office had planned my current tour meticulously, right down to the minute, somehow squeezing twenty-two formal and informal engagements into a span of just sixteen days. It was enough to test the mettle of any conference speaker, including me. No doubt I would sleep well on the plane when it was all over on Monday.

I sat down at my desk and switched on my laptop. The news out of Frankfurt on the subject of coronavirus was ominous. I was skimming over the headlines when my phone rang. It was Karin Straβheim calling to inform me that the first of my four upcoming events had just been cancelled by the organiser, no longer able to justify the risk of a packed venue. The second and third cancellations followed shortly.

'All right,' I thought, 'I'll have a bit of a break before I head back to Peru.' My phone rang again. This time it was Doris Manco calling from Peru. 'Klaus, the President has just ordered that Peru's borders be shut from this weekend.' I sat up straight in my chair, wide awake. 'If you want to get back here, you'll have to leave now!' she said.

'OK,' I responded, 'I'll try!'

Within seconds of hanging up from the call with Doris, I was on the line with Mr Fett from the travel agency in northern Germany of the same name. He immediately understood the urgency of the situation. All around the world, countries were battening down the hatches, locking down in a rapid chain reaction that brought public life as we know it to a grinding halt.

While Mr Fett combed through flight options, I started packing a carry-on bag with underwear, socks and three additional shirts. I expected I would be required to quarantine for two weeks in a hospital or private home once I arrived in South America. Unfortunately, my large suitcase would need to stay behind – I needed to leave immediately to get on a plane while that was still possible. I discussed the options with Mr Fett. I would need three plane tickets to increase the likelihood of getting back into Peru. If Peru shut its borders to Europe, it would be easier to get in from another South American country – so I needed a single ticket to Brazil. If Peru was shut to its neighbours as well, Brazil could send me straight back to Germany. That had to be prevented by another flight ticket. Mr Fett booked me on a Qatar Airlines flight to Doha for 30th March. I would use the two weeks between scheduled flights to make my way overland to Peru, 2,500 miles of adventure through the Amazon. I had no other choice; I had to get back to Curahuasi at any cost. Tina and I needed to weather this crisis together.

Despite my expectations, my journey to Peru went smoothly. I was even permitted to quarantine in my own home in Curahuasi. I could make phone calls at home just as well as at the hospital, and I did so like a champion.

There were many precautions to set in place. We needed to double the oxygen production of our generators. More ventilators would undoubtedly be required. We didn't have enough blood gas testing kits either. Karin Straβheim somehow persuaded a Lufthansa pilot to transport a thousand of these test kits in his personal luggage. Lufthansa had discontinued flights to Lima years earlier, but in the interest of repatriating some four thousand Germans in the wake of the coronavirus threat, the German government had arranged a number of flights. I reached out to the Löwenstein and Bauder medical companies, which then gifted us with thirteen new ventilators, both invasive (tube) and non-invasive (mask), valued at more than €70,000.

On Sunday 22nd March, I felt a massive tightness in my chest and wondered if I might be developing coronavirus. I had no idea. More likely, it was anxiety owing to the recent visit of the governor and head of the health department. They had shown up with less than an hour's notice. I had a bad feeling as Tina and Dr Thomas Tielmann gave them a tour of our facility. President Martin Vizcarra had declared a state of emergency only a week prior. In the burgeoning crisis, it was only a matter of time before there was a shortage of ICU beds and ventilators. No potential solution for addressing this need would be out of bounds – even the forced nationalisation of private hospitals.

The regional authorities were impressed with our resources. We had the capacity to ventilate ten patients simultaneously in our ICUs and forty on our regular ward. As it soon turned out, our hospital would offer half the ICU capacity of the entire state of Apurímac. They left after about ninety minutes, with no indication of impending government encroachment. But less than two days later, Dr Omar Merino Lopez, a congressman from Apurímac, introduced a concerning bill to Parliament. He proposed that the government be allowed to assume control of Peru's entire private medical sector. I could only imagine how this would play out – under the pretext of 'state service', local doctors would be smirking with satisfaction as they commandeered the valuable equipment that had been donated to us. I was continuously on the phone with the Olaechea lawyers, who confirmed my assessment of our vulnerability. The Minister of Health, Victor Zamora, evidenced Marxist leanings and had previously supported the nationalisation of private institutions. He was now in a seat of power, right next to the President.

Tina and I were concerned not only about protecting the autonomy of Diospi Suyana. As the days went by, patients stopped coming. We were used to hundreds waiting in long queues to get help. Now there was a yawning void. The police and the army had blocked all interstate roads. The government had ordered all hospitals to prepare for a flood of coronavirus patients, effectively stemming non-emergency operations. And schools were closed throughout the country; more than 10 million children were now spending their days at home. Our income plummeted by 80 per cent, but our expenses actually increased. The 217 Peruvian employees at Diospi Suyana were dependent on their wages. Our utilities ran at about 400,000 *soles*, or US$130,000, per month! And we had just purchased several hundred thousand *soles* worth of various PPE and medicines.

Our missionaries watched horrific stories from northern Italy and Madrid, as chronicled on YouTube. Dying patients, hospitals overwhelmed and unable to keep up with the demand for care, exhausted and weeping doctors – it all definitely caused one to question the wisdom of trying to fight the virus in a developing nation such as Peru. Staff were legitimately concerned for the well-being of their families. Team morale was also on the line. We sent out a detailed memo to all staff, noting the unprecedented challenges that lay before us and encouraging everyone to take advantage of the opportunity to evacuate through the European embassies. Despite our urging, forty-three missionaries elected to remain and serve alongside their Peruvian colleagues. Tina and I breathed a sigh of relief. With great determination, we banded together to prepare

Diospi Suyana for the inevitable deluge. Oebele de Haan and Matthias Kügler led a team to shore up our oxygen supply. In the orthopaedic clinic, others found a new purpose for the 3D printer: making protective shields. And still others set to work sewing plastic overshoes for ICU staff.

The Olaechea team were instrumental in drafting a contract with the Apurímac state government to provide us with legal protection and prevent government appropriation of our private assets, including staff and equipment. A great weight was lifted when the governor and health director added their signatures to the document after substantial discussion. We had no idea what was headed our way.

We admitted our first coronavirus patient on 25th April, a forty-two-year-old truck driver from Cusco. On a long journey from Lima to Quillabamba, he suddenly found himself gasping for air as he approached the exit to Curahuasi. By the time he got to our emergency room, his oxygen levels were at only 75 per cent, and an X-ray of his lungs clearly revealed the severity of his illness. He received oxygen, medication and life-saving treatment for eleven days in our isolation ward.

We upheld our part of the government contract and prepared to take in more coronavirus patients. Unfortunately, the state did not provide the agreed-upon financial supplement. We called regularly, but there was always some excuse, deferral or vague promise. Lawyers from both sides met again to amend the contract, providing critical clarification of responsibilities. We naively thought this would set everything right, but once again, the state failed to follow through. In May, the state called for a new contract that would give the government authorities the right to intervene in the management of our hospital. It would be suicide to accept such a proposal. If the state filled our wards with its patients and refused to pay its bills, we would be bankrupt within a matter of days. In addition, this change could end up being the 'open door' we had previously feared, giving our opponents the perfect opportunity to sabotage our work from the inside. Apart from a small group of us, few realised that the very existence of Diospi Suyana was in jeopardy.

On 29th May, Tina and I drew the line and addressed the Peruvian people via our own radio station. The message of our twenty-minute broadcast could not have been more explicit: 'This far and no further! We will not be exploited by corrupt politicians!'

Immediately after our broadcast, we sent our written statement out via the press distribution lists for the entire country. On our own station, we were likely preaching to the choir, those listeners who tuned in by choice. We needed to get the word out to everyone else – especially those with authority. President Martin Vizcarra himself read our statement before 11pm that night. And that was just the beginning. Over the next few days, 1.5 million Peruvians visited our website and social media pages. Thousands commented on the woefully inadequate state of the country's healthcare system while simultaneously voicing support for Diospi Suyana. Our phones rang non-stop!

On 1st June, Head of Administration Steven de Jager and I drove fourteen hours to Lima to meet with the most powerful politicians in the country. With the support of the people giving us traction, the President of Congress, Manuel Merino de Lama, carved out two hours of his time for us. We presented our concerns to Prime Minister Antonio Zevallos as well as the Minister of Health. We did many radio and television interviews and received more requests to meet with congress members than we had time to honour. Diospi Suyana had become a federal priority and a political hot button almost overnight.

For Diospi Suyana, COVID-19 was a challenge of historic proportions. We bore the acute risk to our staff, the immense financial loss and the latent threat of government appropriation for months on end, clinging to God's faithfulness time and time again.

45

Tying up loose ends

As an attentive reader, you have no doubt noticed that some stories in this book still need to be given closure. Rest assured, any lingering questions you may have are about to be answered. Most puzzle books provide solutions at the very end, so I shall do the same.

What happened with our logo issues? In December 2017, we re-registered our logo in Germany, this time with 30 per cent shading on the components. The German Red Cross has rescinded the allegation of infringement, and our modified logo has been trademarked since 9th July 2018.

We were able to completely clean up the extortion that had occurred in our optical clinic. Americo V had to reimburse nearly two-thirds of the injured parties.

Professor Schlickewei had strongly cautioned Dr Tim Boeker against going to Peru. He was certain that the Freiburg resident would have neither the essential equipment nor the prostheses he would need if he went to the mission hospital. He was wrong. In October 2015, Dr Booker attended the German Congress of Orthopaedics and Traumatology in Berlin. While in the exhibition hall, he struck up a conversation with Mr Orschler, head of Königsee Implante. The company donated a complete set of brand-new orthopaedic implants and related materials worth six figures, bringing traumatology at Diospi Suyana up to a European level of care. In August 2017, Dr Boeker published a seven-page article in the specialist journal *Der Unfallchirurg* ('The Trauma Surgeon'), describing the successful development of the Traumatology department at Diospi Suyana Hospital.

Christiane Klatt underwent extensive cancer treatment in Germany. In January 2019 the family arrived in Peru, one year later than initially planned. Both Christiane, a surgical assistant, and her husband Markus, an electronics technician, served in critical roles at Diospi Suyana. In August 2021 the Klatts returned home to Germany.

Diospi Suyana was at risk of losing our VHF channel in Puno. Our lawyer appealed, and a higher court overturned the initial ruling. Since 2nd April 2019, our fifty-metre tower has been broadcasting 24/7 from the nearby mountain, reaching an estimated quarter of a million listeners in the area.

The INDECOPI patent and trademark office forbade the Hampina Wasi clinic in Andahuaylas from using our logo on its building and advertising. The owner of Hampina Wasi appealed, brazenly claiming that the yellow sun with the red cross had been used by his clinic since 2000. In August 2022, the authorities finally ruled in our favour. They ordered Hampina Wasi to remove all logos similar to ours and pay a fine of 13,600 *soles* (about US$3,600).

Regarding Abraham K, an independent expert legal examination concluded that Diospi Suyana had adhered to international regulations during treatment. The patient's death was caused by a serious car accident and subsequent complications, and there was no evidence of medical negligence. The prosecutors in Curahuasi have been replaced twice since this all started. In 2022 we completely won the case in court.

Our legal action against Ricardo C has been dragging through the court in Lima for more than two years. But we are confident that with patience and prayer, the evidence will be sufficient to bring about justice.

46
Harsh reality

Alpacas graze serenely in the verdant meadows. In the distance, the glaciers glimmer as they reflect the light of the setting sun. The swelling peaks of the cordillera are bathed with a warm, red glow. Quechua in brightly coloured ponchos drive their cattle home along the well-worn paths, their day's work behind them. They will spend their evening comfortably passing the time with some lively music and dancing. They are a people who live in harmony with nature and enjoy the unspoiled utopia in which they dwell. On a plateau not far from Machu Picchu stands a large hospital, distinctly red and white in colour, and with staff known all over the world for their selfless dedication to help and to heal. The German women's magazine *Tina* even referred to them as 'angels' for this reason, and *Lisa* went a step further, claiming that the smiles of their patients were more than enough thanks for their efforts. This is the idyll of the Andes, where love and gratitude flow in abundance. A little piece of heaven here on earth.

It sounds harsh, but the above is a load of nonsense that does not reflect the reality of life in Peru in any capacity. The country suffers from deep-rooted dishonesty and corruption throughout all levels of society and government. Five presidents in a row have been removed for 'moral incapacity' and indicted for related crimes, including bribery, embezzlement, human rights violations and even murder. Some have served time in house arrest or prison or, as this book opened, have even committed suicide in order to avoid facing a jury.

In May 2020, a federal commission investigated 334 Peruvian judges and prosecutors suspected of illegal and/or ethical misconduct. That seems a huge number, but corrupt officials are not the problem in its entirety – they are merely a symptom of it. Ingrained and even systemic rule-breaking permeate Peruvian society. The taxi driver who bribes a police officer to make a parking ticket disappear, and even the parent who intentionally intimidates a teacher into promoting a child to the next grade despite poor performance also contribute to this formidable foundation of injustice.

Some two thousand years ago, Pontius Pilate famously challenged, 'What is truth?' (John 18:38). In Peru, a more appropriate question would be, 'Does truth even exist?' A Peruvian congresswoman went on record saying it was perfectly acceptable to lie, as lying is not considered a criminal offence. Two-thirds of the congress members serving between 2010 and 2015 were eventually prosecuted for acts that *were* considered to constitute criminal offences.

Narcissism is at the heart of such an ideology. The concept of 'the common good' is elusive at all levels of society in Peru.

A taxi driver in Lima once asked me, 'Is it the same in your country, that cars won't let ambulances with flashing lights through?' Appalled and saddened by this, I shook my head in disbelief.

Of course, exceptions exist, but what I have just described reflects the predominant value system and social order here. In Peru, relationships trump the law. People behave badly at the top, skimming off excess and climbing on the backs of their subordinates, but there is a marked 'trickle-down' effect, with those lower in the proverbial food chain also attempting to raise themselves up at the expense of others.

Giving someone your word means nothing. Even official contracts, signed and sealed by all necessary authorities, seldom turn out to be worth the paper they are printed on. Years ago, we signed a detailed agreement with our neighbours above the hospital regarding the distribution of water. The document bore the signatures of nearly all of the sixty affected residents and was even notarised. But five years on, we are still met with apathy and inaction when we insist on honouring the terms of the contract.

There is a massive problem with continuity in Peru. Between 2003 and 2023, I interfaced with thirteen different Ministers of Health. The average term served by each was approximately eighteen months. Every time a new President took office, his cabinet was overhauled. Under such fleeting conditions, long-term policy is essentially impossible.

Our school has been a blessing to Curahuasi. Our hospital has changed an entire region for the better through healthcare, wellness initiatives and job opportunities. People can now access news and positive programming through our media broadcasts. Most of our patients appreciate our efforts, but there are some who respond with an attitude of entitlement that is frankly irritating. On average, every Curahuasino has received care at Diospi Suyana three times. But instead of thanks, we are frequently subjected to complaints about having to join the queue. The locals still have a much easier time than the 80 per cent of our patients who have to travel a long way.

The discrepancy between one's words and actions could not be more pronounced here; there is no point in attempting to sugar-coat that reality. However, this is not to say that Peru has no redeeming qualities. No country in South America has worked through the Odebrecht construction scandal as thoroughly as Peru. And by the end of 2019, Peru will have taken in nearly one million refugees from Venezuela. These deeds deserve recognition, and we will give credit where credit is due.

We would do well to examine ourselves before rushing to condemn the conduct of the Peruvians. Weren't CEOs in Europe and the US awarding themselves bonuses while investors suffered massive losses during several recent financial crises? How about honesty on both individual and corporate tax returns? A little cheating seems to be acceptable – as long as you don't get caught. And hit-and-run vehicle accidents always seem more likely to occur when no one is around to see.

My point is this: selfishness is the real problem. It is not exclusive to Peru but can be found in every society in every era. If we could only conquer the brutal false god of 'self', we would be that much closer to living in harmony with each other and our planet. Unfortunately, we are slow learners with bad memories. We may be able to modify some external behaviours through effort and education, but we have yet to find a way to engender lasting internal change.

The Bible tells us of a power that can control our self-interest-run-wild. The Holy Spirit miraculously changes attitudes and qualities as it dwells in us. Paul wrote about the fruits of the Holy Spirit: 'love, joy, peace, forbearance, kindness, goodness, faithfulness, gentleness and self-control' (Galatians 5:22-23). We all fail to live up to our own standards. We all fall flat and struggle to get back up. It seems the more we try, the more we fail, and ultimately come to understand that we need God and His forgiveness. It is precisely for this reason that Jesus Christ gave His life for us on the cross.

At Diospi Suyana, I have personally met many employees and patrons who effect positive change in their respective environments. These unique individuals love God more than they care about money or status. This kind of faith is 'not from [them]selves, it is the gift of God' (Ephesians 2:8).

47

Has God been hiding?

In the film *Expelled: No Intelligence Allowed*, comedian and political commentator Ben Stein interviews notorious atheist Richard Dawkins. During the interview, he asked Dawkins to imagine the scenario of having to stand before God as the Almighty asks, 'Why didn't you believe in Me?' Drawing on the words of British mathematician Bertrand Russell, Dawkins said he would flip the question and ask God why He had hidden Himself so well. A valid point. Why doesn't God show Himself on television? He could address the entire world, calling out, 'Here I AM! Anybody have any questions about my existence now?'

Both the Old and New Testaments of the Bible are replete with accounts of God speaking and acting throughout the world. He can be found by those who earnestly seek Him. No matter where I travel, people always share their own divine encounters with me after hearing the Diospi Suyana story. I have come to the firm conclusion that God works in everyone's life with the aim of drawing us to Himself. Christians, atheists, followers of other faiths – we all may experience the hand of God in ways that cannot be explained away by luck or coincidence.

An ambassador from a Western land shared with me how this common thread ran through his personal history. We were in Zwickau, Germany, and I was just about to begin my presentation when a stranger approached and told me what he had experienced when he was just twelve years old. 'I was riding my bicycle down a steep hill. I lost my grip and went over the edge in a freefall for several metres. Suddenly, I saw a figure of light next to me. The figure held me and set me down gently at the bottom of the slope.'

In Mannheim, a wealthy socialite who had little to do with church or faith relayed the following incident: 'I lost my first child through a miscarriage. When I became pregnant again, I was terrified that I would miscarry again and lose this child too. In my anguish, I went to see a priest, hoping for some kind of consolation. He gave me a little book of Bible verses and sent me home. I sat in my lounge and opened the book to a random page. My eyes went straight to a line that read, "God will not despise a mother's prayer". Suddenly, the walls of the room shone with a supernatural light. I felt so safe and comforted!'

As is often the case, I was on a plane, flying between Europe and South America. The woman seated next to me was going on holiday to the Galapagos Islands. I soon learned she was a retired biologist from England and had previously worked as a school inspector. She assured me she was a committed atheist, reason enough for me to share tales of answered prayers at Diospi Suyana during our long flight across the Atlantic. I tried hard to convince her that there was more to life than meets the eye, but she remained resolutely sceptical. Finally, I proposed that many people experience unexplainable phenomena surrounding the time of a loved one's death. And now my seatmate acquiesced, 'Yes, you're right. I can confirm that!'

My maternal ancestors lived in Pomerania until shortly after World War 2. One evening, while my grandmother's family was having dinner, they heard the front door open and heavy footsteps sounded up the stairs. Who could it be? The family investigated but found no one there. Strange, even eerie. They just happened to glance at the clock on the wall and notice the time. A few days later, the postman delivered a letter bearing tragic news – my grandmother's favourite brother had passed away in another location at the exact time they heard the mysterious footsteps.

I indulged in running with a partner for almost thirty years. Whenever the opportunity arose, we would run several miles around a sports field just to prove to ourselves and the groundskeeper that we still could. Now I have trouble with my knee and Uli with his feet, but we like to imagine we are as fit as we were 'in the old days'. In 1996, Uli's younger sister was hospitalised in the Horst Schmidt Clinic in Wiesbaden with a terminal illness. Uli, his older sister and their mother planned to visit her in the hospital one afternoon. According to the doctors, the sick woman's condition was poor but stable. Around 10am, Uli felt inexplicably restless. He was instinctively drawn to go to the hospital early. Uli, his mother and his older sister all arrived at the hospital at the same time, independently, each having been overcome by the same feeling of urgency. When they entered the ICU, the attending doctor said, 'You've come at the right moment. We are losing her.' Half an hour later, Uli's sister breathed her last.

We have an inkling, an intuition, deep inside us about the unseen world surrounding us. Our own experiences, as well as family stories, confirm our gut feeling that there is more life beyond our earthly death.

In the Bible, we read that Jesus is the image of the invisible God. His words and deeds are unparalleled in accumulated world literature. Even non-Christian historians speak of His crucifixion. Hundreds of eyewitnesses confirmed His resurrection two millennia ago, and millions have since testified to the power of the risen Lord.

My books contain more than one hundred illustrations of extraordinary events through which God became visible. My wife and I, and so many of our friends, have prayed countless times in faith for God's help and intervention. He has never let us down. The results are plain to see and objectively verifiable. It is often said that we believe what we want to believe. Many of us admittedly gravitate towards a fixed mindset. Questioning one's beliefs, especially if they have been held for a long time, is never easy or comfortable. And still I urge, with no offence intended, if you have rejected the idea of the God of the Bible up until now, it is time to give Him a chance!

On 31st August 2006, I was sharing the Diospi Suyana presentation with a discussion group in Wiesbaden-Sonnenberg. One participant, a businessman I will call Mr Vogel, found our experiences completely baffling. 'These are educated people,' he thought to himself. 'How is it that they are so naive to believe that a God would hear and respond to their prayers?'

But our story contains numerous examples of divine intervention beyond anything we could ever ask or imagine. A modern hospital came into being literally out of nowhere. 'Hearing about Diospi Suyana flipped a switch in my head,' Mr Vogel recalled. 'I was still thinking about it all days later. God and prayer – these were very alien concepts to me. I finally pushed past my doubts and started to pray in particular terms. And indeed, the very next day, God unmistakably responded to my prayer!' Since that moment, Mr Vogel himself has been trusting in God.

More than a decade later, in February 2018, Tina and I stood before the same discussion group, sharing our testimony that the miracle of Diospi Suyana had not been a flash in the pan, but that the living God has continued to hear and answer our prayers.

I encourage you today, if you have not yet dealt with the question of God, please do not delay. The boat in which you sit is in a pitiful state and won't hold up much longer.

48

When the 'lifeboat' springs a leak

I don't know what makes you tick, ideologically. Perhaps you don't see your personal circumstances as requiring something as radical or dangerous as walking on water. It may be enough for you to stay comfortably inside your metaphorical 'lifeboat', enjoying the gentle lull of the waves. You know what I mean: enjoy life's pleasures and let the rest take care of itself.

But you will need to settle the question of whether or not you *can* walk on water. Sooner or later, the storms of life will come. The wind will pick up, your perceived tranquillity will be turned on its head, and you will find that your little boat is taking on water. Despite all your efforts to remain afloat, your once safe haven is now sinking, and you will inevitably go down with it – unless you can walk on water.

No one is spared hardship. It may come in the form of a family tragedy. We may receive a devastating diagnosis from a doctor. It may be a personal loss. We often realise too late that placing too much faith in our financial 'security', which can change overnight, plummeting millions into ruin, is unwise. The truth that suffering is universal became even more real during the recent pandemic. When we start to get carried off by rough currents, sometimes those we had considered friends are nowhere to be found. We may feel very much alone.

I remember one of my classmates from primary school with whom I unexpectedly crossed paths again some twenty years later. We spent a pleasant evening catching up and philosophising about our futures. Not yet thirty, we had a bright outlook and felt ready to take on the world. My mate was an entrepreneur who was into 'wealth management' and had a clear idea of how to set himself up comfortably for life. He spoke of the importance of diversifying investments. 'You mustn't put all your eggs in one basket,' he advised, 'or you may find them all broken at once!'

Two years later, I learned he had died from a sudden heart attack. He was here one minute and gone the next.

It's no use clinging to a ship that can never save you. Another schoolfriend of mine recently lost her father. The man was over ninety years old, hospitalised in the ICU, and desperately trying to stay on this side of eternity. He had begged his doctors to save his life by any means necessary. His family knew his earthly life was over, but he himself had no faith in an afterlife – and he was terrified. A flat line on the ECG would indicate his descent into nothingness. What an awful thought!

You may object that death is simply part of life. Each of us will one day have to bid this earthly realm farewell, whether peacefully in our sleep or violently in an accident. Our time will be up, we will disappear and one day we will be forgotten. I am very grateful to know this is not true.

Now I found myself on the road to southern Germany. My schedule was tight and really did not allow for this diversion, but it was important to me to make it work. I drove two hours out of my way for a thirty-minute visit, foot down all the way.

I was off to see a young lawyer named Nicole Otto, whom I had met several months earlier at one of my presentations. She had recently undergone treatment for pancreatic cancer, but tragically the cancer had returned and metastasised throughout her body. There was no hope of a cure. Death was imminent.

When I finally arrived at her bedside, I wished we had more time and that my words could ease her pain. I prayed silently and entrusted the young woman to God's care.

As a doctor, I have seen many people die. It's not something I will ever get used to, though – facing the fragility of life and human suffering can easily cause bitterness. 'What kind of God would let a young woman suffer like this?' her oncologist lamented aloud.

But the atmosphere in that hospital room was far from hopeless. I could discern that even over the phone when I called to tell her I was coming.

Nicole's body was swollen, wracked by the illness that would end her life, yet she smiled brightly when I entered the room. 'Surely you have your ups and downs?' I asked.

I was taken aback when she beamed, 'No, I feel sustained by God all the time!'

Like so many in my generation, I know the tacit fear of a cancer diagnosis. A lump that appears but doesn't hurt, an unexplained visual disturbance – we often assume the worst before tests put our mind at ease. The woman before me was in a state that anyone would dread, and yet a deep peace emanated from her.

I called Nicole later on from the Frankfurt airport. It was the last time we ever spoke. She died four days later. I asked her how she was doing. Her answer will stay with me for ever: 'I'm fine. God is with me. He is just awesome!'

Nicole had chosen a Bible verse to be included in her obituary: 'You hem me in behind and before, and you lay your hand upon me' (Psalm 139:5).

Often, a dying person's last words reflect sorrow or hopelessness. Not Nicole's. She knew the truth about God, entrusting herself to Jesus Christ and holding to His promise that, 'The one who believes in me will live, even though they die' (John 11:25).

With unshakable faith, Nicole got out of the boat and walked on the water. And in doing so, she learned that the water carries you. Miraculous, comforting, and 100 per cent real.

49
A personal statement

Now you have reached the end of my third book. The events carefully chronicled throughout these pages took place over the course of forty years. My goal has been to show that faith in God is more than a platitude; it is a very real power, far beyond our understanding. Diospi Suyana exists today because of God's action, not our wishful thinking.

In the autumn of 2004, I was invited to present the Diospi Suyana story at the German Ministry of Economic Cooperation and Development. Minister Heidemarie Wieczorek-Zeul and the other officials present were interested in learning how they might support our endeavour, but when they understood the faith basis of our work, their attitude changed from curiosity to condescension. I can still see their mocking faces. 'You've got your work cut out for you,' they smirked, 'but you're hoping for help from above, right?'

These distinguished ladies and gentlemen had no concept of the omnipotence and faithfulness of the Most High, not a mere illusion but a tangible reality.

It's asking a lot of a PowerPoint, but I ached to be able to truly convey the marvel of how Diospi Suyana developed from a rough idea to one of the best-known and well-respected mission hospitals in the world. And now we have our school and broadcast centre too. All of this has come into being without financing from the government or backing from the United Nations. The productivity and sustainability of Diospi Suyana are unparalleled.

At this point, I would like to make a confession. Despite appearances, I struggle with doubts and anxiety, just like everyone else. Those who know me well can attest to this humbling truth. I worry often for my wife and children, and I have spent many sleepless nights worrying about the work we have built with God's help. Tina and I have taken numerous risks over the past twenty-five years in particular. It's been a roller coaster of an adventure, euphorically riding the 'highs' and frantically trying to avoid being overcome by the 'lows'.

In this book, you have read about a myriad of diverse believers who left all comforts and safeguards behind in order to step out boldly with faith in God. The cover depicts my wife and me walking on the surface of a churning, stormy sea with a multitude of hungry sharks eyeing us from below. Peruvian artist Eunice Espinoza has captured our reality masterfully. There are many who wish to destroy Diospi Suyana, some because of our success, some because of what we stand for. Corrupt politicians, indifferent bureaucrats and even criminals have threatened our very existence.

A Peruvian doctor invited me to come to Lima on Friday 19th July 2019 to share the story of Diospi Suyana with his extended circle of friends. For me, this was an event like hundreds of others. But the evening before the presentation, things took a disturbing turn. Dr Kcam received an anonymous email seeking the exact location of the event. The tone and content of the message were unsettling and raised red flags. Who were these people, and what were they up to? Did they plan to disrupt the event somehow, or maybe even plan to kidnap me? Earlier that week, I had posted on our website that a large donation had recently been made to our surgical department. Perhaps they saw an opportunity to exact some financial gain or notoriety. The police looked into the matter immediately. The sender's email had been deactivated and their Google account deleted. There was no way to track down who was responsible.

Dr Haβfeld was still awake when I called. 'No matter what happens,' I charged our deputy director, 'Diospi Suyana does not pay ransom demands as a matter of principle!'

That night, I could hardly sleep. I tossed and turned on my pillow. At around 4am, Tina and I prayed together, turning the situation over into God's hands.

On the day of the presentation, the venue was moved to another part of town. Five plainclothed police began patrolling the area several hours before I was scheduled to begin. While I was inside talking about our missionary work to a welcoming audience, a solid security presence had the entire building under surveillance, working overtime to ensure my safety.

It may well be that one day we will become victims of a violent crime. Or perhaps some dark night, a lorry will hit a curve too fast, cross the median and cause a horrible collision like the one I survived in December 2008. Rough waters are a regular occurrence at Diospi Suyana, and we often get our feet wet. Sometimes we are overcome by the sight of the crashing waves, and we cry out just like Peter did, 'Lord, save us!'

When we speak of faith, we don't mean a cultural leaning, theological debate or inspirational quote on a coffee mug. What we are talking about, what we are passionate about, is faith in action for life. The events at Diospi Suyana continuously exemplify the fact that we are indeed walking on water. Our hearts are full of hope and longing to someday see – face to face – the One who called us out of the boat.

Thanks

'God, where are You? I want to see You!' I cried out one stormy November night. It was decades ago, yet that prayer echoes through my life to this day. God, in His grace, continues to answer it. I will never be able to thank Him enough.

More than 220 long-term volunteers have faithfully served alongside my wife and me throughout this incredible journey. Diospi Suyana simply would not exist without their sacrifice. We will always cherish each of them in our hearts, especially Barbara and Udo Klemenz.

Our friends in the Diospi Suyana Association, notably Olaf Böttger and his sister Annette, have been unwavering in their commitment. Whenever I try to credit the Böttgers' contribution, they wave me off. Modest to the core and preferring to remain in the background, they have nonetheless been shining stars in the story of Diospi Suyana.

Thousands of supporters, sponsors and friends have shared our vision. May God repay them for their selfless generosity.

Last but not least, thank you, Tina. I know no other woman with whom I would want to share this walk across the water. Hand in hand and looking ahead. Come what may.